The Science of Dreaming

Why We Dream, What Dreams Mean and How to Lucid Dream

Case Adams, Ph.D.

The Science of Dreaming: Why We Dream,
        What Dreams Mean and How to Lucid Dream
Copyright © 2014 Case Adams
LOGICAL BOOKS
Wilmington, Delaware
http://www.logicalbooks.org
All rights reserved.
Printed in USA

Publishers Cataloging in Publication Data
Adams, Case
The Science of Dreaming: Why We Dream, What Dreams Mean and How to Lucid Dream
First Edition
1. Health. 2. Medicine.
    Bibliography and References; Index

ISBN trade paper: 978-1-936251-49-0
ISBN ebook: 978-1-936251-32-2

Table of Contents

Introduction

While we sleep for several hours each night, and dream during a portion of that, most of us don't know why we sleep, let alone why we sleep.

The meaning of dreams, and dream interpretation has been accepted for thousands of years. We find the Bible full of discussions of dreams, for example. Daniel was known for his prowess of dream interpretation. Other prophets and writers of scripture have reported that their dreams revealed future events. Many since, including the Egyptians, Greeks, Romans, those of Chinese and Indian cultures, and many other ancient peoples have investigated and interpreted their dreamscapes.

For thousands of years, humankind has speculated on the meaning of dreams. The mysteries regarding dream meaning and origin have continued to capture our attention to this day. In 1899, Sigmund Freud published his classic *Interpretation of Dreams.* This treatise proposed that dreams provided windows into the mind, and the "road to the unconscious."

Researchers have gained significant information over the past few decades about dreaming. Using advanced methods of brain analysis such as computed tomography (CT), magnetic resonance imaging (MRI), single photon emission computed tomography (SPECT) and positron emission tomography (PET), researchers have been able to monitor the location, movement and quality of neural activity. This has allowed dream research to advance quickly, enabling a number of windows into our dreamscapes.

By monitoring brainwaves of sleep subjects, and waking them up at strategic moments, these researchers have unveiled some of the secrets of sleep and how dreaming fits into sleep. By studying how dreaming affects problem solving, cognition and the ability to deal with stress, researchers have put together many pieces of the puzzle.

Other researchers have dived into the aspects related to lucid dreaming and the ability to steer our dreams. This has led to some exciting breakthroughs with regard to our ability to control, to some degree, our dreamscape.

These advancements have led to a greater understanding of the relationship between dreaming and our waking lives. They have not given us, however, a full understanding about what our dreams mean and why we have them. This research has indeed brought us newfound knowledge of the dreamscape and quite possibly, at least part of the understanding of why we sleep.

Yet there are still many questions remaining about dreaming. One critical question is whether dreams have any meaning at all. A number of researchers have asked this question, and concluded that dreams are simply brain cell impulses being intermixed and jumbled up in our brain—as we try to find some meaning to this seemingly chaotic world.

Other researchers are convinced the purpose of dreaming lies deeper. There is a deeper level of learning taking place while we dream. While this deeper level is not fully understood by modern science, there is increasing evidence this is related to the same type of learning processes that take place during our waking lives.

This book is meant to crack open the research, and explain the real meaning of dreaming from an even deeper perspective. This comes from a deeper understanding of our real identity and our purpose for existing.

Chapter One

The Anatomy of Dreaming

Every night we lay our body down and slip into another world. We hand our body over to our autonomous nervous system. Our body becomes paralyzed as we drift into a realm completely unlike our waking world. This is a world with a different set of rules. In this world, we can fly. In this world, we can swim underwater for hours. In this world, we can achieve riches and fame and lose it all in a matter of minutes. In this world, we can accomplish things we could never achieve during our waking hours.

As we wandering through distant lands, our body cruises on autopilot, breathing deeply and fully—as we lay oblivious to our external environment. During this state, our brainwaves cycle from one sleep stage to another with almost clockwork accuracy.

As we cycle, our body's immune activity increases, as our cells and tissues are cleansed. Our breathing is rhythmic and deep. Our body adjusts position when necessary without any awareness by ourselves. Sometimes we even get up and walk to the bathroom or elsewhere without any awareness. As we sleep, our memories become consolidated and prioritized.

As we go deeper and fall into the REM-stage, our neurons begin to fire as though we were awake. Our eyes dart around as though we were watching something moving under our eyelids. Just what is going on here? Magnetic resonance has discovered that during this period, our visual cortex is processing information precisely in the same way at this stage as it does during our waking lives. We are seeing something and watching something, but our eyes are closed.

Just what is dreaming and why do we dream? Part of this is understood by knowing what happens when we don't get enough sleep.

The Need to Sleep

According to a poll done by the National Sleep Foundation in 2000, almost two-thirds of American adults experience a sleep problem a few nights per week or more, and

43% say that they are so sleepy during the day that it interferes with their daily activities.

Reports have shown that up to half of all Americans report having insomnia at some point. One out of ten adults will change their jobs in order to sleep more.

Drowsy driving causes over 100,000 car crashes each year, and more than 50% of adults report that they have continued driving while sleepy during the past year. From a financial perspective, sleep loss is costly. Some 40% of adults have reported that lack of sleep forces a decrease in work quality, with over two-thirds saying lack of sleep interferes with concentration and the ability to handle stress.

Our technology-driven, accelerated society has shifted into high gear. The distinction between day and night has become blurred with the advent of the internet, 24-hour shopping, and the unending pressure to do it all now. As a result, sleep has fallen victim to the technical phantasmagoria of smart phones, laptop computers, MP3 players and televisions—all with remote high-speed access and satellite communications. The prospect of slumbering down to a relaxing night of deep dreams and soothing silence seems to have escaped into the shrieking lights of digitalland.

While there is some debate whether these have significantly decreased sleep among our population, it is certain that these at the very least present a strong deterrent to good quality sleep, as these media devices favor our waking attention.

Most researchers agree that sleep represents a systemic recharging and resetting of the body. This consists of metabolic renewal among cells and tissue systems around the body combined with the consolidation and sorting of the memories stored within brain cells. It is quite easy to observe the importance of this resetting and recharging feature of sleep, and most of us know this all too intimately.

This still brings up many questions: Why do we need sleep every night? Do we all need sleep? If so, how much do we need? And what happens if we don't get enough?

These are a few of the mysteries that have plagued scientists and physicians for centuries. While research has progressed significantly over the past few decades, some of these questions are still being debated.

Sleep by its very nature is rhythmic. Sleep is circadian: We need it daily, and we feel better if we get it at the same time and length each day. Most people sleep between five hours and nine hours per night. We find reports of people sleeping only one to three hours every night, while some seem to need ten to twelve hours per night to feel rested. Sleep researchers have concluded that most of us sleep an average of seven to seven-and-a-half hours every day (Meddis 1977).

It also seems that we need to fall asleep and wake up at about the same times each day for some reason.

Considerable research has concluded that many of us do not get enough good quality sleep. Ron Kramer, M.D. of the Colorado Neurology Institute's Sleep Disorders Center has said:

> *"There is growing medical literature showing that many of us in today's 24/7 society are not getting the basic sleep we need every day. At the same time, there is increasing evidence from human sleep research that chronic lack of even a few hours of sleep a night can result in significant health consequences. These consequences include an increased risk of accidents; fatigue that makes you prone to depressive symptoms or not enough energy to exercise; and even chemical changes that stimulate your brain to eat more and to eat more salty and sugary food."*

How do we know if we are not getting enough sleep and thus dreaming enough? There are several signs, according to sleep research. These include:

- ❖ increasingly forgetting things
- ❖ drowsiness while behind the wheel, at work or class

❖ losing concentration
❖ making simple mistakes that could easily be avoided
❖ feeling depressed
❖ becoming easily frustrated
❖ being anxious about non-critical things
❖ becoming angry for little reason
❖ frequent illnesses
❖ feeling extremely drowsy as we wake up

Regarding the last item, most of us awaken slightly drowsy and would rather sleep some more. However, if we cannot readily rise and become alert within a few minutes (without coffee or other stimulation) then we likely didn't sleep enough, slept too much, or didn't get enough good quality sleep.

Sleep research has unveiled a lot about the mechanics of sleep over the past five decades. Recently, sleep research has gained increased funding. Governments, universities and private research foundations are all conducting sleep research now. And there is good reason for this increased focus.

Though it may sound simple, this is not a simple question. Why? Because sleep itself is complicated. Sleep has a number of facets, and each of those facets has a purpose. We know from research that without the right amount of sleep we will die of heart diseases and other ailments a lot sooner. We also know from research that a lack of sleep can cause a variety of psychological issues. These include cognitive dysfunction, memory loss and increased anxiety. Without enough sleep, we will become more stressed and less productive. Without enough sleep, our immune systems will become weakened.

These together render at least five reasons for sleep. The first is to conserve and rest cellular metabolism, allowing the immune system to accelerate. This enhanced state of immunity is supported by studies that have shown increased levels of interleukin-1, tumor necrosis factor (TNF) and other immune cells during sleep. Studies on intestinal microflora confirm that probiotic activity also increases during sleep. Probiotics provide upwards of 70% of the body's immune response system.

Why does the immune system go into high gear when we sleep? When the body enters the paralysis of sleep, the immune system can more easily clear out pathogens and toxins. We can see this by the fact that bacteria loads increase within the lymph nodes of those who have been sleep-deprived. This is also the reason we are more prone to illness when we are not sleeping enough.

A second reason we sleep is cellular regeneration. This is the process of cell repair and cellular division. These processes are stimulated while we sleep. Just as road crews can get more highway paved with asphalt at night when they can block lanes, the body can heal damaged tissues and grow new healthy ones when the body's metabolic activity slows down.

Cellular division is stimulated by growth hormone. Growth hormone release into the bloodstream is stimulated by GMRH, or growth hormone-releasing hormone. Research has illustrated that both GHRH and growth hormone levels increase as we sleep. Actually, it is more complicated than that. GHRH actually helps stimulate sleepiness along with the release of GH.

The third reason we sleep is memory consolidation. While we are in non-rapid eye movement sleep, our neurons begin to sort through the various images and stimuli that have been taken into the sensory organs and brain cells. This information is stored as short-term memory at first. When we sleep, through a process involving the hippocampus, our brains sort through the information and store away for later retrieval those memories we consider important. Memories we'd rather not keep, on the other hand, are tossed away and left to our sub-conscious self. These are typically events that we'd rather not face in the future, or events that we simply haven't come to terms with.

The fourth reason for sleeping has to do with problem

resolution for those events we haven't come to terms with yet. During certain NREM sleep stages, our mind reflects upon the various events of the day (and previous days) and works through the confusing or uncomfortable issues or images. We ask the mind to reconcile problematic areas. Why did this happen? Why did I see this? What can I do to fix this? How can I avoid a bad thing from happening? These are questions the mind is asked by the self to fix. When we go to sleep, our sensory systems all shut down. This gives our minds the time to sort through the events of the day and help find resolution within them. It is for this reason that people who don't sleep enough end up becoming confused and depressed. They aren't regularly coming to terms with the things that are going on around them.

The fifth and last reason we sleep is for escape. As we'll focus on later, every night, for some reason, we slip into a fantasy dimension. This is the dimension of our wildest dreams. This is a place where we can rearrange people, places and things in such a way as to live out our fantasies.

This dream-state typically occurs at a particular stage (REM, discussed later) of our sleep. During this stage, we subconsciously play out any and every variance of the physical world we can imagine. Why we do this is debated, but researchers know that we need this type of sleep so badly that if we don't get enough REM-stage sleep, we'll somehow rearrange all of our other sleep stages to specifically allow us to catch up on our REM- stage dreaming.

This brings up the notion of lucid dreaming, which is somewhat misunderstood. Lucid dreaming is often confused with the vivid and imaginative dreaming of the REM stage.

Actually, lucid dreaming describes a type of dream where we become conscious that we are dreaming. This means that we first become conscious of our dream as we are waking up—or remain conscious as we continue to watch or even steer the activities of the dream. Should we see a wall in our dream, we may decide to leap it. Or we decide to break it down. Either way, we utilize conscious choice to move within the dream. This is often regarded as a "hybrid state of consciousness," which is both physiologically and mentally different from REM-stage dreaming.

Furthermore, some researchers, namely Stephen LeBerge, Ph.D., have determined methods by which one can be trained to increase their ability to dream lucidly. We'll discuss this further in our chapter on dreaming.

Our Sleep Stages

Three relative sleep parameters quantify and define sleep. These are the *sleep stages,* the *sleep cycles,* and the *sleep brainwaves.* While each of these is interrelated, they are measured through separate readings. These can be a bit confusing, so let's review each of these individually.

The sleep stages are the depth of sleep that a person experiences during a night's sleep. The convention most sleep researchers agree upon now is that there are three stages of non-REM sleep, and two stages (or types) of REM stage. REM means *rapid eye movement,* which we will discuss in further detail later.

Then there are the sleep cycles. Sleep cycles are periods of deeper sleep separated by short periods of reduced sleep.

Then we have the brainwaves that occur when we sleep. These help us classify and categorize the type of brain activity occurring at any particular time, which helps us measure sleep cycles and stages. The sleep stages are often referenced to by their dominant brainwaves. We'll discuss these more specifically later.

There are two general categories of sleep: Non-rapid-eye-movement (or NREM) sleep, which covers about three-quarters of total sleep; and REM sleep, which covers the remainder in healthy adults. Healthy adults thus get about two hours of REM-stage sleep per might. Adolescents get more REM-stage sleep. Children and especially infants have significantly more REM sleep.

Sleep researchers used to classify sleep into five stages, including REM-stage sleep. However, there were some grey areas within the third and fourth stages. As a result, the American Academy of Sleep Medicine decided to combine the third and fourth stages of NREM sleep (the theta and the deep-theta) into a single third stage. The first two sleep stages are now called N1 and N2, and this third consolidated sleep stage is called the N3 stage. N3 is also sometimes referred to as slow-wave sleep.

A healthy night's sleep consists of between four and six cycles. Each cycle often approximates about 90 minutes in length, but this can be different from person to person and can change periodically. In general, the first cycle proceeds from a light, stage one (N1) sleep to a stage two sleep (N2). During this first sleep cycle, our breathing increases, our body cools, and our mind begins to drift into slumberland. During this phase, the mind is still somewhat aware of the surroundings, but not completely aware. Sometimes, this phase will be characterized by some twitching, as the muscles progressively begin to lose their tone.

Most good sleepers will drop into a stage two sleep during the first cycle. Others might stay in the light stage one sleep during the whole first cycle. This, however, sets up the possibility of *sleep stage latency,* or a delay of the deeper sleep stages.

After about ninety or so minutes, the first cycle ends, and our sleep depth gets shallower for a few minutes. During this period, we are practically awake, but not fully conscious of our environment. Here we can readily wake up and fall back to sleep (into the next cycle) without missing much sleep quality. After a few minutes of this practically awake period, we should fall into another sleep cycle.

During this second sleep cycle, we hopefully become firmly established into stage two sleep. During stage two sleep, we lose awareness of our environment along with the ability to control muscle motion. Our breathing becomes deep and rhythmic. During this stage, we can also begin to have some reveries and light dreams that are closer to reflections on our waking life.

Later in the second sleep cycle, a good-quality sleeper may move into the deeper, stage three (N3) sleep. During this deeper NREM sleep, our mind completely detaches from our body, as we drift through reveries, thoughts, problems and further reflections. These can sometimes have disastrous results, as we can talk in our sleep, sleep walk and experience nightmarish reflections (also called *night terrors*). During stage three sleep, our body is on automatic, as we breathe deeply and adjust our position every so often. From this stage, we can merge into the deepest stage of sleep, called REM-stage sleep.

During REM-stage sleep, something mysterious happens. Following a jolt of electrical activity in the brain, our brain wakes up. While our muscles have all but paralyzed, brain activity becomes significantly active—very similar to the brain activity found during our waking hours. As our brain becomes engaged, our eyes begin to move around in our sockets as if we were watching action swirling around us. Because the pupil and iris protrudes a bit from the eyelid, our eyeball activity is distinctly noticeable. It is almost as if we are looking around us, but with our eyes closed. During the REM-stage, the rest of our body becomes catatonic and motionless.

NREM type sleep (without rapid eye movement) is typical during our early and later sleep cycles. N1 and N2 stages occur during the first few cycles, intermittently through the night and during the last cycle. REM increases during third, fourth and fifth sleep cycles and we may have a last REM-stage period just before waking in the morning. These later REM-stages may be short, however. They won't be as long as we might experience during the third sleep cycle.

It was once thought that all dreaming occurs during REM sleep, but this assumption partially depends upon what is considered dreaming. During our NREM stages, we are sorting through memories and problem solving. While some might consider this dreaming, others might consider it akin to filing away stacks of paperwork and solving word problems. REM-stage dreaming is more like the classic dreaming people talk about. This is also sometimes called slow-wave dreaming. REM-stage dreaming involves strong visuals and a fantasy world born of our imagination. We'll discuss dreaming in more detail later.

REM-stage sleep is thought to be one of the most critical stages of sleep, and without it, we will not feel rested. During REM sleep, our body is immobilized, but our eyes and brains are as active as they are during our waking lives. This is because during REM-stage sleep, the larger-wave signals that drive large muscle motion are blocked at the spinal cord. Occasionally a person might mutter something or move around a bit during REM-stage, but this is rare. During healthy REM-stage sleep, the body is paralyzed.

Sometimes people become aware that their body is becoming paralyzed as they doze into deeper sleep. This is fairly normal, and should not be a cause for alarm.

REM-stage dreaming also often engorges the genitalia. Research shows that this is not necessarily due to sexually oriented dreams.

People with less REM sleep tend to suffer from irritability and anxiety. Decreased REM-stage sleep can also lead to progressive insomnia. Sleep studies have indicated that a lack of REM-stage sleep can also cause psychosis and hallucinations. This theory has been debated by sleep researchers, as NREM-stage sleep deprivation has also been connected to these types of mental issues.

If a healthy sleeper's REM-stage sleep is disturbed, the sleeper will typically rearrange sleep cycles to accommodate more REM sleep during successive nights. If a person is deprived of REM sleep for a period of time, they may immediately fall into REM sleep in an attempt to recover the REM they missed.

Interrupting REM-stage sleep with any consistency will cause a progressive deterioration of sleep, leading to insomnia. Harvard researchers (Barbato *et al.* 2002) established this as they woke up subjects repeatedly when they were in, or entering into REM-stage sleep. They found that NREM sleep was progressively disturbed with REM-stage interruption. The researchers concluded that REM-stage sleep provides a controller or governor for the rest of our sleep patterns.

NREM-stage deficiency can produce health problems, mental instability, chronic fatigue and delirium. During NREM-stage sleep, our mind and brain cells are sorting and prioritizing the memories and events of our waking lives. We store away those memories that can be put in the past, and we try to work through those issues that are problems or inconsistencies. This process is called consolidation. Consolidation is a necessary function we must do nightly.

Curiously, if we don't get enough sleep, however, we will easily give up the NREM stages in lieu of trying to get sufficient REM-stage sleep. While we have an innate need for both REM-stage and NREM sleep, functional NREM sleep is put aside by the sleeper in favor of the more enjoyable REM-stage sleep.

Body temperatures also fluctuate with sleeping cycles. Core body temperature gradually drops with increases in melatonin and adenosine levels through the evening. Core body temperature drops substantially in the deeper sleep cycles, often falling as much as two degrees Fahrenheit from waking temperatures. In contrast, people with difficulty sleeping often show elevated core body temperature in the evening and during sleep.

Sleep research has indicated that healthy sleep is dependent upon the full completion of each sleep cycle, and sufficient amounts of both REM and NREM sleep. The more complete each cycle is; the better, more restful sleep we will experience. Yet like fingerprints, each of us has unique sleep cycle particulars. We each fall in and climb out of each cycle slightly differently. Some of us have abrupt and defined cycles, while others show less definition. The period and depth between each cycle can also vary from person to person, as does our stage progression and length through the cycles. In addition, the amount of relative REM and NREM sleep needed to feel rested varies from person to person.

Critical neurotransmitters known for balancing moods and nerve activity are produced during REM sleep. These include dopamine and serotonin. A lack of these brain neurotransmitters can result in mood disorders and sleep dysfunction.

For example, Parkinson's sufferers typically produce less dopamine. Increasing dopamine levels relaxes the symptoms of Parkinson's. For example, in one study (Willis and Turner 2007), bright light therapy increased dopamine levels among Parkinson's patients—elevating their moods and increasing their sleep quality.

Furthermore, studies have confirmed that REM disorders often precede Parkinson's and dementia by a few years. Cognitive impairment, schizophrenia and hallucinations have also been associated with a lack of REM-stage sleep (Arnulf *et al.* 2008).

Brainwaves of Sleep and Dreams

As we examine some of the expansive research done in the field of brainwaves, we will see how both brain function and the mind are measured by wave mechanics. The electroencephalogram measures the voltage potential differences among different regions of the brain. These voltage differences result in a wave formation with particular wave qualities. These include wavelength, frequency and amplitude. Brainwaves indicate the predominant activity occurring within the brain and nervous system. They are a measurement of collective neuron firings.

In other words, brainwaves are the cumulative electromagnetic pulse activity of our brain's neurons. We might compare this cumulative effect to the roar of a crowd at a ballgame. Each individual fan may be clapping or yelling differently. As a whole, however, the stadium crowd roars at a certain pitch. In the same way, while each neuron may be firing slightly differently, the combined frequency of all neurons together is considered a brainwave.

This means that brain cell firings tend to resonate to a particular frequency. This resonating frequency reveals a particular type of information processing amongst brain cells. This is especially applicable to neurons within the same processing regions—called cortices (plural for cortex).

Waves are measured by frequency: cycles per second or hertz. The main three frequency ranges found in sleep are delta, theta and alpha.

The first and part of the second sleep cycles will typically consist of alpha waves. N1 sleep is dominated by alpha waves. Alpha waves have frequencies that range from eight to thirteen cycles per second. In our waking lives, alpha waves are seen dominant during observation and memorization tasks, especially those related to words, persons and visual impressions. Alpha waves are also present in some meditation states and periods of relaxation.

After early alpha-dominated sleep cycles, theta brainwaves (5-8 hertz) begin to appear, as our sleep becomes progressively deeper. These signal N2 stage sleep. Theta waves dominate during middle night sleeping. Theta waves are elusive during our waking lives, but are seen during memory retrieval, creative endeavors and behavior modification. Theta waves during sleep indicate memory consolidation. Neurons within the hippocampus actively fire as information is transduced and transmitted to resonate within memory neurons. EEG readings confirm that theta waves accompany peak hippocampus activity. The hippocampus is associated with spatial recognition and short-term memory consolidation.

The third cycle will typically descend us into delta stage sleep. This is considered slow-wave sleep. Delta waves cycle in a very slow range of one to three cycles per second (or hertz), and are the deepest NREM sleep. During our waking lives, delta waves are rarely seen, except perhaps during some deep states of meditation. During delta or N3 sleep, dreaming is minimal and the body can twitch, roll over or make other motions.

Brainwaves

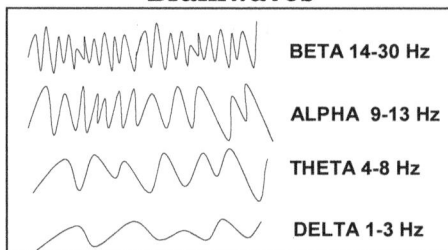

This does not mean that delta sleep isn't important. Delta waves tend to resonate more actively in the frontal cortex. Delta waves correlate with an increase in the production and circulation of growth hormone. One of growth hormone's important attributes is its ability to advance the healing and regeneration process. This means, therefore, that delta sleep is critical to our cells' ability to heal and recharge. This prepares our body for the next day of physical stress. A lack of delta sleep has also been associated with higher stress levels and lowered immunity.

While we're on the subject of brainwaves, let's review our waking brainwaves. This will give some contrast to the waves that drive our sleeping lives. Our waking brainwaves are dominated by the higher frequency—faster and shorter—beta and gamma brainwaves.

Beta waves cycle at fourteen to thirty hertz and are dominant during active thinking and problem solving. These waves tend to be prominent towards the front of the brain—where the frontal cortex is located—and on the sides—where the motor cortices are located. Beta waves reflect a state of focused attention. A lack of beta waves during waking hours—or lower frequency beta waves—tends to occur when we have a lack of focus or concentration. This often takes place during creative or 'spacey' moments. On the other hand, brainwaves toward the higher range of beta will reflect an increased focus on problem solving.

Gamma waves are higher frequency brainwaves, and are sometimes referred to as high-frequency beta waves.

Gamma waves predominate during intense problem solving and focused learning. Gamma waves range from thirty to sixty hertz. Gamma waves occur during increased visual cortex activity and the brain's sorting processes. They also occur during reflection and light meditation.

High gamma waves cycle from sixty to two hundred hertz, measured by sensitive EEGs. High gamma brainwaves occur during the most intense cognitive brain functions. In one study of eight subjects, for example, high gamma brainwave activity increased during the practice of *pranayama*—a method of concentrated meditative breath control (Vialatte *et al.* 2009).

The bottom line with regard to our brainwaves is that while we are sleeping, our brain cells fire much slower and longer. This allows them to *process information.* This processing includes sorting memories and visual stimuli, and consolidating those memories we want to keep in long-term storage. This also includes tossing out those memories we prefer not to keep, and prioritizing those that need resolution.

The other part of this process is critical: Our brain cells work to help us resolve issues. This means coming to grips with certain events or situations, and learning to work around them. Our brainwaves present to us a shadow of the complexity of these events.

Neurotransmitters and Hormones

After just a few weeks of life outside the womb, we begin to process periodic light signals. As we process these signals, our bodies systematically produce several neurotransmitters and hormones that regulate our energy levels and moods. The neurotransmitters that most affect our sleeping cycles are melatonin, adenosine, dopamine and serotonin. Furthermore, hormones that interact with sleeping include cortisol, thyroid hormones and growth hormone. Each of these are produced by the body through enzymatic protein assembly using available nutrients in orchestration with daily rhythms of light, activity, food and sleep. Amazingly, these substances are all interlinked in a symphony of orchestration.

Neurotransmitters are produced among the nervous system. They are active within the tiny space between two neurons; or between a neuron and any other cell. This space is called a *synapse*. Neurotransmitters occupy a fluid within the synapse, appropriately called the *neurotransmitter fluid*. This fluid provides the medium through which the exchange of signals between the two cells flows.

We might compare this fluid to the role water plays when we cook. Say we are cooking pasta. We first pour the water into a pan, and heat the pan. This heats the water to a boil. We then add salt into the water and add the pasta (some also add a little oil). The salt water (and maybe oil) cooks the pasta a certain way. When the cooking is complete, the pasta is soft and a little salty, which adds to its flavor. If we didn't add the salt to the water, the pasta would taste a little bland.

Now if we put sugar into the water instead of salt, we would find an altogether different tasting pasta. It could barely even be called pasta. Furthermore, if we cooked the pasta in milk, it would also turn out differently. Or if we cooked the pasta in vinegar water, we'd probably not want to eat the pasta at all.

In each of the examples above: salty water, plain water, milk and vinegar, the pasta was still cooked mostly in water. But the addition of the salt, vinegar or milk changed the finished product—possibly disastrously.

In the same way, the neurotransmitter contents within the synaptic fluid will change the way signals are processed between neurons or neurons and cells.

The neurotransmitter **serotonin** allows for a balanced flow of moods, memory and activity through the nervous system. A good supply of serotonin among the brain's cells will allow the body to relax and conduct itself with composure. A lack of serotonin will increase anxiety and restlessness. Serotonin deficiency has also been associated with nervous disorders.

Serotonin is produced in the brain and nervous system. It is also found in the digestive tract. Serotonin binds with receptors in the prefrontal cortex and amygdale neurons, making its deficiency critical to controlling thinking and regulating fear.

Serotonin's levels in the brain are dependent upon a receptor called SERT, which clears serotonin from the system. When SERT is activated by a different molecule, however, more serotonin is left in circulation. This is the mechanism behind the selective serotonin reuptake inhibitor inhibitors, or SSRIs.

5-HTP is a precursor for serotonin production. When there is a deficiency of the amino acid tryptophan in the diet, there are usually low levels of serotonin. We'll discuss serotonin availability and 5-HTP in more detail later on.

Serotonin is also a precursor for the critical neurotransmitter called **melatonin.** Melatonin is produced in a cyclic process driven by the reduction of light and the availability of serotonin.

Melatonin is one of the most powerful hormones relating to sleep. Melatonin levels are highest as we fall asleep, and least during our waking daylight hours. Melatonin production is also greatest during infancy and tends to decrease as we get older.

Like melatonin, REM-stage sleep falls in a parallel fashion as we age. REM sleep decreases from levels of 60-80% of sleep for fetuses to 50% of sleep for infants, and levels of only 15-20% for elderly persons. It is thus not surprising that children tend to sleep more than adults do. Our body's melatonin production decreases as we begin to be able to get by with less sleep. This decrease in melatonin levels also signals the body's start of puberty. This is notable, because melatonin given to young persons is not advised, simply because it can delay the onset of puberty.

Dopamine is a neurotransmitter/hormone that facilitates cognition together with the body's pleasure/reward responses. It is produced in the hypothalamus and other regions of the brain. Should the nervous system lack dopamine, cognition is interrupted, and the processes related to memory, learning, muscle control and movement are disturbed. Parkinson's disease, for example, is characterized by a lack of dopamine among the brain and nervous system.

Dopamine is also critical to sleep. Its availability is critical to the body's cycling through the sleep stages, with their characteristic changes in muscle control and rapid eye movement. Dopamine is also critical to the processes of memory consolidation.

Dopamine also balances sleepiness. Dopamine levels are increased during wakefulness, and it actually helps us stay awake and keep from dozing off when we should be awake. Research has found that a night of poor sleep will stimulate an increase in dopamine levels, as the body seeks to stay awake.

Energy-related hormones such as cortisol, testosterone, thyroid hormones, estrogen, epinephrine and other energy hormones serve to balance neurotransmitter flow. Hormones are produced by endocrine glands, which are stimulated by 'master hormones' released by the pituitary gland. The pituitary gland in turn is stimulated by the pineal gland, which is stimulated by the rhythms of light exposure. The pineal gland, together with special cells called SCN cells, provides a foundation for the body's biological rhythms.

Cortisol and related corticosteroids are directly associated with sleep because they are the anti-sleep hormones. Cortisol increases energy production, and along with testosterone, glucocorticoids, epinephrine, norepinephrine and others, stimulates blood flow and metabolic activity. The pharmaceutical form of cortisol is also better known as cortisone.

Most people have two peaks in cortisol production: one in the mid-morning and another in the early evening time. Some of us have stronger morning production and some of us have stronger evening production. Some might refer to this as the "morning person" or "evening person" syndrome. In healthy-rhythm people, cortisol release begins to slowly increase around 2 a.m. After peaking in the mid-morning (between 8 a.m. and 10 a.m.), it drops off in the early afternoon (the "siesta"). It again slowly picks up at about 3:30 p.m. and peaks again in the early evening, when it falls off dramatically. If we have built up a significant sleep debt, we will become sleepy in the afternoon during the afternoon cortisol dip. Once the afternoon cortisol pulse resumes, we can easily stave off our sleep debt with the surge of early evening hormones.

Hormones are also linked to the sleep stages—many to the early delta (N2) stages. **Growth hormone** (GH) release, for example, is associated not only with development, but also with cellular repair. Thus, we find that GH circulation is greatest during delta stage sleep.

Adenosine is also an important biochemical for sleep. Adenosine could be considered a hormone, but probably best described as a neurotransmitter. Adenosine has the distinction of slowing down corticoid secretions, which lower the level of cortisol release. This works to preserve sleep as the night goes on as melatonin levels begin to wane. Adenosine does this by modulating the adrenal gland through special receptors. Away from its active anti-cortisol role, adenosine also combines with phosphate molecules to form adenosine triphosphate and diphosphate, which are part of the cellular energy cycle.

Fat utilization and energy production are closely aligned with sleep cycles. Insomnia and sleep dysfunction have been associated with decreased leptin hormone levels and increased ghrelin levels, for example. The rhythms associated with leptin and ghrelin production are connected with the cycles of blood glucose and hunger. Thus sleep deficiency is linked to increased hunger and increased appetite, especially for high calorie, high carbohydrate foods.

More recently discovered hormones include two brain proteins called **orexin** and **hypocretin.** These proteins are produced in the hypothalamus and bind to receptors that signal wakefulness within the brain. They also stimulate an increase in core body temperature. Tests have shown that those who have narcolepsy (excessive sleepiness) have either a lack of these proteins or a reduction in their receptors.

In a healthy circadian rhythm, after sunset, our melatonin levels begin their rise, peaking around midnight supported by adenosine. That is, unless we have otherwise deranged our natural body clocks.

Light and Sleep

Our bodies are rhythmically synchronized to light. The dimming of light during the evening signals to our body's clocks multiple hormonal and cellular responses, drawing us toward sleep. As the sunset fades and darkness creeps into our respective caves, our SCN cells provide the switching signals. As they receive the photoelectric change, they trigger phosphorylation reactions and genetic bonding adjustments. These changes stimulate a release of the hormone melatonin into the bloodstream. As this takes place, our cortisol levels lower and our parasympathetic and sympathetic systems become primed for relaxation and the gradual glide into sleep.

Core body temperature levels are reduced progressively until about three in the morning. After about three, cortisol stimulates a rise in body temperature. Our sleep cycles begin to respond to this change, and our body prepares itself for waking up. Once eyes open to the daylight brought by the rising sun, our CLOCK genes are reset. Melatonin production halts as adrenocorticoid hormones surge through the blood. We are awake.

Research has shown that as little as 180 lux (lumens per square meter) of light can reset our body clocks. One lux equals the light of one candle, and a 100-watt light bulb glare at 10 feet away causes about 190 lux. We'll focus on light in more detail later.

We must be careful not to reset this CLOCK during the evening, however. Evening bright lights or computer screens can reset CLOCK if they are bright enough—restarting our flow of higher-energy biochemistry. Anxiety can also trigger a cortisone increase.

Our rhythm cycles and body clocks have been trained over millions of generations to reset with the rise and fall of the sun. A repetitive destruction of that rhythm can upset the CLOCK and disrupt various hormonal and neurotransmitter levels. Should our melatonin cycle be disturbed for example, we will have a hard time getting to sleep. Or if the cycle amplitude isn't high enough we might find ourselves waking in the 2am-3am zone as our body's cortisol levels begin to trickle into our bloodstream.

Should our evening rhythms be confused and we find ourselves in cyclic turmoil—combined with overthinking and anxiety—we may begin the bumpy ride of insomnia. We also face the potential of a double-reset cycle the next morning. Once the sun shines through in the morning before we are fully rested, our CLOCK system will reset for cortisol production.

After sunset, if our rhythms are not regular, our CLOCK undergoes a melatonin reset. Within these resets, our cells calculate our sleep-debt. An irregular pattern, however, increases the number of resets needed. This adds stress to the cells as they readjust.

If we are prone to stress responses and bright lights into our late nights, or turning on the television, computer or other stimulating activity past the melatonin peak, we risk our night rhythms being delayed, and running into the beginning of the new cortisol production phase. Should we pass this point awake—typically between two a.m. and three a.m.—we risk having a tough time getting to sleep because our cortisol cycle starts our cells whirring again before our melatonin cycle had a chance to come into full swing.

Once our rhythms are thrown off like this, a number of other disturbances can result. This is evident in sleep studies of shift-workers. Shift-workers suffer higher levels of mood and energy difficulties, decreased work performance, increased social and family relationship problems, deterioration of general health and wellness, and increases in disorders related to the gastrointestinal system, the cardiovascular system, and mental health (Costa 1996).

Our multiple body rhythms are harmonious in healthy persons. They pulse together in a symphony of synchronization. In a person with a deranged body clock, however, these cycles pulse at conflicting rhythms, negatively interfering with each other. This creates—literally—mixed signals throughout the body's metabolism.

As night falls, our pineal gland and hypothalamus coordinate to secrete melatonin. Say we get to thinking about a stressful subject during this period. We turn on some glaring lights to study the situation or write an email.

The stress stimulates our adrenal glands, and cortisol levels are punched up. Our cells switch to "alert" rather than "rest and revitalize" mode. As a result, our heart rate, breathing rate, brainwaves, cerebrospinal fluid, blood pressure and lymph circulation are all stimulated. Cellular conflicts between these cycles and melatonin's instructions to calm things down create the bleary-eyed insomniac. We cannot turn our mind off but we cannot function very well either.

Our hormonal rhythms become conflicted during stress, toxins, or nutritional deficiencies. Inadequate nutrition can weaken hormone production. Toxicity can also weaken or halt hormone production, as the body surges to eliminate the intruders. Each of these cumulates to set up a unique paradigm of conflicting cycles, moods and energy levels.

Each of us deals with a unique combination of body type, mental approach, motivations, environment, and people around us. As a result, we each foster a uniquely different array of body clock patterns and hormone cycles, just as each of us has a unique set of fingerprints.

These fingerprints translate to how our dreamscapes cycle along with our REM and NREM stages. As the light of dawn lights our eyelids, our cycles shorten and prepare us for exiting the dreamscape and entering the reality of physical life.

This can lead to some vivid dreaming because we often become more conscious of the fact that we will need to awake from our slumber. This often merges the context of our dreams with our concerns for the coming day.

How Much Dreaming Do We Need?

As we'll discuss later, there is a psychological purpose to our dreams, and research shows that if we don't get enough dreaming in, we will feel unrested and stressed through the day.

Thus we can directly relate this to sleep, because the amount of quality sleep directly relates to the amount of quality dreaming we will have.

And just as each of us dream unique dreams, our sleep requirements are unique to each of us. Some of us need more sleep and others need less sleep. To force a different sleep pattern upon someone can have disastrous effects. Lowered immunity and difficulty concentrating are just a few of the results from dramatically changing our sleep length or sleep parameters too quickly or without the proper guidance.

Still, there are patterns among us. Several large studies have found that optimal sleep duration for staying healthy is substantially less than the eight hours traditionally recommended by so many health experts, parents and others over the years.

In a study by researchers from the University of California-San Diego and the American Cancer Society (Kripke *et al.* 2002), 1.1 million adults were followed between 1982 and 1988. Survival rates (from death for any cause) were highest among those who slept an average of 7 hours per night.

Those who slept more than 8.5 hours per night had a 15% increased chance of death. Those that slept less than 6 hours also had an increased risk of dying. Those who took prescription sleeping pills also had increased mortality rates.

In another study (Ikehara et al 2009), 98,634 adults between the age of 40 and 79 years old were tracked for about 14 years. Mortality rates were compared to those who slept an average of seven hours per night. Those who slept under four hours per night had more than double the likelihood of dying from heart disease and other non-cancer deaths.

Those who slept an average of more than ten hours per night had nearly double the risk of dying from heart disease and other non-cancer deaths—again compared with those who slept an average of seven hours per night. Interestingly, there was no correlation between sleep duration and cancer incidence. When the total deaths were graphed against sleep duration in this study, the result was a U-shaped curve, with seven hours at the apex—meaning that seven-hour sleepers had the lowest risk of mortality.

Other studies over the past few decades have confirmed that lower mortality rates occur amongst those who have good quality sleep in the range of seven hours per night. In a review of twenty-three sleep-mortality studies from the Weinburg Center for Women's Health and Medicine (Gallichio and Kalesan 2009), both long sleepers (over 8.5 hours per night) and short sleepers (under 6 hours per night) had increased mortality rates from heart disease or cancer. Again, about seven hours was optimal.

Sleep research has also identified that long sleepers and short sleepers tend to have higher rates of obesity, stress, mental diseases and cognitive issues (Grandner *et al.* 2009).

Furthermore, those with sleep disorders such as restless leg syndrome (RLS) or periodic limb movement (PLM) have an increased risk of cardiovascular diseases and kidney disorders (Portaluppi *et al.* 2009).

Sleep among the elderly has other considerations. In a study from Okayama University's Graduate School of Medicine (Suzuki *et al.* 2009), 11,395 elderly adults between 65 and 85 years old were followed for seven years and analyzed for mortality risk. In this study, short sleep was not associated with a higher risk of cardiovascular mortality. Longer sleep duration was, however. Those sleeping longer hours, when compared to those who averaged about seven hours per night, had a greater risk of dying of heart disease.

Most of these studies were based on self-reports. In other words, the test subject answers a questionnaire about his/her sleep habits. A revealing study regarding self-reporting versus actual sleep duration is worth considering with sleep research statistics. The Department of Health Studies at the University of Chicago (Lauderdale *et al.* 2008) studied 669 adults for two years and measured their self-reported sleep averages against their actual sleep duration—obtained through sleep observation. They found that the average self-reported sleep duration was 6.8 hours, while the actual sleep duration averaged 6 hours.

This means that most of us calculate that we are sleeping more hours than we actually are. It also indicates that since most of the epidemiological studies on optimal sleep have measured sleep duration using self-reported sleep, there is a strong possibility that the real optimal sleep duration is closer to 6.25-6.5 hours of quality sleep per night. This is measuring the time between when we actually fall asleep and the time we actually wake up—which may be difficult for us to determine ourselves.

Even with this variance, seven hours is still a good number to remember. Since most of the above-mentioned studies utilized self-reported surveys from sleepers, our perception of sleep duration is likely to be equivalent to their self-reporting. Therefore, seven hours of sleep is still a good target, measured from our perception: when we think we fall asleep and wake up. After all, sleep includes quite a bit of relativity all the way around.

These studies of course apply to adults. Children should sleep far more hours than adults, depending upon their age. A healthy infant can sleep anywhere from 10-20 hours per day. This decreases with age, to 10-15 hours after one-years old, 9-12 hours until the age of twelve, and 8-10 hours during the teenage years. Less sleep during these formative years can have drastic consequences upon development, both physically and psychologically—for reasons we'll discuss in more detail later.

Nevertheless, we each have unique biological clocks, and thus have slightly different sleep requirements. This fact is supported by research from Harvard Medical School (Aeschbach *et al.* 2003) that showed that short sleepers had different biological clocks than did long sleepers. They studied 24 young adult volunteers, ten of which were long sleepers and 14 of which were short sleepers.

They found that the short sleepers and the long sleepers had similar relationships between their physiological conditions (such as body temperature and hormone levels) and their sleep particular duration. In other words, the length of their "biological nights" was relative to their sleep duration regardless of how long they normally slept.

At the end of the day, as a rough rule of thumb, the best duration of sleep is the minimal level before daytime sleepiness takes hold. If we are falling asleep during the day, especially when trying to stay awake, we are not getting enough sleep. Let's look at this angle a bit deeper.

What if We Don't Get Enough Dreaming?

Regardless of our age and biological clock, if we do not get our accustomed sleep and dreaming during a particular night, we will develop what is called sleep debt—but this is directly related to what we will coin in this text as *dream debt.*

Sleep debt is a cellular record of sleep obtained versus sleep required. Dream debt is the absence of enough healthy dreaming to accommodate the brain and the mind's needs.

Sleep debt is balanced against the backdrop of hormonal cycles, metabolic cycles and cellular regeneration programming. There is also immune system memory and genetic triggers for sleep debt, but determining these with precision is quite difficult.

Even an infant sleeping twice as much as an adult will build up sleep debt should the infant be kept awake or otherwise be prevented from getting their nominal hours of sleep per night.

Likewise, if the adult were to be sleeping an hour a night less than their functional minimum, then sleep debt would begin to build up in the form of cellular exhaustion. This sleep debt requires that we sleep additional hours to bring our metabolism back to a functional balance.

Sleep and dream deprivation causes a number of physical, emotional and mental problems. These can include brain fog, reduced memory, reduced immune function, slower healing, reduced productivity, daytime drowsiness and inhibited cognition. Sleep loss and especially dream deprivation can also cause psychosis and hallucinations.

Two studies have provided the foundation for our understanding of sleep debt. The first was a study conducted at the U.S. Naval Hospital in Maryland. In this experiment, Navy seamen were incubated in small, dark chambers for one week around the clock. They had no sense of time, and no external stimuli, including light or technology. They were also attached to electrodes, which measured their sleep parameters.

The study found that during the first few days, most seamen sleep up to 25 hours straight. But after a few days, they settled into a sleep duration approximating 8 hours for the remainder of the study (Dement and Vaughan 1999).

The experiment was not solely about sleep, but sleep researchers gained an awareness of sleep debt. During the first few days of the study, the seamen worked off their sleep debt. Once their sleep debt was worked off, they settled into fairly normal cycles that approximated their circadian clocks.

Another study had a similar result. This study was conducted by researchers from the National Institute of Mental Health (Wehr *et al.* 1998). This study focused more specifically on sleep debt. Sixteen volunteers went about their normal days but reported to a sleep laboratory at 4:00 p.m. everyday for 14 weeks. Their sleeping quarters were darkened and had no lights. From 5 p.m. to 7 a.m., they would lie in their beds with no stimulation: Just darkness for 14 hours every day.

As in the Navy study, for the first few weeks, the subjects slept long and hard, up to 12 hours a day. After about the fourth week, and through the end of the study, their sleep hours settled in at 7.5 to 9 hours of sleep.

Eventually the researchers reduced the hours of darkness from 14 hours to 10 hours per night. What this means is that when they entered the study, they brought in plenty of accumulated sleep debt. The researchers calculated the average sleep debt to be about 30 hours each.

Note that these volunteers were healthy when they began the study. This indicates that they (and likely most of us) are carrying around a significant amount of sleep debt.

The question this brings up is whether sleep debt is such a bad thing. Multiple studies have shown that some sleep debt is necessary to bring about normal sleeping patterns (Duncan *et al.* 2009). In other words, sleepiness is brought on by sleep debt: We need it to fall asleep. Every day we accumulate some sleep debt while we are awake.

The question is how much debt we can accumulate from previous nights before we are fighting daytime drowsiness. Some sleep debt is necessary to fall asleep each night. This influence of sleep debt on getting to sleep is called *sleep pressure* or *sleep inertia*. Without sleep inertia, we are faced with random bouts of insomnia, depending upon our moods and physiological factors.

Over time, our bodies have become adjusted to unique sleep patterns, complete with certain sleep cycles and stages. Our optimal sleep pattern to maintain a healthy state depends upon our body's metabolism, diet, age, cellular and genetic makeup. For example, a healthy infant might be healthy sleeping 15 hours per night and waking every hour or two, while a healthy adult's healthy sleep is a continuous seven hours per night. For discussion-sake, let's call the difference between optimal sleep and actual sleep, *sleep variance.*

Sleep debt is not exactly like credit card debt, where the exact amount that is charged needs to be paid back with interest. It is not an exact hour-for-hour loan account.

If anything, the amount of sleep debt is far less than the actual sleep variance. This means that a person could short an hour of sleep every night for a week, and they may only need an extra two hours a night for two nights (four hours) to catch up on their sleep debt.

This relates directly to dream debt, but with even more flexibility. While a person may only require four sleep hours to catch up on a sleep loss of seven hours, they may only need one or two hours of deep REM-stage dreaming in order to recover their dream debt.

The calculations on payback for both sleep debt and dream debt are highly individual. The determinants are not consistent among everyone. In the example above, another person may only need an extra two hours for one night to be caught up on his or her sleep debt, and may require only a half-hour of REM-dreaming.

Sleep debt will typically also occur with REM-stage sleep deprivation. If we are short on our REM-stage sleep, we will also need to catch up by getting more REM-stage dreaming. This REM variance catch-up might not affect the total hours slept, however.

But during the REM catch-up period, NREM-stage sleep might lag, which may create some additional stress and anxiety. This in turn might have to be resolved by sleeping an hour or more each day to catch up on NREM-stage sleep. Without this, our REM-stage and NREM-stage sleep cycles will be out of balance, disrupting our entire cycle.

Sleep debt and thus dream debt can accumulate for a very long period: Years in fact. A person who is missing sleep and dreaming for a full year may fall into a state of exhaustion due to their accumulation of this deprivation. As a result, they may end up sleeping an extra 2-3 hours per night for a month or two to catch up on that sleep debt. Again, it is highly individual. The catch-up period depends upon how much sleep was missed combined with current sleep quality and hygiene; along with the person's relative stress levels, traumatic experiences and how they individually deal with problems.

Sleep Debt Calculation
(Using Epworth Sleepiness Scale)

0 =	Would not doze
1 =	Slight chance of dozing
2 =	Moderate chance of dozing
3 =	High chance of dozing
_____	Sitting while reading
_____	Sitting while watching television
_____	Sitting in a public place (inactive)
_____	Sitting in a car (as a passenger)
_____	Sitting while talking with someone
_____	Sitting alone after lunch
_____	Lying down to rest in the afternoon
_____	Driving, or stopped at a stoplight or in traffic
	TOTAL SCORE

Sleep Debt Rating:

0-5	Little or no sleep debt
6-10	Moderate sleep debt
11-20	Heavy sleep debt
21-25	Extreme sleep debt

(Adapted from Dement and Vaughan 1999)

Calculating Our Sleep Needs

This question may sound odd to someone who has some sort of insomnia, but it is a pertinent piece of information to have as we begin our journey back to optimal sleep. We each need a unique amount of sleep, depending upon a number of factors:

Summary of Sleep Variance Factors

Age	Younger people need more sleep than older people
Gender	Women tend to need more sleep than men, especially during pregnancy, nursing, or menstruation.
Genes	Sleep patterns tend to move in families (could also be family habits)

Season	Colder weather and winter-time tends to increase sleep need
Physical exertion	Days with more physical activity require more sleep than days of low activity
Sun	Increased sun exposure tends to increase sleep quality and decrease sleep requirements
Stress	People leading more stressful lives tend to need more sleep than those leading lives of minimal stress
Health	Healthier people tend to need less sleep than those burdened with toxicity
Sickness	Lower immunity/illness tends to increase our need for sleep

Summary of Dream Variance Factors

Age	Younger people tend to dream more than older people
Gender	Women tend to dream more than men, especially during pregnancy, nursing, or menstruation.
Genes	Dream patterns tend to be relative to body type and ancestry rather than direct genetic variances.
Season	Spring and fall periods tend to increase dreaming
Physical exertion	Days with more physical activity produce greater dreaming than days of low activity
Sun	Increased sun exposure tends to increase dream quality and decrease dream requirements
Stress	People leading more stressful lives tend to need more dreaming than those leading lives of minimal stress
Health	Healthier people tend to need less dreaming than those burdened with toxicity
Sickness	Lower immunity/illness tends to increase our dream needs

One of the best ways to calculate our *current* sleep requirements was developed by renowned sleep researcher, William Dement, M.D. His method is called the Multiple Sleep Latency Test, or MSLT. Here is how the test is calculated:

The subject lies down in bed in a dark, quiet room with the intent of falling asleep for up to 20 minutes. Optimally the test is performed for multiple periods at least two hours apart, from 10 a.m. to 6 p.m. The number of minutes it takes to fall asleep is the score. If the person falls asleep after the first minute, this is a score of 1. After five minutes, this is 5. After ten minutes, this is 10. After twenty minutes, the score is 20. If the subject is not asleep in twenty minutes, the sleep test is discontinued and the score is 20.

In his many years of research, Dr. Dement determined that if a subject has a score of 0 to 5, they likely have severe sleep debt or a sleep disorder. A score of 10-15 minutes is fairly healthy. A score of 20 is unusual. A score of 20 indicates unusual alertness.

This test can gauge the quality and quantity of our sleep. We just need someone to watch the clock and check in on us every few minutes (quietly) to see if we have fallen asleep yet. To get a good fix on our sleep, we can do two tests in an afternoon to rate our current sleep quality. If we fall asleep within five minutes, we know that we need to be getting more sleep. If we fall asleep within the first minute or two, our sleep debt is likely extremely high, and/or our latency (time it takes to get to sleep) is at an unsustainable level and needs to be corrected.

Using the MSLT on a regular basis by picking at least one of those time periods (10, 12, 2, 4 or 6 p.m.), we can monitor our sleep debt and latency by taking note of our sleep hours each night, and also our MSLT number. Over time, we can determine how much sleep we need to be rested (at least 10 on the MSLT scale), and possibly even determine our optimal sleep requirement (15 or higher on the MSLT scale).

Note that a MSLT score inside of five indicates danger.

We should not be driving. We should not be operating heavy machinery. We should not be doing anything that could result in the injury of others or ourselves if we were to fall asleep or otherwise slip up as a result of delayed reaction times.

Sleep Disorders

Sleep issues are often related to other conditions, just as dreams are. These include depression, hepatitis, cancer, alcoholism, migraine, post-traumatic stress disorder and many others.

There are also a number of insomnia-related sleep disorders: These include sleep apnea, restless leg syndrome, narcolepsy, cataplexy, circadian rhythm disorder and others. Types of circadian rhythm disorders include time-zone change, shift-work sleep disorder, irregular sleep-wake pattern, delayed sleep-phase syndrome, advanced sleep-phase syndrome and 24-hour sleep-wake syndrome. Other sleep disorders include such obvious issues as inadequate sleep hygiene, environmental sleep disorder (heat, cold, noise, light, etc.), adjustment sleep disorder (temporary stressful event), nocturnal eating or drinking syndrome, and hypnotic-dependent sleep disorder. Here is a summary of the major sleep disorders and their underlying issue:

Sleep Disorder	Issue
Sleep apnea	Sudden awakening
Restless leg syndrome	Motion/discomfort in legs
Narcolepsy	Lack of sleep control
Cataplexy	Lack of muscle control
Shift-work sleep disorder	Inability to handle shifts
Irregular sleep-wake pattern	Sleep timing problems
Delayed sleep-phase syndrome	Sleep phase problems
Advanced sleep-phase syndrome	Sleep phase problems
24-hour sleep-wake	Sleep timing problems

syndrome	
Sleep hygiene disorder	Sleep pattern problems
Environmental sleep disorder	Inability to adapt to environment
Adjustment sleep disorder	Inability to adjust to sleep change
Nocturnal eating syndrome	Eating too late
Nocturnal drinking syndrome	Drinking too late
Hypnotic-dependent sleep disorder	Requiring pharmaceuticals to sleep

Sleep studies have defined insomnia as either difficulty falling asleep for greater than 30 minutes (extreme sleep latency); difficulty sleeping enough by 85% or more (sleep efficiency); or erratic or disturbed sleep (sleep disturbance) for more than 3 times per week and for longer than one month.

There are a number of scales used to establish and gauge the existence and severity of insomnia. Validated questionnaires such as the Pittsburgh Sleep Quality Index (PSQI), the Sleep Associated Monitoring Index (SAMI), and various sleep log formats help assess the presence and severity of insomnia. The SLEEP L system is a diagnosis tool, while the Structured Clinical Interview for DSM-IV (SCID), the Short-Form 36 (SF-36), and the Epworth Sleepiness Scale (ESS) each examine consequential and adjunctive issues. Sleep labs usually use polysomnography to reveal specific tendencies. These tools have been useful to sleep researchers in gauging sleep disorders over the last 40 years.

Chronic diseases increase the likelihood of insomnia. This is illustrated by decreased levels of plasma TNF (tumor necrosis factor) and interleukin-6 during insomnia bouts, which increase with healthy circadian rhythms. Because these two factors are immune activators, their decrease is associated with a weakened immune system and subsequently, a variety of illnesses.

Studies have shown that insomnia is greater among those with greater alcohol consumption, those on regular medications, those with psychiatric disturbances, and/or those in noisy nocturnal environments. A number of medications have been found to interrupt or disturb sleep, including corticosteroids, decongestants, ß-agonists, ß-blockers, diuretics, antidepressants, and H-2 blockers. Many of these drugs also have been known to inhibit the absorption of nutrients from our foods, some of which are necessary for serotonin and melatonin production.

Most of these disorders affect our dreams negatively. Quite simply, they prevent us from having deep and productive dreams. Therefore, they are disruptive to our ability to dream. Here is a discussion of a few of the most disruptive sleep disorders.

Obstructive Sleep Apnea

If we are a loud snorer, and find that we are extremely sleepy during the day—even when seemingly sleeping enough hours—there is a good possibility we have sleep apnea. A person with sleep apnea will typically stop breathing for several seconds—up to 30-40 seconds several times per hour. This can occur sometimes up to 15 times an hour. They may also wake up in a panicked manner, almost out of breath, feeling like they are choking. They may or may not be aware of this—most likely not. Should our sleeping mate tell us we stop breathing while we sleep, we should seriously consider talking to a health professional about sleep apnea. Sleep apnea is a very serious sleep disorder that can be life threatening. It can also be at the root of a number of chronic ailments.

Sleep apnea is the obstruction and narrowing of the upper airways, often occurring in those who are obese and/or those who sleep supine (i.e., on the back). The cause may be rooted in throat tissue obstruction, a tumor, or brainstem issues in the medullar portion of the brain. Complications and effects of sleep apnea include daytime sleepiness, headaches, mental slowness, cardiac and pulmonary infections and immune deficiency (getting sick often). Depression and cognition difficulties have also been seen among people with sleep apnea.

Recent research has indicated that patients with a body mass index over 35 have a greater than 70% probability of having sleep apnea (Ringdahl *et al.* 2004). Another study on 1,166 apnea patients concluded that women are more likely to remain undiagnosed for sleep apnea (Quintana-Gallego *et al.* 2004).

By far the greatest danger of sleep apnea is the restriction of air supply to the point of suffocation. Outside of suffocation, brain damage or heart attack may occur due to the lack of oxygen. During the day, another danger exists. This is the danger of falling asleep while driving, operating machinery or other hazard during the daytime.

Narcolepsy and Cataplexy

Narcolepsy is a condition whereby a person has seemingly little control over their sleep habits, notably falling asleep during odd times during the day, and sometimes while conducting physical activity. A person with narcolepsy may fall asleep while they are working, eating or even driving.

This can become a dangerous proposition, especially when driving. The severity of narcolepsy can be variable. It can range from a mild case of falling asleep during periods of relaxation to falling asleep during more stressful or active times. Should we be repeatedly falling asleep and dreaming during the day, narcolepsy should be investigated.

Furthermore, the narcoleptic almost invariably falls directly into REM-stage sleep. This can create other problems. Falling directly into REM-stage sleep will bypass the all-important NREM sleep stages. This will inhibit our problem solving and resolution. Falling directly into REM-stage can create rather stark breaks between REM and waking as well. Without the gradual lowering of consciousness into the REM dream stage, REM dreams can dramatically incorporate waking realities. Waking directly out of REM dreaming can also be startling for the narcoleptic. This is often the reason for some of the bizarre oc-currences among narcoleptics.

Cataplexy sometimes accompanies narcolepsy. Cata-plexy occurs in approximately 30% of narcolepsy cases. Cataplexy is accompanied by a sudden loss of muscle tone and strength. This can result in a sagging of the body; fal-ling down; or a loss of the ability to move while awake. Because a complete loss of muscle control is a normal part of REM sleep, the narcoleptic experiences this loss of con-trol at any time of the day. And because the transition between REM dreaming and waking is so abrupt in the narcoleptic, the narcoleptic can often exhibit the catatonic state while awake.

Shift Work Sleep Disorder

This disorder is caused by a shift in sleeping rhythm. This may be caused by a change in work schedules or some other trauma: Any activity or stressor that substan-tially changes a person's sleeping cycle. A shift in sleep cycles can have a traumatic effect upon the body in many ways. This disorder is so named because it is typically caused by a change in shift work schedules. Regardless of whether caused by a work schedule or trauma, the result is the same: A difficulty sleeping, and then a difficulty waking at a desired time.

For example, let's say that we normally work a 1 p.m. to 9 p.m. shift. We get home at 10 p.m. and get to bed at 12 midnight, and awake at 7 a.m. The boss suddenly asks us to begin working the 9 p.m. to 5 a.m. shift. So we begin working this shift, but instead of being able to fall asleep at 7 a.m. and sleep until 2 p.m. (our normal 7 hours), our hormones prevent us from sleeping at this time of day. We end up sleeping lightly five hours a day if we are lucky. We now have shift work sleep disorder.

Circadian Rhythm Disorder

Most insomniacs have some sort of circadian rhythm disorder. Circadian rhythm disorder may well be the root cause of our sleep issues. Or another disturbance may create our circadian rhythm disorder.

The central theme in this disorder is that our daily sequencing of waking and sleeping hours have been severely discombobulated. Let's say we stay up late a few nights to cram for an exam. Once the exam is done, our timing has become messed up and we can't sleep at our normal bedtime. This is because our circadian clock has been altered.

An important thing to understand about circadian rhythm disorder is that if we cannot fall asleep on time for a few days in a row for any reason—such as stress or a financial problem—this may be enough to change our circadian rhythm. This will make it harder to get to sleep every day thereafter. It is important in this case to readjust our biological clock, as we'll discuss in detail.

Delayed Sleep Phase Syndrome

This sleep disorder is thought to be caused by our endogenous circadian pacemaker freezing at a late phase, causing a modulation in the sleep and waking cycles. DSPS is poorly understood by medical and research science, and research is ongoing. Here the phases of early stage and REM-stage sleep are slowed, with more than the typical 90-minute cycles in between. Advanced sleep phase syndrome will have the same problems as other phase issues, except the correction measures may require a more advanced approach.

REM Sleep Behavior Disorder

Rapid eye movement is critical for healthy sleep, as we will investigate further. While we might fall asleep and sleep reasonably well through to the morning, our sleep may not have sufficient rapid eye movement sleep. This results in a reduction in REM-stage dreaming. This has a number of consequences to our waking life stability.

REM sleep behavior disorder is also commonly referred to as RBD. It has also been described as parasomnia. Once considered to only occur among older men, sleep studies have indicated that many children also have RBD:

Especially those children with poor sleep hygiene or an abundance of nightmares.

The lack of REM-sleep causes the sleeper to be unable to complete acting out dreams to completion. This results in anxiety, depression and a variety of other behavioral disorders. Some researchers have found that RBD is associated with self-infliction and bullying among children. In adults, various neurodegenerative disorders have been linked to RBD, including Parkinson's, epilepsy and various mental disorders.

Irregular Sleep-Wake Pattern

Most of us have a regular pattern of hours we sleep. We also have a semi-regular time that we feel tired and fall asleep. We will then awake at a time that is typical for the hours of sleep we typically get. For example, if we normally go to bed at 11 p.m. and rise at 7 a.m., and then we stay up Friday night until 1 a.m., it would be normal for us to awake at 9 a.m.

If, however, we fall asleep at different times of the night, and then sleep five hours some nights and seven hours on other nights, we have an irregular sleep-wake pattern. This means that we have deranged our body clocks.

Non-24-hour Sleep-Wake Syndrome

Here there is a significant discrepancy in our circadian rhythm with regard to sleeping. Instead of being tired at around the same time each night, we will be tired an hour or two earlier or later each night. This means that our cycle will soon move all around the clock. This can in turn result in a complete loss of sleep on days when we have to wake in the morning to go to work.

Sleep Hygiene Disorder

Here the person does not adequately prepare for sleep, and/or cannot fall asleep using typical scenarios. Sleep hygiene is the preparation and control of the environmental and physical conditions that promote a restful sleep.

For example, if we cannot fall asleep unless we have a light on, then we may have a sleep hygiene disorder.

Sleep hygiene is critically important for consistent sleep. SHD can lead to a host of other sleep complications should our hygiene conditions not be met.

Environmental Sleep Disorder

This is similar to sleep hygiene disorder, except that it is related specifically to the external environment, rather than a combination of sleep preparation components.

For example, if we cannot fall asleep when the house is quiet and dark, but we can fall asleep in a noisy living room full of kids, we may have environmental sleep disorder.

Adjustment Sleep Disorder

Here we find it difficult to fall asleep in any kind of changing situation. In other words, if we can only sleep in our own bed, or if we sleep late one day and cannot fall asleep that night, then we may have this disorder. We need to be able to fall asleep even if there is a minor adjustment to our schedule. If we are hamstrung to a stringent schedule in order to sleep, we likely have this condition.

Nocturnal Eating Syndrome

As indicated, this condition is simply feeling the need to eat late in order to fall asleep. Some refer to this as 'midnight snacking' but this condition takes eating much further. Having to gorge on two large bowls of ice cream with all the toppings and feel 'full' before we can fall asleep is more than a 'midnight snack.'

This also applies to alcohol. Nocturnal drinking syndrome addresses not being able to sleep unless we have drank a certain amount of alcohol. This can also apply to drinking non-alcoholic drinks, but this is rare.

Nightmares

Research from the Department of Clinical Psychology of Utrecht University has classified nightmares as a sleep disorder. Frightening dreams can disrupt sleep by wakening the sleeper. They can then prevent the sleeper from falling back to sleep. Polysomnographic recordings illustrate that nightmares can be either idiopathic or post-traumatic in context.

Either of these can cause distress and lessen sleep, although post-traumatic nightmares tend to cause more wake-ups and prevent falling back to sleep. Nightmares also can cause mental pathologies, creating phobias and other types of problematic behavior (Spoormaker *et al.* 2006).

We'll discuss this topic in detail later.

Parasomnias

Parasomnias refer to a range of sleep disorders that typically combine with some type of physical motion. These can include sleepwalking, bruxism (teeth grinding), and restless leg syndrome. They can also include talking in ones sleep, or even shouting and yelling during sleep. Parasomnia types are divided between REM-stage parasomnias and non-REM-stage parasomnias.

REM-stage parasomnia means that a person begins to move around during a deep REM-stage sleep. This often results in bizarre activities, which the sleeper is not aware of and does not remember. There is some controversy as to whether this is true REM sleep, however, because during REM sleep, the body is considered atonic, or motionless.

Non-REM sleep parasomnia often takes place between sleep stages, as the sleeper moves from one stage to the next. For example, the sleeper may move from N1 to N2, and during the transition, begin to clench the jaws and grind the teeth.

Restless Leg Syndrome

RLS is a type of parasomnia. This is a condition where a person jerks, twitches, kicks or restlessly moves the legs around while trying to sleep. This condition affects millions of Americans, and is often a cause of insomnia. In this condition, people often experience leg cramps and fatigue. There are a number of variances in the condition, including leg extension and flexion; toe and ankle extension; knee bending and extension; and even arm spans. Some say that dopamine deficiency is a central cause. Nutrient deficiencies, including iron deficiency, calcium and magnesium deficiency, B vitamin deficiency and others have been seen in RLS as well. Hypoglycemia has also been linked to RLS, and certain medications have been shown to aggravate RLS symptoms.

Recent research (Minai *et al.* 2008) has shown that pulmonary hypertension increases the risk of RLS. In this study, 54% of PH patients also had RLS. RLS occurred among hypothyroidism patients at a rate of 64%. The mechanism appears to be that venous weakness can result in increased temperatures in the legs. This causes the leg sweating and irritability characteristic in RLS.

Sleepwalking

Sleepwalking, or somnambulism as it is known in the medical world, is a parasomnia that is typically associated with non-REM sleep. It is typically seen when the sleeper is deep in slow-wave sleep, which mostly occurs in the later part of the sleep cycles.

Sleepwalking has been associated with chronic sleep deprivation. This is also sometimes accompanied by mild dementia or the taking of psychotic drugs. Quetiapine and olanzapine are examples of drugs that have at times resulted in sleepwalking.

The onset of Parkinson's disease has also been followed by sleepwalking. Currently researchers are perplexed by this association. In one study done by researchers from the Zurich University Hospital (Poryazova *et al.* 2007), 165

Parkinson's disease patients were followed for two years. Six of these 165 began sleepwalking—a much higher rate than occurs amongst the normal population.

The maximum onset timing for sleepwalking was four years after developing Parkinson's disease. The researchers analyzed the medications the PD patients were taking. The sleepwalking patients were all taking levodopa. Four of the six were also taking dopamine agonists, and three were taking selective serotonin reuptake inhibitors and hypnotics. The association between these medications and sleepwalking appear quite similar to the sleepwalking side effect reports that arose from the medications mentioned above.

Childhood sleepwalking, in contrast, often subsides during adolescence. Thus, many physicians and medical researchers have concluded that sleepwalking in children is not necessarily something to be concerned about, unless the child is causing harm to himself or herself, or to others.

There are many other types of sleep disorders. These are the most common, and those that are the most likely to affect our ability to dream.

Chapter Two

The Reason We Dream

Dream Theories

There have been several theories of dreaming that we ought to discuss. These are peer-reviewed researchers, many of which spent many years performing sleep studies and interviewing subjects.

Freud's Unconscious Mind Dream Theory

This theory was proposed by Freud in his 1900 book, *Interpretation of Dreams.* Freud suggested that our dreams allowed us to explore our unconscious mind, a secret identity that had desires that were otherwise hidden from the conscious mind.

The theory was interwoven with Freud's proposition that our identities contain several layers, including the ego and super-ego, which are our socialized selves and idealized selves, respectively. Beneath these dwells the id, which he described as our primitive self.

Freud's dream theory had many followers, and they supposed that there was a storehouse of latent desires—primarily sexual in nature—that were played out during our dreamscapes. These, he believed, were repressed by the conscious mind because they are so outlandish and socially unacceptable. In our dreamscape, Freud theorized, we could exercise libido desires without endangering our social self.

Jung's Theory of Collective Unconsciousness

Carl Jung, a Swiss psychiatrist who was a peer and research partner with Freud, eventually broke with Freud's dream theory.

Jung surmised that during our dreams, we could access a collective memory database of all humanity, including an ancient memory archive, which he called the collective unconsciousness.

The idea is that the experiences and desires of other humans, along with the memories of those who lived before us, creates some sort of pool, which can be swum through during our dreams.

This theory has been largely rejected by scientists, who call the theory unverifiable.

Gustavus Miller's Future Dreaming

Gustavus Hindman Miller was a celebrated author and dream interpreter around the turn of the 19th century. His dream research utilized dream recall of many people, who would write him and travel many miles to visit with him for dream interpretation. His view was that within most dreams were symbols that foretold future events in our lives and in the lives of others. According to Miller:

> A dream is an event transpiring in that world belonging to the mind when the objective senses have withdrawn into rest or oblivion. Then the spiritual man is living alone in the future of ahead of objective life and consequently lives man's future first, developing conditions in a way that enables working man to shape his actions by warnings, so as to make life a perfect existence.

Miller met with so many people, documented in his writings,

As indicated here, Miller put significant emphasis on the spiritual aspect of a person. His writings on dream interpretation emphasized that dreams gave warnings about the future. These ranged from family problems, to wealth, health and longevity.

Activation-Synthesis Theory

This theory was proposed by Hobson and McCarley in 1977. The theory states that dreams are simply random neuron firings from the brain. They supposed that since the brain's neurons record events from the senses, during sleep the brain fires back those images sequentially. The brain's activity during REM was thought to be spontaneously active, making "neural noise." The brain is supposedly trying to make sense of the sequential firings.

According to the theory, this activation step of neural noise is then synthesized together with external stimuli coming in from the senses during sleeping. The brain supposedly synthesizes the external stimuli together with the neuronal firing.

The portion of the theory supported by observation was that many dreams will incorporate external sounds, temperature and other external stimulation. This was shown in Dement and Wolpert's 1958 dream research, where they woke up sleepers while they were in REM-stage sleep.

The Restoration Model

Research from the mid-sixties to early 1980s, Oswald surmised that the purpose of dreaming was to restore the brain's supply of neurochemistry. It was supposed that during the day, the body exhausted the brain's supplies of neurochemicals such as dopamine, serotonin and others. For example, baby's and fetuses appear to have significant amounts of these chemicals, and thus have more REM-stage sleep. It was also surmised that this explains why exercise seems to increase the duration of REM-stage sleep and dreaming.

The criticism of this theory is that it fails to explain why a person has definite dream architecture and so on.

The Rubbish Model

Dr. Francis Crick and Dr. Graeme Mitchison came up with this theory in 1983. Dr. Crick is the Nobel prize winner for his participation in the revelations on DNA.

This theory supposed that dreaming is simply the brain's disposal mechanism. They surmised that what is dreamed is being discarded by the brain. The unwanted "rubbish" is tossed out by assembling it into a throwaway process.

Their concept is based upon a popular theory that was supported by Evans (1984) that memories were equivalent to files being stored away in a computer memory, and this memory must be periodically purged to allow for room for new memories.

Crick and Mitchison's theory also suggested that remembering our dreams could thus be damaging to our mental health because these are memories that are being dumped.

This of course contradicts Freud's theories that remembering and working through our dreams provided a facility for mental health.

This also seems to be contradicted by the observation by scientists that new neuron connections are made with new memories, and older neuron connections have not been observed to be destroyed and replaced by new memories.

The selective process of which memories are discarded (considered rubbish) and which ones are not appears implausible in the face of this theory, in the opinion of many researchers.

One thing to also consider is that some animals, like dolphins, do not appear to have REM-stage sleep. Yet they do not have enlarged brains, as would be the result if REM-sleep were needed to discard neuron connections.

It also does not answer why fetuses and infants have fabulous REM-stage dreams with little if any external stimuli to process as memories worth removing or retaining. Infants will typically sleep three hours for every one-hour awake at the early stages. About half of this sleep has been observed as being REM-stage sleep.

And how about those "novel" dreams that we have, such as falling or flying or otherwise. These are obviously not memories to be thrown out, because they are not memories at all.

Mental Reorganization

Another theory, put forth by Dr. Robert Ornstein in 1986, supposed that during our dreaming we are reorganizing our memories and consolidating them. This supposes that our synapses are being altered so that the memories will be more efficiently accessed. Meanwhile, more room for new memories is being developed through the reorganization.

This reorganization and consolidation process, according to the theory, takes place almost exclusively during REM-stage sleep, and this is composed together with any new external stimuli during the dreaming.

This theory is of course conflicted by infant and fetus dreaming, much of which is decidedly REM-stage sleep. What would the fetus and infant need to reorganize and consolidate?

Some have proposed that infants and fetuses are actually trying to develop their synapse pathways during their dreaming. Maybe, it has been supposed, they are trying to prepare their synapses for new memories.

Cognitive Theory

This dream theory was suggested by Dr. Richard Evans in 1984. It aligned with the notion that our brain comes pre-programmed, and our personal experiences afterward must be reconciled with this pre-programming.

The dream-state, according to this theory, is a time when the brain can go "off-line" and test out the notions of our experiences that lie outside the ordinary programming. They theory states that during this period, the brain also performs efficiency processes of filing away and organizing memories. In this respect, the theory incorporates the reorganization theory just discussed.

The theory also states that we try to make sense of our memories during REM-stage dreaming.

Chapter Three

NREM and REM-stage Dreams

Many of the theories discussed were conceived by scientists who have either been directly involved in sleep research or have investigated sleep research. They are the central theories of dreaming according to science. They of course also lie outside of traditional theories relating to dream interpretation.

The sleep study is a more scientific approach to sleep and sleep research. It is also used to diagnose sleep disorders in individuals. During a sleep study, the researcher attaches a variety of wire electrodes to the head and parts of the torso. These are connected to a router that connects the electrodes to different physiological measuring devices. With these attached, the subject lays down for a hopefully restful night of sleep, while the equipment monitors the body's metabolic and electrical physiology throughout the night.

This is called *polysomnography,* or PSG, better known as a *sleep study.* The test result is called a polysomnogram—also abbreviated as PSG. The name is derived from Greek and Latin roots: the Greek *poly* for 'multi-channel' or 'many,' the Latin *somnus* for 'sleep,' and the Greek *graphein* meaning 'to write.'

A polysomnographic recording combines readings from an electrooculograph (EOG), an electrocardiograph (ECG), an electroencephalograph (EEG), an elctromyograph, (EMG), a pulse monitor and a respiratory monitor. These together collect data measuring eye movement, heart activity, brain wave and electrical activity, muscle activity, pulse activity and lung function, respectively.

Because each part of the body is active during different stages of sleep, the combination of data readings from this equipment allow the researcher to correlate sleep depth and staging. This allows the researcher to determine the quality and functionality of the sleep, and diagnose eccentricities from the normal patterns of most sleepers. These are often called *sleep disorders.*

Thus, polysomnographic recordings offer researchers a

comprehensive recording of the bio-physiological changes that occur during sleep. It is usually performed at a sleep center, where the subject cuddles up in a sterile bed inside a laboratory environment.

While sleep research can be very reliable, sleeping in a strange bed with wires attached to the head and torso does not exactly create a replication of a typical night's sleep for most of us. This in itself prevents many people from undergoing a sleep study. This of course, keeps most of us in the dark (no pun intended) about the quality of our sleep—and whether we have any sleep disorders.

New devices have been invented to screen sleep without as many electrodes and head attachments. Some have also been designed for the sleeper to use at home. One of the more popular of these is called the Watch-Pat 100®, developed by sleep researcher David White, M.D. This small device takes readings from the hand and fingers and stores them on a removable disk, which can be put onto a computer. This allows a person to do a home sleep study in the comfort of his or her own bedroom.

The Dream Stages

During our first light stage sleep (N1) we begin to sort through the visual stimuli and memories of the day. Our brains and minds are processing information. As they do this, short-term memories and long-term memories are sorted and compared.

We prioritize their importance, and store away or trash them as appropriate. During N1, we ponder problems and sort through priorities. This has been termed *hypnagogia,* which characterizes the state at sleep's edge where we have short, partially visual dreams. These have also been called *dreamlets.*

The mechanics behind this include the processing of prefrontal neuron contextual memories through the hippocampus. This processing produces the memory consolidation process mentioned earlier.

During the second N2 stage, we get more serious about our consolidation process. Here we try to work through problems, and seriously reprioritize our event memories. During this stage, we complete the conversion of memories into long-term and short-term. We also eliminate many images and memories at this stage: By *eliminate,* we mean *forget.*

So is forgetting a conscious process? This depends upon our definition of consciousness. If by consciousness, we mean the conscious living being or self within the body, then yes, forgetting is a process driven by con-sciousness. If we mean conscious by being mentally aware of the process: then no. It is a process that takes place at a sub-awareness level: our minds participate in this proc-ess as a matter of protocol.

Meanwhile, our conscious self drives the process of forgetfulness according to our innate goals and desires. It is our inner objectives and desires that drive consolida-tion. Within the limitations of our brain capacity, images that do not yield our objectives are thrown out, while im-ages that do are kept in memory to recall later. We might compare this to sorting mail: We keep the mail that fur-thers our objectives, and toss out what we don't feel we need.

Most researchers divide dream stages into NREM and REM. Others disagree, and propose that the NREM (which include the N1 and N2 consolidation process) are not real dreams. They are like cleaning up a desk piled up with paperwork. This is consistent with the results of research, which shows a mass sorting of information through the limbic system during this stage—with the limbic system lighting in magnetic imaging studies.

On the other hand, there is no reason why we cannot have reveries during this stage. Let's say for example that we are cleaning up our desk that is piled up with paper-work. As we are going through our papers, we land on one that reminds us of a project that we are supposed to do right away. So we stop the sorting process and focus on getting the project done.

The NREM stage can also allow this. As we sort through the day's information, something reminds us of an interesting topic or something requiring resolution. So we'll focus on that for awhile. This means we might rehearse the situation, or

We will discuss dreaming with more detail later on. For now, we should realize that dream study has substantially progressed: Especially in the realm of REM sleep. REM-stage dreaming is the peak dream state. Some dream researchers have classified REM-stage dreaming as the only true type of dreaming. Others simply categorize it as a different type of dreaming.

Dream study is conducted by researchers who awaken sleepers and ask questions about what was being dreamed. These can be quite revealing, because we forget our dreams almost immediately otherwise. Contextual images are collated and sorted during REM sleep dreaming. This process transmits synapse-maintained information to the hippocampus. After the sleeper is awakened, the information is retrieved as episodic memories stored in the hippocampus.

Research has confirmed that REM dreaming is a necessary component of quality sleep and mental stability.

Good quality REM dreams will help resolve traumatic events. Sigmund Freud called these resolution-oriented dreams *biographical dreams*. Past emotional experiences are worked through by playing out events as they might have occurred, or perhaps could not have occurred no matter what we did. These suppositions can take us to conclusions that teach us lessons about our experiences—allowing us to live with our physical realities.

REM Dreaming

Dreaming peaks during REM-stage sleep. REM-stage sleep has also been associated with higher quality sleep, and better health. On the other hand, those lacking in REM-stage sleep have problems dealing with their waking lives. This indicates that REM dreaming is not simply essential for getting sufficient rest: It is essential for a balanced outlook of our waking world.

As we've mentioned earlier, various nervous disorders

can result without adequate REM-stage dreaming. Cognitive impairment and hallucinations have been associated with REM stage deficiency. Parkinson's disease and dementia have also been linked to a lack of REM-sleep. REM-stage deficiency often precedes Parkinson's and dementia occurrence by a number of years (Arnulf *et al.* 2008).

Non-REM sleep also will contain dreaming, but of a different sort. NREM sleep dreaming does not have the deep architecture, resolution quality and vividness that REM sleep dreaming has. Some researchers have characterized NREM dreaming as more like hallucinations than dreams. Still, NREM sleep provides the important tasks of detail sorting and priority management. This is critical to the next sleep stages, because we need to sort through details and prioritize the things of the waking world before we can start consolidating memories and resolving issues.

Rapid eye movement sleep behavior disorder (RBD) has been seen increasingly among both adults and children. Children with RBD can have dramatic behavioral development problems. These include self-affliction, or the practice of hurting oneself by cutting. Depression, narcolepsy, epilepsy, and other nervous disorders have also been associated with RBD.

During our deepest REM-stage sleep, our cells become busy flushing toxins out and removing proteins that are no longer operable. During our REM-stage sleep, our probiotic activity also increases. Probiotics make up an important part of our immune system. They toss out microorganisms that threaten healthy metabolism and manage many epithelial areas.

During REM-stage dreaming, hippocampus stimulation regulates the body's production of critical neural hormones and neurotransmitters. These include cortisol, acetylcholine, dopamine, serotonin and norepinephrine. When REM-stage sleep is inadequate, these critical biochemicals become imbalanced. This imbalance leads to a distortion of our moods and emotional responses to the waking world. This is one reason a lack of dreaming is associated with mood disorders such as mania, depression and anxiety.

Indeed, when REM-stage sleep is disturbed, a number of distortions can occur. In narcolepsy and sleep apnea, for example, dreams can become increasingly bizarre in their content. REM-stage interruption is also associated with negative and even haunting dreams. In the case of Parkinson's disease sufferers, 15% to 60% will laugh, shout, and even fight dreamscape enemies in their sleep. They are often seen kicking, punching and writhing while they sleep (Cochen De Cock and Arnulf 2008).

Sleep research has more recently revealed that often the subjects of our REM-stage dreams are the more contradictory or stress-related areas of our waking life. This indicates the rationale for some of our more intense REM dreams. Those who subject themselves to stressful, complex and problematic situations during their waking life are also more prone to having intense dreamscapes.

Melatonin, Cortisol and REM Sleep

Melatonin sets or stimulates many of the clock processes around the body, and it is critical to good quality sleep. The biochemical synthesis of melatonin within the body begins with a hydroxylation of tryptophan to 5-hydroxytryptophan. 5-HTP decarboxylates to serotonin, which is then converted to N-acetylserotonin. N-acetylserotonin is then methylated to melatonin. Melatonin affects the cellular biological clock in a number of ways. It directs the body's metabolism to prepare for sleep. It lowers body core temperature. It helps stimulate the constriction of blood vessels. It also relaxes nerves and moods. Melatonin reduction also stimulates the timing of puberty among adolescents.

Melatonin is also essential to health. Abnormally low endogenous (produced by the body) levels of melatonin have been linked to a higher risk of cancer, notably breast cancer (Oh *et al.* 2010).

Melatonin levels begin to climb as the evening darkens. Raised melatonin levels slow metabolism and reduce core body temperature drops. Assuming a regular cycle and a relatively calm and low-lit household, melatonin will begin to surge around 9 p.m. or so—as our body moves into "rest and revitalize" mode. Melatonin levels tend to peak around midnight or 1 a.m.

During the early morning hours (midnight to 2 a.m.), melatonin levels begin to drop and core body temperature rises. During the early morning period, about 90% of melatonin levels are metabolized out of the body through the liver.

Other hormones also drive core body temperature, such as thyroid hormone, growth hormone, adrenaline, cortisol and others. Thus, we know that melatonin does not work in a vacuum: It works in a cooperative role. Therefore, as we will discuss later, simply taking melatonin as a supplement won't replace the need for the body's production.

Over the past five decades, sleep scientists have been studying the effects of the body clock by incubating people with and without the benefit of light. The implications of melatonin production in response to light change have been well founded. They have repeatedly illustrated that the reduction of sunlight stimulates the melatonin cycle. On the other side of the coin, bright lights at night can disrupt melatonin release.

As the night wears on, and body core temperature rises, the adrenal glands begin to secrete cortisol. Cortisol levels will be high when melatonin levels are low. Cortisol stimulates faster circulation and increased brain activity. Cortisol also slows down the immune system and speeds up the processing of glucose into energy. These in turn raise body core temperature. Melatonin is like the anti-cortisol: It ushers in slower metabolism, stimulates the immune system, and cools body temperature. Glucose metabolism is also slowed, and brainwave activity slows with melatonin.

Interestingly, the gradual release of cortisol into the bloodstream during the early morning sleep hours also helps progress our sleep cycles into productive REM-stage sleep and dreaming.

Cortisol typically climbs and peaks a couple of times a day. Its natural rhythm peaks during the morning and early evening. If a person goes to sleep at 11 p.m., cortisol levels will slowly begin to climb between 1:30 a.m. and 3 a.m. Cortisol levels increase with more dreaming and more REM stage sleep. This slow climb of cortisol continues through to the morning hours. In the mid-morning, cortisol levels begin to spike, and typically peak somewhere between 8 a.m. and 10 a.m., depending upon our waking time, metabolism, breakfast (coffee) habits, and so on.

However, let's say we get to thinking about a stressful subject around midnight, or we turn on the computer or TV or some glaring lights after bedtime. Suddenly, cortisol production is stimulated and our cells are switched to "active" rather than "rest and revitalize." As a result, our heart rate, breathing rate, CSF rate, and circulation start increasing.

Our various rhythms are on "alert," stimulated by the release of cortisone. This status conflicts with the instructions of melatonin to the cells: Rest and relax. This conflict is what typically produces the bleary-eyed insomniac who can't turn his mind off, yet can't fully function either.

Thyroid hormone cycles alternate with melatonin cycles. Both melatonin and thyroid hormones are regulated through the hypothalamus and pineal gland as they respond to light. Thyroid hormones T3 and T4 cycle conjunctively with cortisol and other corticosteroids—as they alternate with melatonin (Wright 2002).

Not surprisingly, deficient melatonin levels have been linked to lowered immunity and heightened levels of cancer and other diseases. A number of pro-inflammatory cytokines are produced when the body is not sleeping enough or is operating on an irregular cycle. Pro-inflammatory interleukin-6 is one of these, and its release correlates with irregular sleep patterns.

Another pro-inflammatory trigger, tumor necrosis factor (TNF), is often seen increased in persons with inadequate or irregular sleep cycles. Heightened levels of these cytokines have been particularly evident during daytime sleepiness episodes (Vgontzas *et al.* 2005).

Slow brainwave sleep is related directly to heightened levels of melatonin, relaxation, and enough sleep time. These all tie to sleeping with the sun's rhythms, as melatonin is linked to darkness.

The relationship between daily cortisol levels in the Van Cauter study also related to sleep quality. Rapid eye movement sleep or REM sleep was associated negatively with evening cortisol levels among the subjects. In other words, independent of age, less REM sleep equated to more evening cortisol. However, this trend also did occur with age:

The older men had progressively lower REM sleep and thus higher evening cortisol levels. This in turn would also reduce melatonin levels, thereby keeping core body temperatures up and lowering sleep quality. Both higher cortisol levels and lower REM sleep are directly related to stress. This is consistent with other sleep studies confirming that REM sleep tends to fall as we age—and even further with higher stress levels.

In one study (Evans *et al.* 2007), fifty active seniors at the University of Westminster were continuously measured for cortisol levels through a forty-eight hour period in their homes. Before and after exams showed that ultradian cortisol cycles significantly correlated with changing impressions of psychological well-being. This was significant during the first 45 minutes after awaking from sleep. Those with lower morning cortisol tended to experience increased feelings of well-being.

Many other daily secretions are not only circadian, but are affected by stressors such as reduced sleep and increased occupational stress. In one study (Persson *et al.* 2006) of 75 workers, those who involuntarily worked over 80 hours in a week experienced dysfunctional levels of cholesterol, cortisol, melatonin, prolactin, and testosterone levels on day seven of the workweek.

In fact, both groups (the 40-hour workers and the 80-plus-hour workers) experienced decreased levels at the end of the workweek when compared to the beginning of the workweek. This would suggest these hormones are destructively interfered by stress. This would be consistent with research connecting low-quality sleep with practically every illness and disorder. Sleep requires balanced hormonal rhythms. And the body needs sleep for detoxification, rejuvenation, and focused immune response.

A preponderance of the research on the human circadian cycle seems to indicate that bright lights are the significant driver for maintaining the body's circadian rhythms. In the absence of bright light enough to entrain the body each day, some metabolic rhythms can cycle variously. The circadian rhythms of melatonin and body core temperatures cycle variously without the cues of the sun, often settling in around 25 hours. The sleep-waking cycle, however, can vary to a larger degree without solar entrainment—up to more than 30 hours (Yamanaka *et al.* 2009).

For most of us, by around three a.m. our adrenal cortex is quietly pumping cortisol into the bloodstream. With cortisol comes higher body core temperatures and increased metabolism amongst the cells. This process subtly orchestrates our multiple sleep cycles—which are ultradian. Our sleep cycles increase in REM-intensity toward the morning as our cortisol levels rev up. A healthy last cycle can dive deep into REM and then glide into a final delta stage as we anticipate our awakening.

As awareness increases after waking in the morning, our body's cortisol levels should increase as our body temperature rises with greater activity. This cortisol surge should peak about an hour or so after waking, tapering off towards the late morning. This results in a late-morning decline in energy. This cycle of lower energy continues into the early afternoon, as our bodies head into 'siesta' mode (researchers call this the *lunch challenge*). After our digestive cycle-down (as blood is diverted to the intestinal tract for digestion), cortisol levels again begin to rise. Depending upon our exposure to the sun, eating habits, stressors, and environment; another rise in cortisol—not usually as high as the morning's—will begin sometime in the late afternoon.

Cortisol levels will also rise during a situation of stress or urgency. This spike can occur at any time of day, and it will usually be accompanied by increases in epinephrine, acetylcholine and other hormone/neurotransmitters.

These all work together to orchestrate changes in metabolism to respond to the urgency. They facilitate increased blood flow and nutrients to the muscles, eyes and brain cells, along with a decrease in blood flow and nutrients to organs like the liver, immune system and the digestive system. For this reason, a physiology pushed by constant stress will usually result in digestive issues, liver problems and lowered immunity.

Should a person have an abundance of these stressful or anxious situations over extended periods (called *chronic stress*), the morning spike in cortisol levels may be absent or flattened. This will usually lower energy throughout the day. This is often diagnosed as chronic fatigue syndrome or fibromyalgia, often traced to the adrenal gland being overtaxed due to over-activity.

In the later afternoon and early evening, cortisol levels again rise, giving a healthy person a burst of energy at the end of the day and into the early evening. The extent of ultradian cortisol secretion and the amplitude (or slope) of the cortisol cycle is related to internal and external environmental conditions in addition to conscious factors. These include levels of estrogen, lutein phase, inflammation, physical fitness, weather, sound, color, oxygen, anxiety and the range of intentions from within.

The artificial suns of today's modern electric world disrupt our natural rhythms of both sleeping and dreaming. Light with even moderate lux levels have been shown conclusively to lower circulating melatonin levels.

By design, our bodies produce less melatonin if the lights are left on too long after the sun's setting because lights signal to the body the need to keep working. Unnatural late night lighting also increases circulating levels of cortisol at abnormal times. Increased cortisol levels late at night decrease the amount of REM-stage sleep we get. This in turn reduces the amount of quality dreaming we can have.

REM-Stage Dreaming and the Sun

Sleep and cave studies have shown that the body's biological clock seems to naturally be set for a cycle of about 24 hours and 10 minutes. However, without the entrainment of the sun, the biological clock will become corrupted. Some studies have shown that without light 'cues,' the body will first manifest a 25-hour body clock. As time goes on, sleeping hours will become disoriented, and the body clock becomes variable and erratic.

In other words, a lack of sunshine disrupts our body clock and our sleeping cycles. This specifically affects our REM-stage sleep and our ability to dream.

Sunlight is specifically related to body core temperature, and body core temperature in turn is related to the release of neurotransmitter/hormones like serotonin, dopamine, cortisol, melatonin and adenosine. Body core temperature is like a delayed intermediary between sunlight and the release of these biochemicals. This is why body core temperature is significantly related to seasonal affective disorder (Schwartz *et al.* 2001).

In the long and short run, body core temperature is relative to the consistency or our sunlight exposure.

In other words, body core temperature follows with a delayed response to sunlight quality and duration. This might be compared to a shadow following a movement. A person who does not receive adequate sunlight for a long duration will have disrupted body core temperatures. Body temperatures will remain high into the evening when they should be falling. This will in turn disrupt our release of melatonin, and our ability to fall into REM-stage sleep.

REM-stage dreaming and sleep in general relates directly to time, which relates directly to the sun.

In a study done by Folkard in 1996, for example, a woman was isolated for twenty-five days without daily light cues. While her temperature cycle stayed close to twenty-four hours long, her sleep cycle was closer to thirty hours. This study indicated that over time, the clock tends to stretch out without any sun. It also indicates individuality among responses to a lack of daily sun waves. Without the daily resetting mechanism of the sun, we might be going to bed later and later each night. After a few days, some of us might be doing all-nighters and sleeping during the daytime. Others may not.

The consistent issue among these various studies on the body clock is how predictably the body's clock mechanisms reset with sunlight. For example, in the late 1980s, Dr. Charles Czeisler performed studies with the Naval Health Research Center on Trident nuclear submarine crewmembers. Submarine crew schedules required an 18-hour body clock.

Dr. Czeisler's results found this just was not possible under the current conditions. The onboard lights were simply too weak to entrain submarine personnel body clocks to that schedule. Dr. Czeisler and others established that bright light from between 7,000 and 13,000 (typical daylight) lux was necessary to produce a resetting of the body clock to this extent (Boivin *et al.* 1996).

The body clock can also be disturbed by lower intensities of light, however. In another study, Dr. Czeisler and Boivin (1998) studied eight healthy men with eight control subjects. They found a mere 180 lux of light (typical office lighting ranges from 200-400 lux) had the ability to alter the circadian body clock, together with an increase in body core temperature. In another test, Dr. Czeisler found that 100 lux of indoor light has about half the alerting response 9100 lux of outdoor light has (Cajochen *et al.* 2000). In a study of twelve adults, Dr. Czeisler and his associates (Gronfier *et al.* 2007) found while 100 lux is sufficient to shift the clock, a 25 lux light was not enough to shift or reset the body's clock.

This research and others indicate that dreaming is irreparably tied to sunlight exposure. After a couple of weeks in temporal isolation chambers—meaning without sunlight, but only artificial light and no time signals—

subjects will sleep highly irregular hours.

Some days, a subject might sleep up to 19 hours a day, while other days, the sleep length might be as few as four hours. Interestingly, on days with as little as four hours sleep, sunlight-less subjects did not recognize that they had too little sleep. They might even remain awake for as many as 30 hours in a row without apparent sleepiness (St Hilaire *et al.* 2007).

Most of us know what takes place when we sleep longer or shorter hours in terms of our dreams. Our dreams also get extended or shortened. When we sleep longer hours, we will play out a greater number of scenarios. When we sleep shorter hours, our dreams are also abbreviated.

This means that our daylight hours will also have a variance in terms of how we deal with others, how we deal with stress and so forth.

There is also a cognition variable to consider in sunlight rhythms. Isolation chamber subjects will quickly become disoriented with respect to time once their light cues are taken away. Subjects may perceive that 2-3 weeks went by during a month, for example.

Despite this confusion, subjects without sleep cues will typically make sleep adjustments in a cyclic way, eventually falling into a new rhythm. Even then, isolation-chamber subjects still illustrate a residual 24-25 hour clock with variances cycling at a 127-day rhythm. Meanwhile their sleep rhythm cycles often return to a resetting rhythm driver.

A number of ultradian cycles are working continuously within our bodies. Many also interplay (or interfere) with cortisol cycles. For example, multiple daily temperature fluctuations were illustrated among babies by Bollani *et al.* (1997). In a study on cognition by Klein and Armitage (1979), it was shown that study participants' verbal and spatial skills cycled at about ninety-six minutes.

Other studies have confirmed several other body rhythms that rotate at intervals close to 90 minutes each. The length of these rhythms correlate closely with the close-to-ninety minute cycles of REM and non-REM stage sleep and dream cycles, as discussed previously.

Research has connected brainwaves to a number of ultradian rhythms occurring throughout the body.

Brainwaves are also ultradian. Slower brainwave rhythms have been connected with the neural activity within the thalamus and cerebral cortex. This also means that our dreams during this stage will be processing those memories encoded in these locations—ranging from short-term to long-term memories.

An oscillation of spindle complexes among these ganglia pathways drive rhythmic pulses through the brain, reverberating throughout the body (Burikov and Bereshpolova 1999). These complex switching neurons have been called *corticothalamic neurons,* and they transduce slow delta waves (Timofeev and Steriade 1996).

Meanwhile, the faster alpha waves respond to conscious optic nerve firings from visual input moving through the LGN and visual cortex. This function has been tested by measuring subjects' brainwave responses in these brain regions while they observe and recognize a variety of image shapes and sizes.

With the processing and recognition of visual information, alpha waves are generated (Shevelev *et al.* 1991). This and other research has illustrated that alpha waves are responsive to images and light reflected within the visual cortex.

The slower theta rhythms, moving at between four and ten cycles per second, are associated with states of relaxation and sleep. In waking adults, theta waves are crowded out by focused consciousness.

Some tests have shown that theta waves will also occur with certain short-term memory tasks; episodic and semantic memory recalls; and spatial navigation tasks (Buzsaki 2005). Relaxation and semantic memory utilize the brain's nerve centers with more elegance.

Slower theta waveforms are thus reflective of a deeper, more abstract awareness. Several studies of theta waves have concluded that they often reflect activity within the hippocampus—a central player in the human limbic system. Theta waves have also been associated with rhythmic movements such as dancing, and certain auditory mechanisms during both waking and sleeping episodes. They have also been noticed during attention shifting (Gambini *et al.* 2002).

The somewhat mysterious theta rhythm may also provide a link to the programming mechanisms required for autonomic function. Pedemonte and associates (2005) also found that theta rhythms substantially affect the heart rate and many reflex movements, including programmed functions related to responsive memory. Theta waves are also more pronounced around sunset and sunrise.

All of these relative brainwaves also reflect our dreamscape movements and activities. Theta brainwaves will accompany serious REM-stage dreaming episodes—those episodes that are critical for our processing of those inputs picked up by our senses or acted out during our waking lives.

The bottom line is that our dreamscape mirrors our physical activities not only in the specifics of the type of events and sensual inputs: Our larger biorhythms correlate with those brainwave rhythms to reflect and play out the consciousness that we portray during our waking lives.

It is not as if these two phases of consciousness are independent. They are linked together. For example, if we watch horror movies, our dreams will likely contain more scary, horrific images. If we play lots of sports during our waking lives, our dreams will also have more sports involvement and more motion.

This association is played out from a memory processing standpoint which is reflected through the transmission and reception of particular waveforms that reverberate through the electrical bionetwork of the brain.

This means that we can affect our dreams by our daytime activities, and we can accommodate our dreamscape by shifting our waking hours more closely with the rising of the sun. This will generate more early morning cortisol, and less evening cortisol. This will allow our melatonin levels to go up at night around bedtime, which will in turn escort us into a nice, deep sleep, enabling healthy REM-stage dreaming.

Chapter Four

Dream Hygiene

If we want to dream well, we need to also sleep well. Here are a few things we can do to help us fall asleep easily and quickly, and sleep deeply.

- Trying to go to sleep and awaken around the same times each day
- Taking a few minutes to go outside into the sun each morning and evening before and during sunset
- Getting a healthy nourishing diet with adequate nutrients and plenty of drinking water
- Getting adequate and sometimes vigorous exercise daily, preferably in the morning
- Avoiding drugs, caffeine and alcohol
- Turning the lights lower as the evening progresses;
- Avoiding late-night television or computers;
- Scheduling 6-8 hours of sleep or relaxation each day
- Eating early in the evening, with a high-fiber/dairy snack an hour or so before bedtime
- Avoiding eating or drinking too much just prior to bedtime
- Dressing in loose-fitting sleeping wear that does not snag or otherwise bog us down as we move around the bed when sleeping
- Sleeping on a firmer mattress
- Keeping room well-ventilated and slightly cool
- Keeping room dark or wearing eye covers
- Using adequate bedding for warmth, but not too much warmth
- Maintaining our privacy while sleeping
- Waking at about the same time each day
- Avoiding waking by alarm clock if possible

Staying asleep is critical to our dreamscape. If our body is not comfortable, it can wake us or keep us in a lighter dreamscape. Better to establish clear and regular sleep hygiene habits, so our bodies can run on automatic while we are asleep.

Let's discuss a few of these points in more detail.

Alarm Clocks and Dreaming

An alarm clock will often interrupt our current dream and sleep cycle. The 90-minute or so sleep cycle is important to maintain, because we dream through the deeper part of the cycles. As the end of the cycle nears, we naturally rise out of the deeper sleep stages into a lighter sleep stage. This process prepares our mind and body for waking. It also brings us to a natural end to our dreaming, providing for better dream resolution.

The alarm clock can zoom us from the depths of a dream into sudden waking consciousness. It shuts off whatever dream we might be having. This may interrupt our brain's consolidation processes and our ability to resolve problems.

The best way to awaken is with natural light. The new light of the dawn has a way of creeping into our sleep cycle and moving us along towards waking, but not too fast. This helps our physiology and mind complete consolidation and resolution, and prepare for the waking day.

How do we assure we'll wake up on time?

We can still set the alarm. But the goal is not to use the alarm to wake up. The alarm should be a safety net for the possibility that we don't wake up beforehand.

The key is to plan out the sleep session accurately before we fall asleep. We can calculate our sleep cycles and determine what time we want to wake up. Simply the determination of a plan to wake up at a particular time will often reinforce our waking up at almost precisely the time we predetermine.

Most of us do not realize this. Even though we might be asleep, we still have a great amount of conscious control of our sleeping patterns—believe it or not. We simply have to first realize this fact, and then make a confident determination to exert control. We will be surprised by how much we can control sleep through suggestion.

If we do choose to set the alarm clock, we might want

to consider setting it to a CD of music that we like, or a recording of our own voice saying that it is now time to get up. This is a great alternative to the annoying beeping of a digital clock or the shrill of an alarm.

Another alternative is to put a timer on the cord of a bright lamp that shines in our face. When the lamp goes on, we are awakened. Waking up to light is the most natural way to wake up.

An even better alarm would be to sleep near a window and wake up with the morning sun rising as it shines through the window. This, together with hearing the sounds of chirping birds and our predetermination to wake up, is by far the best alarm clock.

Dream Body Temperature

Body core temperature relates to cortisol and melatonin levels. It also relates closely with our REM-stage sleep and dream cycles. A hotter body core temperature usually means shorter dreams and more waking.

One of the ways to regulate body core temperature is to control our bedroom temperature. The best environment is slightly cool—well below body temperature and just below room temperature. Many find that about 55-60 degrees F is a good cool temperature for sleeping. However, this is extremely individualistic. Our best sleeping temperature will depend upon our normal rate of metabolism and our sleep metabolism. It may also depend upon the season and the temperature outside. In other words, it may take some experimentation.

Note also that men and women often have different metabolic rates. While not a rule, often women have lower body core temperatures at night and thus require more blankets than the faster metabolic rates of men.

Using a room thermostat, heat pump and central heating may be helpful for regulating room temperature. However, central heating can also come with some risks. One is that the ducting system can be full of mold, bacteria and viruses. These can interfere with our sleep and our health. This can be especially true in an older apartment building with a shared central heating system. If we wake up to clogged sinuses or sore throats, we should suspect dirty heating ducts. In most locations and seasons, we barely need heat outside of some good blankets, pajamas, socks, and maybe a beanie.

In the summertime, things may heat up. Many people use the air conditioner at this point. If at all possible, air conditioners should be avoided. A fan would a better choice, as the fan allows the body to regulate its own temperature with moisture. A small amount of sweat will cool us down dramatically with a fan. The combination will lower the body's temperature to the desired state. Air conditioners, on the other hand, tend to force the body's temperature down too quickly. This can lead to an alternation of overheating and over-cooling through the night as we cover with blankets.

Our body temperatures tend to go way down as we fall deeper into sleep during the first few cycles. Then they start coming back up with REM-stage sleep. Towards the morning, our core body temperatures are significantly higher. This means that between 1 a.m. and 3 a.m. we need to be concerned about supercooling, which can lead to suppression of the immune system. Starting off with a cool environment is great as we are cruising off into sleep. We just need to make sure we don't become over-cooled during the night.

Dream Beds and Pajamas

A study by researchers from the University of Milan (Kircheimer 1993) reported that people sleeping in linen sheets reported falling asleep faster and slept longer than did those who slept in other types of fabrics. They also woke up in a better mood than did people sleeping in sheets of other fabrics. This indicates that they had longer dreams.

The researchers concluded that linen dispersed body heat better than other fabrics. In other words, linen 'breathes' better. This 'breathing' allows the heat of the body to dissipate, away from the body.

While mattress softness is highly individualistic, a firmer bed will allow a balance between circulation and movement—both necessary for comfortable sleep and deep dreams. Ease of movement is necessary for comfortable sleep, and too soft a bed can inhibit movement. Too firm a bed (or sleeping on a hard surface), on the other hand, can also reduce circulation.

Again, sleepiness is promoted by a cooling of core body temperature. Sleeping with too many blankets or with sheets that do not breathe will interrupt the cyclic changes in body temperature when we sleep.

Blankets are best used in layers. We can reduce blankets as we feel warmer. Should we begin to feel clammy, we can remove all blankets and stay inside the sheets. This can cool the body quickly.

Our sheets should be changed frequently, at least every other week if not every week. Dirty sheets can attract mites, which are virtually invisible to the naked eye. They can also attract lice.

Loose-fitting pajamas that breathe are also suggested. Some people like to sleep naked. There is nothing wrong with this, except that it could lead to over-cooling during the middle of the night. Very thin cotton pajamas (or a cotton-polyester combo) are probably a better option, as they will let air in and out, yet still supply some protection against over-cooling.

In the wintertime, we may want to opt for flannel pajamas and sheets. These can be helpful assuming chilly nights and mornings. Practically any heat in the room will likely cause our flannels to overheat our bodies, however. Even the slightest overheating can disturb sleep and cause insomnia.

Because we lose heat quickly through our feet, managing socks can be a great tool to regulate body temperature. During colder weather, we can wear socks into bed. As the weather warms, we can wear socks in the evening, but then remove them as we climb into bed. This will help cool down the body quickly.

Ventilation

To maximize deep sleep and REM-stage dreaming, our bedroom should also be well ventilated with fresh air. To sleep in a closed off room with nothing but ducted air can cause allergy issues and a lack of oxygen, simply because the air must travel through the ducts and filters of a ventilation system and these may be lined with mold and other toxins. Keeping our filters and ducts cleaned may avoid much of this, but an open window, assuming fresh air outside, is suggested for maximal oxygen availability.

Again, fans are better than air conditioners, even in the midst of summer's heat. A fan will cool the body by cooling the moisture on the surface of the skin. This is better for the skin's health, and better for our health. The air conditioner will dry out the skin and cause over-cooling. This will reduce circulation and cause blood stagnation. Over-cooling can also result in depressed immune function. For best results during a hot night, sleep almost nude (underwear is suggested) under a light linen sheet with an overhead fan going and our screened windows open. Fan is best set at a slower speed to prevent sleep disruption.

Keeping outdoor air flowing through the house also reduces the amount of radon within the house. A closed up house draws radon into the house because of the pressure gradient.

Hotel rooms are notorious for having no ability to open the window for fresh air. However, not all are like this. We might want to call the hotel ahead of our reservation to find out whether we can at least crack the window to sleep with some fresh air. Nothing is worse than waking up with a sore throat after a terrible night's rest in an unventilated hotel room.

Our bedroom air should also be free of any irritating chemicals or substances. Fabric softeners should not be used on our sheets and bedding. We should not keep perfume or cologne in the bedroom. Incense or air fresheners are also not a good idea. Chemical cleaning products should not be used in the bedroom close to bedtime. All of these can leave chemical irritants in the air that can disturb our sleep. Mold and dust should be removed from the bedroom. Mold is best removed with vinegar and lemon. Rubbing alcohol or chlorine (but not together) can be used for more hardy cases.

Modern mattresses are notorious for containing various toxic chemicals, including formaldehyde and various plasticizers. Many of the memory foam mattresses contain formaldehyde. Formaldehyde will slowly outgas into the room air over time, creating an unhealthy sleeping environment. A mattress using as much natural fibers as possible should be chosen for these reasons. Memory foam mattresses should be outgassed in the sun for a few days before use.

Humidity

Our air is full of water in the form of vapor. When water is vaporized within our atmosphere, it is called humidity. Humidity levels are typically measured as *relative humidity*. This is the level of humidity the air can contain at a particular temperature. 100% relative humidity is the highest level of moisture the air can contain at that temperature. Warmer temperatures can hold more vapor than colder temperatures, which is why heat and humidity is especially uncomfortable, and can disrupt sleep.

As most of us have experienced, higher humidity during warm weather is uncomfortable. Too low of a humidity level will also be uncomfortable, as it will dry our skin and irritate our lungs. Our lungs are full of moisture, and a slightly humid environment is healthy for the lungs.

What this all means is that winters are often too dry and summers too humid in many places. This can be exacerbated indoors if we are not careful.

The trick is to create healthy indoor humidity levels. This does not mean reducing oxygen levels, however. It is important that we have a constant flow of oxygen from nature into our indoor sleeping environment.

So how do we create a comfortable indoor humidity? Sleeping is best maintained with 25% to 60% humidity at room temperature. Indoor humidity can be affected by the house's building materials, ventilation systems, occupants, water use, and whatever air conditioning or heating units are running. They can also be affected by our presence. Simply being in the house will increase its humidity.

When we breathe, we send out about a cup of water into our environment every four hours, effectively raising the humidity level by 6-8%. Many heating units will also dry the atmosphere, while air conditioner units will raise the indoor humidity. So even if it is cool enough inside, we may be too humid. This will disrupt our sleep. Also, a shower with the windows closed will raise the humidity levels about as much as four hours of breathing.

To test our humidity level in the absence of a humidity gauge (advisable), we can watch the moisture levels on the surface of a glass of ice water. If little or no moisture forms immediately on the outside surface of the glass, our house is too dry. If we see moisture build up or mold on the ceilings, our house is likely too humid.

Changing our humidity is quite easy if it is too dry. A shower, humidifier or a room full of people will increase the humidity quite quickly. If the air is too moist, opening up all the windows is the simplest method, assuming it is dryer outside. In a humid environment, we can reduce indoor plants, cook under an oven fan, and in general keep rotating the moist air out. Dehumidifiers are now available for extreme environments, but better to create our own dehumidifier by ventilating our home with fans and reducing moisture production.

Our Dream Room

Our bedroom does not simply host a bed: It hosts hundreds of dreams a month. The bedroom should be seen as a dream room. It should therefore be reserved for dream time and not waking time.

Research has shown us that those that a noisy sleeping environment is linked to greater levels of insomnia. This seems obvious, yet it is surprising how many people will sleep with a noisy TV on, amongst traffic outside, or in a noisy house. If disturbing noises cannot be shut out easily, sound earplugs can help.

Our dream room habitat should be sparse. The best sleeping room is one with as little of one's waking life as possible. Desks, chairs, sofas, mirrors, electronics, animals, and phones can be distractions. These can easily remind us of the stresses of our waking life.

Electronics are especially problematic. Electronic items such as MP3 players and cell phones can either be turned off or put away. Their blinking lights and various beeps can stimulate the body's cortisone production. They can also create subtle physiological stress. Studies have shown that even a small beep or pulsing light in the room can reduce melatonin levels.

Computers are definitely a no-no in the dream room. If we have to have our computer in the dream room, better if it is a laptop that we can close and put in a drawer or otherwise out of visual range.

The same goes for televisions, radios and stereos. These should not be in the dream room. If we really need to or want to, then we should set up a console where we can close them off to our visual range.

The lights in the dream room should be soft and of low power—preferably 40 watts or less. Dimmer switches are a great way to gradually lower light levels. With dimmers, we can lower light levels as the evening wears on towards bedtime. Fluorescent lights should not be used in the dream room. The flicker of fluorescents stimulates arousal (Küller and Laike 1998).

Our dream room should be an oasis of tranquility. This means clearing out the knick-knacks. It also means putting away our clothes, shoes, books, paperwork and other clutter. A neat and clean dream room clears the mind and settles the nerves. Dream room doors are best closed or almost closed when we are sleeping.

Unless they are clean and groomed, animals are probably best if not allowed inside the dream room for this reason. Outdoor animals can transport fleas and lice. This said, there has been some good research indicating that pets can reduce stress, anxiety and depression (Jorgenson

1997). So this is a personal preference that largely depends upon the type of pet and the effect the pet has upon our sleep. Are they anxious, or are they relaxed when we go to bed? Do they disturb or help us sleep? These judgments must be made.

Our dream room is best situated within or around a natural habitat to the degree possible. If, for example, we have the choice to sleep in the dream room in the back of the house next to our yard of trees, grass and garden, we should sleep there. This is as opposed to the dream room next to a street of concrete, traffic and glaring lights. A number of studies have shown that a natural environment lends itself to better relaxation and sleep (Kaplan 1992; Ulrich 1981). Indoor plants can help lend this natural environment.

Natural environments also typically contain more negative ions than cityscapes. Negative ions encourage relaxation (Karnstedt 1991). Negative ions (and the perception of natural surroundings) can be accomplished with a small indoor waterfall. The sound of trickling water may also help smooth out outside noises as well.

It is best not to use the bed for other activities outside of sleeping. While we are tempted to lie down and study, work on our computer, watch television or do a plethora of other activities, the bed should be used for sleeping and rarely anything else. This sets up the expectation that when we lay on the bed, we will fall asleep.

Our dream room should be our sanctuary, where we can meditate and feel peaceful, and leave behind the stressors of the world as we fall asleep. We can help generate this feeling about our dream room by minimizing the amount of waking time we spend in the dream room. This focuses our purpose when we enter the dream room. When we go in there, we have one purpose. We don't go in there to be entertained or work. We go into our dream room to achieve one objective: A full night of deep, undisturbed dreams.

Our dream room should be as dark as possible. If there is significant light, wearing eye covers is recommended.

Managing Dream Debt

As we discussed in the first chapter, we develop sleep debt when we miss sleep. When we don't get enough sleep over a period of time, we will accumulate sleep debt and we miss precious dream time. This backlog of sleep debt can add up to dozens or even hundreds of hours of critical dream time if we are not careful. Catching up on a day or two of sleep debt can be managed over a few nights. But a large backlog can take weeks or months of extra sleep each day to unwind.

A moderate amount of sleep debt is not bad, however. We need some sleep debt in order to fall asleep. When we wake up in the morning our sleep debt will be less than it was when we fell asleep the night before. Our sleep debt builds up as we go through our waking day. When bedtime rolls around, we have accumulated some more sleep debt. This reinforces our body's ability (and need) to sleep the next night.

On the other hand, a person who has little or no sleep debt built up—maybe they've overslept or taken a lengthy late-afternoon nap—might find it difficult to sleep that next evening. Because they have little or no sleep debt, they will not have any sleep inertia or sleep pressure.

Too much sleep debt, on the other hand, can produce chronic fatigue and daytime sleepiness. Daytime sleepiness significantly reduces our performance, cognition and problem solving abilities. It can also dangerously lead to the risk of falling asleep while driving or operating heavy machinery. This puts our lives in immediate danger.

The trick is to find the right amount of sleep debt. With a little sleep debt, we will fall asleep each night with little trouble, yet will still be reasonably rested the next day.

In the first chapter, we gave a method to calculate the level of sleep debt to judge our sleep quality. This can tell us whether we have built up too much sleep debt or not enough. But it does not tell us how much extra sleep we need to get to a healthy sleep debt.

The best method is to calculate the amount of sleep it will take to reduce sleep debt to close to zero. In other words, if we have ten hours of sleep debt, it will take us five days of two hours additional sleep to work off our debt.

That ten hours debt may have been built up over weeks, months or even years. This is highly individualistic.

For example, we know that dopamine levels will rise when a person is lacking sleep the night before. Dopamine is secreted in response to a combination of metabolic intensity and nervous system productivity. Nervous system activity directly relates to stimulation from the prefrontal cortex, which is driven by the inner self.

After decades of researching sleep debt, William Dement, M.D. estimated that 10-20 hours of sleep debt was healthy, while amounts greater than this are problematic.

To find out how much current sleep debt we are carrying, we can use our next vacation to do some catch up. We can ditch the alarm clock for a week or two and add up how many hours over our normal night's sleep we sleep. An eye mask would be very helpful for this task. During our sleep debt recovery period, we can simply take note of each night's total sleep hours. When we return back to a normal night's sleep for us (hopefully somewhere in the seven to eight hour range), we can then add up the extra hours, and that will be the cumulative sleep debt we've been carrying around for who knows how long.

Let's say we sleep 12 hours each night for five days, and then begin to sleep 7.5 hours the next couple of nights. The debt payoff is 4.5 hours X 5 nights = 22.5 hours of sleep debt.

This much sleep debt (22.5 hours) is beyond a safe amount of sleep debt, and we've probably been suffering from daytime sleepiness. A sleep debt of 10-12 hours would be safer. Assuming we had been playing sleep debt catch up every so often without realizing it (some late sleep-ins during the weekends, for example) we might be able to approximate that we are sleeping about 30 minutes to an hour too little each night on average. Or perhaps our sleep debt is coming from sporadic sleep shortages. This would be quite simple to fix.

Sleep debt testing is invaluable. It could save our lives. The research we reported in the first chapter on increased mortality speaks for itself. To this, we can add that the U.S. National Highway Traffic Safety Administration reported in 2002 that at least 4% of all fatal accidents were caused by sleepiness. We would add that the real number is likely significantly greater.

Now should we do this experiment and find we have little or no sleep debt built up, this may indicate another problem: too little sleep pressure. If we experience periodic insomnia without a seeming explanation, then this may be why. If we have little or no sleep pressure, we won't be able to easily fall asleep consistently. In this case, we should think about reducing our sleep by a few minutes every night. If we are feeling daytime sleepiness, we should increase a little—to find that sweet spot where we have just enough sleep debt to get our sleep pressure, yet not enough to cause daytime drowsiness.

Naps and Dreams

Naps can be a great strategy to balance sleep debt and regain dream time, especially if we work in the evenings or stay up later. However, naps can also cause insomnia, and not many people will enter REM-stage during a nap.

The depth of our nap depends largely upon our sleep debt/sleep pressure levels. If our sleep debt is significant (say 100 hours or more), we may easily fall into REM-stage sleep. Otherwise, we will not typically catch up on our dreaming by napping.

A nap is still good for the sleep-deprived. A nap in the daytime can dramatically reduce our sleep debt each day, giving us the ability to stay focused and productive during the lazy mid-afternoon period. If the nap is too long or taken too late, however, it may also keep us up that night.

Naps are best taken between noon and 1 p.m.: Any later will interrupt our cortisol and melatonin cycles. The nap must precede the afternoon cortisol dip—which occurs between 2:00 p.m. and 5 p.m. After this period, our cortisol levels begin to pick up into the early evening.

An evening nap is definitely a no-no if we want to fall asleep for the night at a reasonable hour and sleep deeply.

Research on naps shows they dramatically increase our focus, productivity and accuracy. Tests on pilots have shown that naps will increase reaction times by 16% and sleepiness by 34%, for example. Furthermore, the research has shown that this increased focus and productivity is not perceived by the person.

In other words, the seeming grogginess caused by the nap masks the increased focus and reaction times brought about by a short nap.

Chapter Five

Dream Categories

Nightmares

Problematic sleep disorders are sometimes caused by nightmares, and in some cases, a sleep disorder can actually cause the nightmares. Regardless of which came first, the two seem to be interdependent. Like a vicious cycle, a lack of REM-stage sleep can create more nightmares, and nightmares may increase waking and cause breaks in REM-stage sleep.

Treatments for nightmares have become increasingly important, as nightmares in many instances create problematic sleep and psychological issues. In 2008, researchers from the Netherlands' Utrecht University (Lancee *et al.*) studied recent clinical research using non-pharmaceutical measures in an attempt to treat people with recurring nightmares. Their twelve studies utilized different methods, including the recording of nightmares, relaxation techniques, exposure adjustment and guided imagery, and cognitive restructuring techniques. Of these techniques, the pre-dream exposure adjustment and guided imagery had the most beneficial effects, including a reduction of nightmares. Between the exposure and imagery, exposure adjustment offered better results.

This means what we expose our eyes to during our waking lives directly affects the types of dreams we will have during the night. This also relates to our visual experiences. Should we subject our senses to intense movies or realities that include gruesome violence, aliens, monsters and other intense visual experiences, we are most likely to integrate those visual experiences into our dreamscapes.

We must remember that our mind is like a recording device. This means that our visual observations are recorded and played back within our dreamscapes. Avoiding graphic scenes that include senseless violence or horror is simple mechanics. We can simply not attend horror films and close our eyes during grotesque and awful scenes. This does not mean that we should not be aware of the real world: But recording horrible and unnecessary images upon the mind is simply a recipe for intolerable dreams.

Post-traumatic stress nightmares present a similar issue, except that we may have had no choice in the matter. Post-traumatic nightmares may be frightening, but they are necessary for healing. The point is to face those nightmares, and make a determination that we will find resolution—eventually. As discussed above, post-traumatic nightmares can also be mitigated somewhat by carefully managing our new imagery and exposures.

Future Dreaming

Many have reported finding that their dreams took them into a future place, which eventually came true. We can and should accept that the mind and self have some intuitive abilities. What are these future-oriented dreams, and how and why do we have them?

The Preface for Gustavus Hindman Miller's book gives this history of some famous future dreams:

> Ancient history relates that Gennadius was convinced of the immortality of his soul by conversing with an apparition in his dream.

> The Bible, as well as other great books of historical and revealed religion, shows traces of a general and substantial belief in dreams. Plato, Goethe, Shakespeare and Napoleon assigned to certain dreams prophetic value. Joseph saw eleven stars of the Zodiac bow to himself, the twelfth star. The famine of Egypt was revealed by a vision of fat and lean cattle. The parents of Christ were warned of the cruel edict of Herod, and fled with the Divine Child into Egypt.

> Pilate's wife, through the influence of a dream, advised her husband to have nothing to do with the conviction of Christ. But the gross materialism of the day laughed at dreams, as it echoed the voice and verdict of the multitude, Crucify the Spirit, but let the flesh live. Barabbas, the

robber, was set at liberty.

Through the dream of Cecilia Metella, the wife of a Consul, the Roman Senate was induced to order the temple of Juno Sospita rebuilt.

The Emperor Marcian dreamed he saw the bow of the Hunnish conqueror break on the same night that Attila died.

Plutarch relates how Augustus, while ill, through the dream of a friend, was persuaded to leave his tent, which a few hours after was captured by the enemy, and the bed whereon he had lain was pierced with the enemies' swords.

If Julius Caesar had been less incredulous about dreams he would have listened to the warning which Calpurnia, his wife, received in a dream.

Croesus saw his son killed in a dream.

Petrarch saw his beloved Laura, in a dream, on the day she died, after which he wrote his beautiful poem, The Triumph of Death.

Cicero relates the story of two traveling Arcadians who went to different lodgings--one to an inn, and the other to a private house. During the night the latter dreamed that his friend was begging for help. The dreamer awoke; but, thinking the matter unworthy of notice, went to sleep again. The second time he dreamed his friend appeared, saying it would be too late, for he had already been murdered and his body hid in a cart, under manure. The cart was afterward sought for and the body found. Cicero also wrote, If the gods love men they will certainly disclose their purposes to them in sleep.

Chrysippus wrote a volume on dreams as divine portent. He refers to the skilled interpretations of dreams as a true divination; but adds that, like all other arts in which men have to proceed on conjecture and on artificial rules, it is not infallible.

Plato concurred in the general idea prevailing in his day, that there were divine manifestations to the soul in sleep. Condorcet thought and wrote with greater fluency in his dreams than in waking life.

Tartini, a distinguished violinist, composed his Devil's Sonata under the inspiration of a dream. Coleridge, through dream influence, composed his Kubla Khan.

The writers of Greek and Latin classics relate many instances of dream experiences. Homer accorded to some dreams divine origin. During the third and fourth centuries, the supernatural origin of dreams was so generally accepted that the fathers, relying upon the classics and the Bible as authority, made this belief a doctrine of the Christian Church.

Synesius placed dreaming above all methods of divining the future; he thought it the surest, and open to the poor and rich alike.

Aristotle wrote: There is a divination concerning some things in dreams not incredible. Camille Flammarion, in his great book on Premonitory Dreams and Divination of the Future, says: I do not hesitate to affirm at the outset that occurrence of dreams foretelling future events with accuracy must be accepted as certain.

Joan of Arc predicted her death.

Cazotte, the French philosopher and transcendentalist, warned Condorcet against the manner of his death.

These instances are truly significant, and some are historical. However, few of us have these types of dreams. Some of us do and not remember them, however.

And most people relate that they often experience what is called a *déjà vu,* with many believing they are experiencing something first seen or experienced within a dream.

Memory recall is at the foundation of this experience. We use our memory recall to remember people's names, events, places and things. Even speaking and writing involves memory recall, as we reach into our past to draw out what was learned sometimes many years ago.

Yet our fears focus upon the future. We cannot be afraid of our past, because that already happened. What is taking place right now is taking place, and there is no mystery. But our mysteries are drawn from our fear—and sometimes simply anticipation—of events that may or may not occur in the future.

So how do we explore our scenarios about the future?

Another way to look at this is that during our waking lives, we are constantly trying to play out future events. We utilize historical learning experiences to play out our current actions. A chess player does this as he or she makes a series of moves in his head, while looking at the possible opposing moves with each move. In this way, we draw out possible scenarios, based upon our experiences of how things worked out for us in the past.

If we do this intently, we can even picture the future scenario. For example, say we have an upcoming company meeting we must attend. We might imagine ourselves standing up and giving a speech in front our peers. We play out in our mind and even plan out using notes what we might say. Then we consider what our peers will think as we say those words. Then we might change our mind and decide not to give any speeches. Or we might decide to change our speech, or maybe not stand up at all. Maybe we'll just casually make a remark from our chair.

With each scenario, we will play out all the consequences. We might consider saying a joke, and then play out what would happen if the joke doesn't go off. We'll be embarrassed and people might make fun of our bad joke later on. Or maybe our joke will be funny, and we might play out ourselves not being taken seriously after the meeting is over.

We can also play out the positive sides of any future situation. For example, we might see ourselves winning a baseball game, and then going to the championships. We might play out the championships, and see ourselves hitting a home run. We'll imagine ourselves circling the bases in glory. In this way, we play out the positive future scenarios.

We might also play out both, and then calculate the chance of each before we play. We might think about whether we'll swing for the fences, or maybe lay down a bunt, and which one has greater chance of success.

With these scenarios, we'll often visualize each one. We might see ourselves rounding the bases and waving to the fans. Or we might see ourselves striking out and being embarrassed. Either way, we are using our mind to play out the possible scenarios.

This is precisely what we do in dreams. Dreams allow us to play out different scenarios, but this time, we get to perform within a virtual arena of our mind, where there is little interference from reality. We get to bring our imagination to mix together various images, fears and even laughable combinations as we visualize possible future scenarios.

The ability to play out different scenarios objectively through the dreamscape may well be more accurate at times than our waking scenarios. This is because during our dreams we are letting our mind roam free into the future. On the other hand, the pragmatic planning that we do in our waking life may be more accurate at other times, noting that we can be more logical and precise in our measuring risk, reward and consequence.

The difference often relates to the type of activity. Is it an intellectual activity borne of the logical part of the brain? Or is it a conceptual activity borne from the creative part of the brain. The conceptual activities are often taken up in our dreams, while intellectual scenarios are typically more functional when planned out during our waking life, when we can be more practical.

The bottom line is that either process can sometimes play out an accurate scenario. While we might be amazed that we dreamed something ahead of time, we are just as likely to see a future event more accurately by playing out events during our waking lives.

In fact, we do this every day, multiple times a day. We will calculate our options, and choose the one with the most likelihood of achieving our purpose. Even walking across a busy street entails some accurate decision-making based on playing out the scenarios.

Even the most mundane decision requires this skill. We look out to the traffic, and see a gap between cars. We then picture ourselves running across and estimate whether there is a large enough gap to make it. Most of the time we'll be right, and we'll make it across the street just fine.

Our minds can do the same thing when we are sleeping. They can play out the scenarios, and often arrive at an accurate projection of what the future will bring. This, however, is not so amazing, because we might have played the same possibility accurately without sleeping.

So whether we see the future in our waking life through our planning process, or through our dreamscape using our imaginative processes, we are still playing out the future utilizing a combination of past experiences, current desires and intuition.

For example, is it so incredible that Croesus saw his son killed in a dream, or Joan of Arc saw her own death in her dreams? In both cases, there was a strong likelihood the event might happen. The mind could have simply played out the scenario.

The question that comes up is how do people sometimes dream future events with vivid accuracy outside of their typical situation. For example, thousands of people (including the author) dreamed about the 9/11 bombing weeks or even months before the event.

Are these scenarios that the mind is trying to play out into the future? Such an event—and there are so many others—of people seeing things in their dreams that are outside their normal experience seems truly unreasonable that is a simple scenario-playing.

This is one reason for Miller's and Jung's attitudes that the inner person is accessing some outside realm of consciousness. Miller felt the person could access past and future with far less limitation during the dream state. This assumes some sort of continuum. Or a grid of possible choices. Miller called them warnings, suggesting we could access and acknowledge something that will happen in the future.

As for predictive events that are outside of our realm of scenario-development, the essential question is whether we can access the future when we are dreaming. We'll look at the science behind this possibility in the next chapter.

Lucid Dreaming

Another type of dream state has been distinguished from REM-stage dreaming. This is called lucid dreaming. The term *lucid* is taken to mean 'clarity' or 'clear perception.' A *lucid dream,* however, is something a bit different. Lucid dreaming was coined by Frederik van Eeden in 1913, as the realization that we are dreaming while being inside the dream.

In other words, lucid dreaming is a state where we become conscious that we are dreaming. The interesting thing discovered from dream research is that most of us have lucid dreams regularly but we simply don't remember them.

Furthermore, some lucid dream states are accompanied by the ability to direct or steer the dream and/or its consequences and events. In this state, we can bring people we want to face into our dream, act out a particular fantasy, or in general direct our and others' activities within the dream.

The lucid dream state is unique from REM-stage sleep in many ways. While this state has been distinguished from REM-stage sleep only over the last couple of years of sleep research, a recent study from the Frankfurt University's Neurological Clinic (Voss *et al.* 2009) has quantified these differences. The research studied 20 students at Bonn University, who took weekly training sessions to learn to lucidly dream for four weeks. After the four weeks, six students maintained lucid dreams at least three times per week.

They reported that their lucid dreaming began during later REM-stages—several hours into sleeping. These six were chosen to undergo EEG and EOG recordings to monitor their brainwaves and eye movements during lucid dreaming. This allowed the researchers to closely monitor lucid dreaming and conclude the associated brain activity.

The dream researchers found that lucid dream brainwave activity is similar to REM-stage in that it will have strong delta and theta wave strength. In addition to this, however, the brainwave state will have stronger activity in the gamma brainwave portion, which tends to peak at about 40 hertz.

Gamma waves, as we discussed earlier, are typically found among deep problem solving states, meditation or other focused, deeper thinking tasks. This gamma activity will have strong activity within the frontal cortex and the frontolateral area of the brain. This is also distinguished from REM-stage sleeping, according to the research.

These quantifications confirm other studies that have found similar associations with lucid dreaming.

Lucid dream researchers agree that there are two basic types of lucid dreams: the *dream-initiated lucid dream* (DILD); and the *wake initiated lucid dream* (WILD). In the DILD, we are having a normal dream, and suddenly we realize that we are dreaming. In the WILD, we awaken as we realize that we are dreaming.

As mentioned earlier, REM-stage brainwaves resemble brainwave activity during our waking lives. It is almost as if we are awake in the brain, but paralyzed throughout the body.

Most researchers see lucid dreaming as a sub-period of

our REM-stage sleep. They see it as a deeper facet of REM sleeping. However, brainwave activity during lucid sleeping is distinct from REM-stage sleeping, as mentioned.

The brainwaves appearing in lucid dreaming resemble the more introspective moments during our waking lives: in the gamma range. Gamma brainwaves are most prevalent during deeper states of consciousness. This can occur during meditation, problem solving, analysis, or general introspection.

The consistency between these waking moments and lucid dreaming is interesting. When we are lucid dreaming, we are being introspective and analytical with respect to the dreamscape. Once we realize that we are dreaming, we may become aware of the implications of the dream. We may become aware that the dream reflects our perceptions and desires. Just as we do in our waking lives, we may be able to learn from the dream.

This avenue is readily available during our waking lives, but we may only ponder life's lessons occasionally. Our lucid dreaming allows us to ponder life's lessons every night. As we do, we can also play out certain scenarios that allow us to further our learning experiences. This is the magic of lucid dreaming.

For example, during our waking lives we might recognize that when we are rude and hostile to others, they tend to be hostile back to us. Through a problem-solving experience, we can realize there is a cause-and-effect relationship, and make the appropriate changes.

Once we make those changes, the outcome of our waking life can be adjusted. The problem-solving activity that made us realize that our activity had certain ramifications is often a gamma-dominated brainwave state—very similar to the state during lucid dreaming where we are viewing the dream and able to learn from it.

On the other hand, this "power-learning" element of lucid-dreaming sleep is likely why we want and need REM-stage sleep so badly: Quite simply, we become hooked on this type of dreaming. Imagine, for example, that we can climb inside our late model car and experience driving it over a cliff. We wondered how this might feel during our waking lives. Now we get to experience it and learn from it: Was it all that satisfying? Did we get a big thrill or did it just freak us out as we contemplated an uncomfortable landing?

Out-of-Body Dreaming

The out-of-body dream is a subset of an out-of-body experience. It takes place when a person has the experience of being outside their body during a dream. Some who experience this have also experienced or are about to experience a lucid dream. Some report having an out-of-body dream experience just as they are falling to sleep. This is often accompanied by feeling oneself as becoming smaller and smaller, until finally, lifting out and away from the body.

Many people report meeting others in their dreams. Some have reported meeting a relative that had passed away years before in a dream. Others have reported meeting someone who just passed away at the time of the dream.

Still others have reported meeting people who were living in their dreams. For these, there is a lack of science showing a confirmation that the other party also met, but this would require that both parties were able to remember their dreams. As mentioned earlier, remembering a dream is quite difficult, and actually rare when compared with how many dreams we might have in one evening: Some researchers suggest that we can have a handful to even tens of separate dreams every night, and the typical dream only lasts a few minutes.

In such an out-of-body dream, we appear to meet with another party, and share an experience together. While the experience may well be within our minds, we call them out-of-body experiences because both parties become separated from their bodies in order to experience relating with each other.

Could a person actually be releasing from the physical body? Many researchers have proposed that this is simply

a hallucination of the mind brought on by the initial paralysis that takes place when moving into REM-stage
sleep.

A closer review of the science and practical issues relating to identity reveals clarity on this topic.

Chapter Six

The Dreamer

Dr. Laberge realized during his lucid dream research that there seemed to be a correlation between lucid dreams and the *out of body experience* (or OBE). He found that previous research on OBE's reported that most people had their out of body experience while sleeping or near-sleeping. These experiences usually accompany a person floating above his or her body at some point in the dream, or otherwise seeing their body separated from themselves.

Dr. Laberge and his associates at Stanford University then took up the study of researching the connection between lucid dreaming and the OBE. A total of 107 lucid dreams from 14 different people were interviewed, analyzed and tested with polysomnography. The researchers found that 10 of the 107 lucid dreams accompanied an out of body experience—many more than is reported by the general population.

The thesis that dreaming is a random firing of neurons is confounded by lucid dreaming and out of body experiences during sleeping. In fact, the whole process of realizing that we are dreaming means there must be an observer separate from the neuron firings; and separate from the dream, who is realizing that we are dreaming.

Furthermore, this same personality who is able to direct a changing of the mind can also direct the activities of the body. In fact, this same personality who is able to direct the activities of the body and the mind can, we now know from Dr. Stephen LeBerge's research, lucidly see, and direct our dreams. So now we must add to our questions: *Who* is it that can direct our dreams?

These experiences bring to mind the *near death experience* (NDE), which typically includes an OBE. Evidence for the OBE has been conclusive, after thousands of NDEs have been intensely studied by doctors over the past four decades.

In other words, with the advent of resuscitation and medical life-support technologies has come a proliferation of patients whose bodies have clinically died prior to resuscitation. Dr. Raymond Moody, the pioneer of this research in the 1960s, introduced us to the NDE. Dr. Moody presented hundreds of cases documenting NDE's among patients who clinically died in a clinical setting. Dr. Moody found a common experience: After separating from the body, the self often floats above it, viewing resuscitation efforts taking place (Moody 1975).

Dr. Moody's research was followed up by Kenneth Ring, Ph.D. In a well-received study published in 1985, Dr. Ring randomly selected 101 patients who had experienced an NDE. Dr. Ring's patients were chosen randomly to eliminate any bias, imagination, hallucination, inconsistency, suggestion and other elements possibly affecting the objectivity of their after-death experiences. Of the 101 subjects, a third reported out-of-body experiences, and a quarter reported entering the darkness or tunnel with a light at the end. About 60% reported at least a positive, peaceful experience. Those NDE subjects whose death was the result of a suicide attempt experienced no tunnel or light, however. (Ring 1985).

Additionally, when both Moody and Sabom tested the observations of NDE out-of-body observations with hospital staff, they almost without exception confirmed the observations the NDE subjects made from outside of a body that lay clinically dead. While dead and with eyes closed, the patient could hardly be expected to observe those events with the physical eyes. Yet they did observe the events, as confirmed by the rigorous research.

Once again, by far the most logical and scientific conclusion to this evidence is that the self is truly a separate entity from the body and mind. Once the body dies, the self departs—a conclusion also shared by most NDE researchers.

In both REM-stage and lucid dreams, we find the inner personality is mentally and emotionally breaking away from the body. While the body lies paralyzed, the inner self travels through the virtual realm of the mind. This is typically when people experience non-NDE out of body experiences. So we can conclude that the dream state is for all tense and purposes, a virtual reality where the self can travel unencumbered by the restraints of their physical body. In other words, the world of the mind is a separate reality from the physical world of the body.

This makes the mind simply a more subtle body encasing the inner self. Like the physical body, the mind temporarily houses the inner self. With this encasement, the self can travel through its own virtual dimension, just as the physical body travels through the physical dimension.

So can others meet and engage with us inside our virtual mindscape? Certainly, but this 'meeting of minds' would require the two personalities to intently share something common that relates to their goals and desires. Most people have uniquely personal objectives and desires. So most of our dreams are solitary and filled with our own personal 'stuff.'

Those who enter our dreamscape often enter only momentarily, because our dreamscape usually does not have all the 'goodies' their own dreamscape contains for them.

The rules of the mental world are different from those of the physical world. We have fewer limitations in the mental world, yet we are still subject to restrictions. We may be able to fly or shrink in our dreamscape, but there are still limitations. We still negotiate within a world governed by time and consequences. We only have so much time every day to explore our dreamscape, and must deal with its consequences.

These are also attached to the physical world. We also must deal with the consequences of our waking lives. In other words, the results of decisions made and actions taken during our waking lives have consequences. While we may seek to change those consequences, they will play out anyway.

The implication of this understanding is that the inner self is of a different substance or quality. How can we say this? When we are dreaming REM-dreams, lucid dreams or NREM dreams, we are able to observe them. Who is observing them? If we were physical bodies, then there would be no dream observation because our eyes are closed. Because we can watch our dreams, and move within these dream dimensions, we know there is an inner being or personality who dwells above both the physical and mental planes. This being can operate the physical body and observe the events of the physical world; as well as merge into the depths of the mental dreamscape to observe this virtual reality.

This can bring up the question: Which plane is real, the dreamscape or physical plane? To this we would volunteer that both planes are real to the inner self during the experience. Yet at the same time, both planes are temporary: The physical plane lasts a few decades, while the dreamscape lasts a few moments.

These points become very important, as we consider dreaming and insomnia. Anxiety comes from a position of identity: When we consider our physical body the end all be all, issues that concern our physical situation are big problems. When we see our physical body as a temporary vehicle, we can step back from our physical issues and see their temporary nature.

In other words, the solutions brought forth to heal sleep issues should be balanced with a scientific understanding of our core identity: Understanding that the same inner personality who observes life through the waking body also observes the dreamscape conjured by the mind. In other words, while sleep engages certain physiological processes critical to the health of the body and mind, it also allows the self to seek its desires and objectives, while learning critical lessons.

One might wonder: if our dreams are fantasy worlds created by our minds, then why do we sometimes have nightmares?

Again, it is not as if we have full control of our dreamscapes. There are rules and consequences. Most of us have awakened in a cold sweat from a dream we didn't like. We were relieved to find upon waking that it was only a dream. Our dreams get out of hand because these are the consequences of our desires, objectives and fears.

So what could be so fantasy-like about having a nightmare? To answer this, we must solve why a person will to go to a horror movie or watch a gruesome show on television. Some will even pay to see a traumatic horror movie on a huge movie screen. Why? Because the inner personality has developed a desire to experience the thrill of being frightened.

The problem with this desire, however, is that it has its consequences. Our desires can get out of hand in our dreamscape. Our mind can rearrange sensual information in such a way as to *really* frighten us. In other words, there are no props in our dreamscape. We can make our dreamscape as real as reality can get. Our mind may even take what we've seen in a horror movie and put us in a dreamscape that makes us experience that horror movie personally.

As for those who experience nightmares and detest any suggestion that their inner desires are causing their nightmares, we present another side of desire: fear. Because our mind and brain are simple machines, they cannot make a distinction between simple pleasures and frightening scenarios. The mind can take any mix of input that the inner self has been focusing on during a combination of waking life, movies and computer games, and mix it up into a dreamscape.

In other words, our dreamscape is a reflection of a combination of our innermost desires, our innermost fears, the sensual inputs we receive, and the activities that we participate in during our waking lives. These are all mixed into a virtual dreamscape automatically by the programming of our mind, which is driven by our inner self's desire to escape the restraints of the physical world and enjoy without restriction.

Just as in our waking lives, however, there are still rules to the dreamscape. We cannot completely control this virtual reality. We also have to deal with the consequences of our decisions and activities.

In the waking world, if we slap someone for no reason, we will either be slapped back or arrested for abuse. In the dreamscape world, if we slap someone, they could turn into a monster and freak us out completely.

Our consequences can also cross over between the physical and virtual realities. Consider if we slapped someone during our waking life, and somehow got away with not being punished or slapped back. The guilt and shame the inner self feels deep inside would likely create a virtual dreamscape reality where the person we slapped in the face came back and threw acid on our face or burned our house down with us in it: or something else that we might be afraid of.

It is for these very reasons that not remembering our dreams can be a good thing. If we remembered all of the traumatic things that took place during our dreams, we'd be traumatized during our waking lives. Still this does happen sometimes. For people who are awakened during a nightmare to remember it, going back to sleep can be terrorizing.

Again, those dreams we remember are those dreams that during the dream we—the inner self—realize are important enough to remember during our waking life. This might be because the dream is so curious that we want to figure it out. It could also be that the dream relates to something we have been concerned about during our waking life, so the inner self pushes the mind to remember such a dream.

The bottom line here is that there is no mystery involved in sleep or dreaming. We create the concept of a mystery because we like to keep our fantasy world separated from our waking world. Our dreams are our private fantasy world, and we—the inner self—doesn't want to wreck it with reality.

This is also healthy. It is healthy for us to escape into this world because we not only are able to play out our innermost fantasies with little effect upon our waking lives: It is healthy because during that escape we can learn.

We can learn some of the same lessons our waking life teaches us: We can learn that honesty is the best policy. We can learn that when we hurt others we only hurt ourselves. We can learn that when we care for others we are happier. And we can learn perhaps one of the greatest lessons of both our waking and dream states: that the world does not—despite our best attempts—actually revolve around us.

The question comes down to identity. Who are we?

Self-Identification

If someone asks our identity we will most likely describe either our body's physical features or our body's country of origin. We might say "I am American" or "I am black" or "I am five feet tall, weigh 125 lbs, and female with brown eyes." The logical question is: Am I really this physical body? If so, what happens if our body gains 100 lbs of weight? Does our identity change?

Most of us have a hint that our identity runs deeper than our physical body. A person with a black body wants equality with a person with a white body because that person considers that beneath the skin, we are equal. Similarly, an obese person wants to be treated equally with someone of a more slender stature. Why would we request equality unless we are assuming we have deeper identities?

This issue relates specifically to dreaming, because before we fall asleep we are identifying with our body, and when we wake up we are identifying with our body. However, our dreamscape body can have altogether different characteristics from our waking physical body.

Our dreamscape body, for example, might be able to fly. It might be able to swim like a fish underwater. Or it might have the ability to run very quickly even though our current physical body might be elderly or even handicapped.

During our dreams, in other words, our self-identity changes from when we are awake. What does this say about our identity?

Consider Amputation

If someone loses an arm in an accident, no one would consider the person any different. They would remain the same person, but without an arm, correct?

This logic can also be extended to losing both arms and legs. An explosion or other traumatic accident might leave ones torso intact while dismembering the arms and legs. Regardless of losing these appendages, the person is still perceived as a whole person, even though their body cannot function in certain ways.

The person who operates the body still contains the same conscious being with the same ability to think and reason. This is why paraplegic and quadriplegic rights are protected by law, and why quadriplegic Steven Hawking is considered one of the today's foremost theoretical physicists. Physically disabled people are given equal rights because society considers them equal in all respects despite their physical handicap.

The physical organs can be considered using the same logic. It is now commonplace in medicine to surgically remove and replace organs such as kidneys, livers, hearts, hips and other parts in order to preserve the healthy functioning of the body. Some parts—like hearts and hip sockets—are now replaced with artificial versions. Modern medicine has illustrated through many years of organ transplants that a person's identity does not travel with their organ.

Otherwise, we might have—as a few comedic theatrical performances have suggested—people whose personalities reflect their organ donors' personality. Imagine: A person receiving another person's heart assuming an aspect of the personality of the dead donor?

We might compare this to an auto accident: Let's say a car is brought into a repair shop after a collision: The shop determines the car needs the tires changed, the engine rebuilt and various other parts of the car replaced before the car can be put back on the road.

These changes and new car parts do not affect the driver of the car. The driver will still be the same person no matter how many new parts are put on the car.

After the engine is rebuilt, the new tires are installed and the other parts are replaced, the unchanged driver gets back into the car and drives it away.

In the same way, a person who receives a prosthetic leg can continue to walk after losing a leg. The person has not changed despite the change in body parts.

Recycling Chemistry

Throughout its lifetime, our body is continually changing, yet we continue to maintain our core identity and consciousness. Research has shown all living cells in the body have a finite lifespan, ranging from minutes to days to years. It is thought a few cells of the body—such as certain bone marrow stem cells and brain cells—may exist through the duration of the body.

Still there are only a handful of these cells compared to the estimated 200 trillion cells making up the body. By far the vast majority of cells in the body will participate in cell division, with the older cells becoming broken down and replaced by the newly divided cells. Thus, we see a constant sloughing off of dead cells from the body and a constant breakdown and wasting of cell parts through the liver and out the body. We might consider these facts:

Surface gastric cells are replaced about every five minutes. All stomach-lining cells are replaced within a week. Skin cells are all replaced within about a month and a half. The entire liver is regenerated within two months. The bone cells will all be replaced within a year.

Furthermore, the composition of every cell—its atoms and molecules—undergo an even faster turnover. Every cell in the body, including even the stem cells, is made up of molecular combinations of atomic waves. Molecular cell wave-parts make up the nucleus complete DNA, RNA, cytoplasm, various organelles, and a cell membrane. Each of these components is made of molecules, and each molecule is made up of various atomic standing waves. These atomic and molecular cell units are constantly being replaced by the minute with fresh atomic wave rhythms.

Each of our body's cell membranes allows for diffusion, osmosis and ionic channel movement, giving each cell a constant exchange of molecules, atoms and ions.

Active cells will replace molecules quite rapidly. Brain cells will recycle all their molecules within three days. In fact, 98% of all the atoms and molecules in the body are replaced within a year, and most biologists agree all the atoms and molecules within the body are replaced by new ones within five years.

Noting our physical bodies change nearly every cell within days or a few years and within five years; every atom and molecule is replaced from the food we eat, the water we drink and the air we breathe, *the body we were wearing five years ago is not the same body* we are *wearing today*. We are wearing a completely different body.

In effect, we have each *changed bodies* within this period. Every rhythmic element of matter—every vibrating atom—is new. This might well be compared to a waterfall. The water within a waterfall is always changing. From moment to moment, the waterfall will be made up of different water. Therefore, the waterfall we see today is not the same waterfall we saw yesterday.

Since each of us is the same person from moment to moment and year to year within an ever-changing body, logically we each have an identity separate from this temporary vehicle.

We cannot be the physical body, since the body has been replaced while we are still here. Should we look at our photograph taken five years ago, we will be looking at *a completely different body* from the one we are wearing today. The eyes looking at the eyes in the picture will be different eyes.

This is the same for our dream bodies. In one dream we might be an athlete while in another dream we might be an astronaut. Or a schoolteacher. We seem to pick up a new dream identity each time we dream.

What is consistent is that our dream body is typically different from our waking body. These differences can be seen by the activities within our dreams. We might still feel that the dream body is me just as we feel this physical body is me even though it is changing.

When we look objectively at what takes place within

each dream, we can realize that our dream body is typically different than our waking body. Sometimes our dream body is younger than our physical body. Sometimes our dream body is older. Sometimes it is smaller or larger—giving us different perspectives of our dreamscape.

Brain Identity

One might propose that since we have yet to transplant someone's brain maybe we are the brain. Most of us have heard of or seen the famous neurosurgical experiments first documented by Dr. Wilder Penfield, wherein stimulation of the temporal cortex stimulated particular memories. These experiments or their successors might leave us with an impression we are the brain since we feel so close to our memories and emotions.

This assumption is disputed by brain research over the past fifty years on both humans and animals. In many cases various brain parts have been removed, leaving memory and emotion intact. Mishkin (1978) documented that the removal of either the amygdala or the hippocampus did not severely impair memory. Mumby *et al.* (1992) determined that memory was only mildly affected in rats with hippocampus and amygdala lesions.

According to a substantial review done by Vargha-Khadem and Polkey (1992), the past twenty years of surgical documentation revealed numerous hemidecortication operations—the removal of half the brain. In a majority of these cases, cognition and brain function continued.

A few cases even documented an improvement in cognition! Additionally, in numerous cases of intractable seizures, where substantial parts of brain have been damaged, substantial cognitive recovery resulted in 80 to 90% of the cases.

These and numerous other studies illustrate that the person is not reduced by brain damage or removal. They are still the same person. They still have the same personality. Many retain all their memories. The majority of stroke patients go about living normal lives afterward. While sometimes we see memory, cognitive and motor skills affected by cerebrovascular stroke, the person within is unaffected by physical changes in the brain.

Many organisms have memory and sense perception without even having a brain. Bacteria, for example, do not have brains, yet they can memorize a wide variety of skills and events, including what damaged or helped them in the past. Other organisms such as plants, nematodes and others are living replete with memory and recall without having brains.

MRI and CT brain scans on patients with various brain injuries or stroke have shown particular functions will often move functions from one part of the brain to another after the original area was damaged. We must therefore ask: Who is it that moves these physical functions from one part of the brain to another? Is the damaged brain area making this decision?

That would not make sense. Are the brain neurons making the decision? How would the new brain neurons know what functions the old neurons had if those neurons are now damaged?

The retention of memory, emotion, and the moving of brain function from one part of the brain to another is evidence there is a deeper mechanism or *operator* within the body who is *utilizing* the brain, rather than the person *being* the brain. The person *operating* the body is the continuing element. The physical structures continually undergo change while the operator remains, adapting to those changes.

Hormones and Neurotransmitters

In recent years, some researchers have proposed that our identities relate to the chemicals that stimulate our nerves and tissues. These are the hormones and neurotransmitters.

The concept is that emotional responses to environmental stimuli initiate physiology to respond. For example, when we receive an indication of possible danger, our body will respond by activating the hypothalamus to send hypothalamic hormones to the pituitary gland. In response, the pituitary gland releases ACTH (adrenocorticotropic hormone), which in turn induces the adrenal cortex to secrete glucocorticoid hormones such as cortisol. These two hormones in turn encourage the release of biochemicals epinephrine and norepinephrine, which work with the glucocorticoids to stimulate muscle response.

The lungs, the heart and the pancreas are stimulated into action by these and other biochemicals. They stimulate an increased utilization of oxygen and glucose by the muscles for their proper functioning. This entire cascade of chemical release is designed to aid the body in evasion or defense against the impending danger.

Because neurologists and other researchers have seen these neurological biochemicals at locations connected to response to emotional states, the assumption is that these biochemicals somehow contain the emotion. They propose that chemicals such as endorphins, dopamine, serotonin, epinephrine, or acetylcholine each contain particular emotions, and are thus the elements of emotion or life within the body.

While these signaling biochemicals connect with receptors positioned at the surface of particular cells, the response by the cell is due to the emotion somehow being released from the chemical. An example is the famed *opiate receptor,* which has been linked with the cell's reception of morphine or endorphins and feelings of euphoria.

One problem with this theory is that no two organisms respond identically to the same chemical. With opiates for example, some may hallucinate while others may only respond casually. On the other hand, some may have nightmarish experiences.

If these structurally identical neuro-chemicals *contained* the emotion, why would each person respond differently to the same chemical and dose?

The main problem is *who* is observing these euphoric feelings or hallucinations that are stimulated by these neurochemicals? *Who* observes the body's positive or negative sensations?

The perception of pain may offer some clarity. In 2005

Dr. Ronald Melzack, a co-author of the famous *gate control theory* of pain transmission, updated his theory of pain from a simple gateway effect to one of a multidimensional experience of *'neurosignatures'*.

Dr. Melzack's new theory—which he calls the *"body-self neuromatrix"*—explains that the consensus of clinical research on acute pain, behavior and chronic pain indicates an independent perceptual state, observing and exchanging feedback and response with the locations of injury.

Because doctors and researchers have found a good portion of the pain response is unrelated to specific injury but rather a modification of sensory experience, this *neuromatrix* indicates an interaction between the nervous system and what Melzack calls the *"self."*

Elaborating, pain requires two components: 1) The sensory transmission of pain and 2) the observer or experiencer of that pain. Now once that pain is experienced, there may also be a feedback response from the experiencer. This feedback may either be: 1) take action to remove the cause of the pain; or 2) if there is no apparent cause then become extra-sensitive to the pain (Baranauskas and Nistri 1998) until the cause is determined.

This increased sensory elevation may lead to what is called *noiceptic pain,* or pain not appearing to have a direct physical cause. Some might also refer to this type of pain as being *psychosomatic,* although psychosomatic pain is often thought of as not real. Noiceptic pain is considered real, but its cause is not physically apparent.

Regardless of the name, this type of pain is very difficult to understand and manage, especially for doctors and patients dealing with chronic pain appearing unrelated to trauma or inflammation. Because the self naturally seeks pleasure, we would propose the current cause of that pain is always real, from either a gross physical level or a more subtle level.

Regardless of the amount of pain the self experiences, that pain is separate from the self. Why else would the self want to escape it? Furthermore, any biochemical messengers assisting in its transmission would necessarily have to be separate.

The discoveries of new biochemical *ligands* observed during cognitive events have unveiled yet another chemical-identity-based theory, suggesting these biochemicals are the source of memories, and together they form the basis of our personality.

The proposals of some surmise that when certain biochemicals tie with particular synaptic (nerve) cells, the emotional response produces a memory response. They propose since these certain biochemicals are present in larger volumes during memory recall, memories must be contained within them.

Since these biochemicals are present during certain responses or memories, it may make sense that these chemicals have a *role* in physical responses to emotions or memories. However, the proposal that memory and emotions exist *within* the chemicals is not supported by logic or observation. If the chemicals contained memory or emotion, these characteristics should exist in the chemicals both inside and outside of the living mechanics of the body.

Researchers often will remove biochemicals from bodies, putting them into beakers as they draw blood or other body fluids. This theory is tested thousands of times a day by hospitals who transfuse blood from one subject to another. In none of these cases are emotions or feelings being transferred from one person to another. Once drawn, the biochemicals contained in the blood do not display any sort of memory or emotion consistent with the emotions displayed by the previous host.

This is not to say injected biochemicals do not elicit a physical response. The organism receiving epinephrine or another neurochemical may incur a physical response consistent with the cascade related to that biochemical. Injected adrenaline may produce a physical reaction of increased heart rate, for example. But adrenaline drawn from one person during a fearful response will not induce a recall of that specific fear in the person it is injected into.

We must therefore conclude there is someone inside who is either—directly or indirectly—initiating or responding to the body's neurochemicals. In all cases, in order to stimulate any emotional response, there must be a conscious stimulant.

Fuel may ignite a spark in the cylinder of an automobile engine causing combustion, which will push the rods into motion, exerting force on the axel cranks. Fuel is not the driver though. Nor does fuel contain directions for the destination. The driver of the car consciously turns the key and determines its direction using a steering wheel, accelerator, and brakes.

When the living being leaves the body at death there are no emotions exhibited in the dead body. While all the neurochemicals and cells—all the ligands and receptors—are still contained within the body, the body supports no memory or emotional response because there is no longer a conscious driver present. The conscious driver ultimately initiates as well as responds to the neurochemistry of the body.

Emotions elicited from a response to an observation or other sensual stimuli would logically come from someone who separate from those stimuli. Because emotion is integral with interpreting stimuli, an observer would be necessary for that interpretation. Without an observer, there could be no decision-making and no choice. We would essentially all be robots.

This does not mean that all physiological responses require interpretation and decision. For example should we touch the burner of a stove there is programming in place within the neural network to instantly react by pulling the hand away. This will happen often before the self has a chance to make a decision.

However, it does not mean the self cannot decide to resist that reaction of pulling away. A firewalker may intentionally walk on the coals despite his autonomic system screaming to jump away onto the cool sand. These observations lead us to understand the self can be involved in almost any autonomic system should there be determination and intention.

Other stimuli may require the emotional self to respond. Otherwise, no action will take place. Upon hearing the alarm in the morning, the self could choose to do nothing—lying in bed for the rest of the day. The self could also intend to accomplish something that day, and rise to begin the day's activities.

Once sensual stimuli are pulsed to the neural network after being received by one or many of the biochemical receptors, the body forms specific information waves. These waves have been studied over the past fifty years using an apparatus called the *electroencephalograph* (also referred to as EEG). EEG studies have confirmed that the brain's neurons, in response to signals from either the sensory nerves or incoming responses around the body, produce various brainwave patterns.

There are numerous specific wave patterns, but they are generally categorized by their frequency range. The main frequency ranges of brainwaves include *Gamma, Alpha, Beta, Theta and Delta waves:*

Gamma waves are high-frequency waves that range from between thirty and sixty cycles per second. *Alpha waves* have a range of between eight to thirteen cycles per second. *Beta waves* have a range of fourteen to thirty cycles per second. *Theta waves* have a range of four to seven cycles per second. *Delta waves* have a range of from less than one cycle per second to about three cycles per second.

While the higher frequency waves are prominent during periods of higher stress or problem solving, the slower, lower-frequency waves tend to be dominant during periods of relaxation, meditation, or sleep. Still, all of these types of waveforms are typically present.

At any particular point in time, there are billions of brainwaves of various specific frequencies moving around the brain. As the different waves collide—or interfere—they create different types of interference patterns. As confirmed by neurological research headed up by Dr. Robert Knight (Sanders *et al.* 2006) at the University of California/Berkeley and UC/San Francisco, the interaction of these interference patterns together formulate a type of mapping system. This mapping system forms a type of screen, upon which the self can view sensory information coming in from the eyes, ears and other sense organs, together with the feedback from the body.

As the self views the waveform image patterns, it can respond with intention. Intention from the self is typically translated through the pre-frontal cortex and medial cortex to create response brainwave patterns, although other cortices are also sometimes used.

These response brainwave patterns are translated through the hypothalamus and pituitary gland to produce master hormones such as growth hormone, adrenocorticotropic hormone, follicle-stimulating hormone, oxytocin, luteinizing hormone, and others, stimulating the cascade of physical response as mentioned above.

For example, waves in the delta frequency range tend to stimulate the production of growth hormone. One of growth hormone's more versatile effects is its ability to advance the healing and regeneration process.

Researchers have observed during feelings of love or compassion an increase in biochemicals like dopamine, serotonin, and various endorphins in the bloodstream. Did the emotions stimulate the biochemicals or did the biochemicals stimulate the emotions? Many are proposing the limited view that the emotion even created by the biochemicals. This would be equivalent to saying love comes from biochemicals.

We must question the logic of this proposal, however. While dopamine, serotonin, and endorphins are circulating at heightened levels following activities such as laughing eating, sex and post-traumatic stress, these biochemicals are also circulating at other times, albeit at different levels. If they were creating the emotion, they would be present only in and prior to specific emotions. Instead, they are present during a variety of emotions. We also are not seeing different molecular structures between the biochemicals in different moods.

On the other hand, we could logically conclude that the body produces positive (or negative) feedback neurotransmitter or hormonal messengers, which could well stimulate an emotional *response* to those messengers. Considering that biochemical levels change depending upon the condition of the body, it would seem appropriate that the self would be able to respond to this condition.

It would also be logical that once the self did respond to a particular sensory stimulation or physical feedback messenger, that emotional response would also stimulate particular biochemicals. In other words, these biochemicals are messengers. Like current in an electric wire, the process can move in either direction. Biochemicals can be stimulated by emotional decisions as well as potentially stimulate an emotional response. This would reveal these biochemicals as parts of a cyclic balancing process, while the self is the observer and driver of the cycle.

To suggest any one of these biochemicals is responsible for a particular emotion would be to ignore its physiological relationship with the rest of the body's biochemistry. Almost every biochemical process in the body is cyclic, with various operational conclusions. 'Biochemical emotion' would also ignore the presence of an intentional observer—responsible for responding to the body's balance as well as driving its balance towards particular objectives.

We can illustrate this process on another level. Hearing that a friend was hurt will cause an emotional reaction. The emotion was experienced following the aural reception. Upon hearing this and reacting emotionally, a physical response might follow, such as tears or a rush to the hospital. These physical responses were stimulated by the emotion. The initial emotion was stimulated from hearing. This emotion was felt by the self and the self initiated a physical response to those emotions. It would be nonsensical to say that the biochemicals in the tears caused the emotional response.

Biofeedback and the Observer Within

Biofeedback mirrors what occurs between the self and the body, or the self and the dreamscape.

In biofeedback, sensors are attached to various parts of the body to monitor physical responses like heart rate, breathing, brainwaves, muscle activity, and so on. These sensors are connected to a computer, which displays the various response levels onto a monitor for the subject to see. The heart rate amplitude and frequency readings will be displayed on the monitor in waves, bars, and/or numbers.

With a little practice, most people can—once they see their heart rate with graphics clearly on the monitor—consciously lower their heart rate. Biofeedback has thus been used successfully to teach a person to alter various other functions such as muscle tension, hunger, stress, and other autonomic functions. Biofeedback training gives the subject the ability to directly control a variety of physical responses including stomach cramps, muscle spasms, headaches, and other occurrences—many known to be part of a biochemical cascade.

The reason why the biofeedback subject can learn to control certain biochemically driven autonomic functions is that the self ultimately exists outside the biochemistry of the body. It is the self who can decide to influence physical functions. Once the person intends to make a change, the mind will facilitate the stimulation of the biochemicals by the appropriate glands to produce a physiological response.

Even without biofeedback, a person can initiate various autonomic responses. Most of us have experienced how a physiological fear response may be initiated by simply imagining a dangerous event or situation. This happens every day in the professional world, where executives stress over events that have not happened nor may never happen.

This stress increases the heart rate and stimulates stress biochemical release. Most of us have experienced being worried about an event that may never happen. The resulting increase in our heart rate indicates our body's autonomic response to the anxious self.

If the self can affect the body's biochemistry with anxiousness, the self is separate from the biochemistry. Furthermore, if the self can affect the body's biochemistry intentionally, there is no question of the self's ability to direct the body through intention.

And this extends to dreaming. The self can initiate and stimulate certain brain neurons and neurotransmitters which draw particular memories from the thalamus, for example. These can be used to play out particular scenarios based upon past activities.

The ability to stimulate certain neurotransmitters and neurons would be analogous to a computer operator operating a computer. A computer will tabulate, calculate, and memorize data. It will display various graphics and perform various functions, based upon the input of the operator. The software and hardware are set up in such a way to coordinate computer functions very quickly and automatically.

However, these software and hardware functions require human initiation. A computer operator must turn on the computer and input into the machine certain intentional commands in order to initiate and maintain the computer's functions.

In the same way, the physical body, with all of its functional chemistry and various physical responses going on, is ultimately being steered by a personality within: this is the self, the living being—the operator of the body.

It is difficult sometimes to separate the living being inside the body from the various physical and biochemical operations. This is because the feedback-response system is bridging the self with the physical body.

Chemicals influence behavior because they not only stimulate physical tissue response, but they also give feedback to the self about what is going on in the body.

For example, the feeling of thirst is a neuro-chemical signal to the self that the body needs water. The combination of hormonal, osmotic, ionic and nerve signaling all integrate to stimulate *osmoreceptors* located among brain tissue (such as the anteroventral third ventricle wall).

Once stimulated, these receptors initiate waveform signaling through the hypothalamus, which converts into the more subtle waveforms of the mind. Through the reciprocation of the mind, the self observes this feedback, and responds by initiating action to find some water.

A computer will also feed back to its operator in the same way. The computer is not only designed to perform operations based upon the input of the operator, but it is designed to feed back to the operator the results of those operations, signaling a need for new responses from the operator.

This process is called a feedback loop. The body's feedback system is designed to respond to environmental and physical changes around the anatomy. The system is designed to signal to the self on how the body is functioning. This is one of the purposes for serotonin release in the body: To feed back the presence of balance within particular mechanisms.

A diet balanced in proteins, carbohydrates, and fats, along with physiological activities that stimulate the conversation of tryptophan to serotonin such as relaxation, laughter, and exercise. This combined state of balance results in a normal flow of serotonin, which feeds back to the self the presence of balance among certain mechanisms.

Pain, on the other hand, indicates quite the opposite: Some imbalance exists somewhere, and the pain feeds back to the operator the need for an adjustment among those functions. This necessary adjustment could be to the diet, fluid intake, a sitting posture, lack of the wrong type of exercise, or perhaps an infection of some sort. Chronic pain indicates an unresolved lack of balance in the body.

Just as an instrument panel on an automobile tells the driver the running condition of car, we can monitor the condition of our body through these and other neuro-chemical feedback mechanisms. Just as the car driver slows down when the speedometer shows the car is over the speed limit, the self—directly through conscious control or indirectly through the autonomic system—makes the needed adjustment when the body's feedback systems indicate those needs.

Misidentifying ourselves as the body confuses the body's positive feedback mechanisms with pleasure. This misconception leads us to attempt to manipulate our body's neuropathic mechanisms.

Eating, for example, will stimulate positive neurochemicals such as serotonin and dopamine when there is a balance of nutrition and energy. Our taste buds feed back positive neural signals when we eat something sweet or fatty (food providing energy).

In an effort to gain positive neuropathic responses, many of us continue to eat long after the body has enough for its fuel. An ongoing attempt to become fulfilled through eating can result in obesity, frustration, and depression. In the same way, the car driver does not get full when he fills the car's fuel tank.

The Time of Death

By any observation, life leaves the body at the time of death. A living body is full of life, movement, energy, personality, and purpose. We can readily understand these are symptoms of life.

But when death arrives, suddenly the symptoms of life depart. There is no movement. There is no energy. There is no personality existing within the dead body. The body becomes lifeless.

What does this have to do with dreaming? Just consider what happens to the body when we dream: The body becomes practically lifeless. What happens to us when the body is lifeless?

After thousands of years of scientific observation and research on cadavers, no one—not even modern researchers with advanced medical instruments—has been able to find any chemical or physical element that leaves the body at death. The dead body has every physical and material component the living body had. All of the cells are there. The DNA is there. All of the nerves, the organs, the brain and central nervous system—every physical element—that was in the living body remains in the dead body.

One claim of the soul weighing 21-grams was made in 1907. The family physician Dr. Duncan MacDougall attempted an experiment where six patients were monitored as they died upon a table rigged with a scale. While the results of his experiment have been popularized, they have also been taken out of context. The fact is, the experiment was a failure from a scientific perspective.

Of the six test subjects, two were eliminated because of technical issues. Three subjects died of tuberculosis. Two of these were losing weight before and after death by "evaporation and respiratory moisture."

One subject died from "consumption" and seemingly lost ¾ of an ounce in weight as he was dying—later converted by popular media to 21.3 grams. However, Dr. MacDougall admitted that it was difficult to know at what point the patient had died (MacDougall 1907).

A fellow doctor in Massachusetts, Dr. A. Clarke, immediately disagreed with Dr. MacDougal's hypothesis that the 21 grams was lost at the time of death. Dr. Clarke argued that the typical sudden rise in body temperature before and subsequent cooling without circulation indicated that the weight loss was caused by slight weight changes due to evaporation. This was also supported by the fact that the patient had lethal tuberculosis—a disease of the lungs, where fluid often fills the lungs.

While Dr. MacDougal assumed the moment of death occurred when the patient convulsed a bit and then lay still without breathing, modern research shows that brain death must also occur—something Dr. MacDougal was not monitoring. Because the correct time of death was not ascertained by Dr. MacDougal, the proposed weight change likely did not occur at the time of death.

Until his own death in 1920, Dr. MacDougall tried to repeat the results and could not confirm his findings. In one test, he killed fifteen dogs while he weighed them.

Again, he found no loss in weight.

Centuries of intense cadaver research and autopsy has found no gross difference between the living and dead body. No scientific study has corroborated any loss of any physical element, including weight, upon death. Organs, bones, nerves, brains, blood, neurochemistry, DNA and so many other physical aspects of the live and dead body have been analyzed. Nothing physical has been found to be missing after death.

What the dead body is missing is the immeasurable element of life. This is the element that drives the living body. This element gives the physical body personality. This element gives the body energy. This element initiates the urge for survival and procreation.

This element stimulates the factors that drive the healing processes, the digestive processes, the sensual processes, the circulatory processes, and so many other biological and biochemical processes. This element of life is definite. It is not imaginary. Seeing a dead body formerly living will clearly illustrate that this key element is quite real.

For this very reason, people describe the point of death as a "passing" or "he passed away" or "he left us." Why are these expressions used? Because most of us accept (at least deep within) that the person still exists, despite the fact that the body is lying in front of us devoid of life.

The life force has never been seen under a microscope, a CT scan, an MRI, or by any other physical piece of equipment. This is because the living force dwells within another dimension.

Consider for a moment if you were playing a computer video game. You sit down at the computer and you start up the game. The game then gives you a choice of icons, and you select your icon. Maybe it looks more like a cartoon character.

Then you start playing the game. Your icon immediately gets bashed from the game's various elements. Maybe it's a war game and your icon is getting bombed and shot.

At some point in the video game, if your icon gets shot enough, the icon is announced dead. At that point, you have to turn off the game and if you want to play again, you have to start up a new game. Or perhaps you decide that one game was enough and you get up and walk away from the computer.

It is not as if you died when your game icon died. You didn't even get scratched by those nukes and bullets in the video game.

Why?

Because the icon that you took on in the video game was a temporary, fake identity you utilized in order to play the game. The game icon was not you.

Furthermore, let's say that there were other players in the game, and the game was being played online, so that no one could see each other's faces—you could only see each other's game icons. And let's say that you didn't know that the other game icons were run by other players. Let's say you thought the game icons were part of the computer program.

Now in this scenario, where you could only see the various players' icons and not who the actual computer operators were, let's say one of the other game icons was shot and died. What would you see and think as you looked at the screen? You would only see the icon die. You would not see any computer operator behind the game icon—maybe he has simply gotten up and walked to the refrigerator to get some food.

The reason you could not see the other computer operator was because the computer program did not allow you to see them: It limited the extent of vision of the other players to their game icons. This gave you the impression that there was no computer operator behind these game icons.

In this way, when one of the other icons died, you figured that the icon died and that's that. You would certainly identify each of the players as their game icons.

Why? Because you could not see the computer operators behind those icons. Thus, when an icon died, your only perception would be that that was the end of that game icon.

This is no different from the scenario that takes place at the death of the physical body.

Furthermore, since the living force separates from the body at death, yet is not evident in physical elements of living or dead bodies, we can scientifically conclude that the life force is not a physical part of the living body.

Since the personality is also gone when this life is gone from the body, it would only be logical to conclude that each of us 'personalities' *is* this life force, and not the physical body: Just as the car driver is not the car. The car driver can and needs to get out of the car at some point. Therefore, the car driver has a separate identity from the car.

For this same reasoning, when Socrates' students asked him how he wanted to be buried, Socrates' reply was that they can do whatever they want with his body after death, because he will already have gone by then.

So does the self stay in the body while we are dreaming?

Clinical Death

Evidence concluding our identity as nonphysical has been presented by a number of respected researchers over the past four decades. With the advent of resuscitation and medical life-support technologies has come a proliferation of patients whose bodies have clinically died prior to resuscitation. Author and researcher Dr. Raymond Moody pioneered this research in the 1960s, and thus introduced us to the *Near Death Experience* (or NDE).

Dr. Moody presented hundreds of cases documenting common experiences among patients declared clinically dead in a clinical setting. Dr. Moody's research reviewed a cross-section of thousands of cases of patients with a variety of religious and socio-economic backgrounds.

Dr. Moody discovered a common experience: After separating from the body, the self floats above it, viewing the various resuscitation efforts taking place on the body.

This is often followed by the self remotely traveling to and viewing loved ones. Often traveling at the speed of thought to their homes or locations, the self often tried in vain to communicate with their loved one.

Afterward, many subjects detailed being drawn into a darkened tunnel with a bright light at the end. At the end of the tunnel, many either entered or saw a dazzling light or personality. Many reviewed their lives in an instant. Many went on to meet with this personality.

In many cases the personality indicated it was not "their time yet." Following this, many instantly returned to their body. This usually coincided with the revival of the body. While specific experiences were often different, most NDE subjects experienced separation from their physical body and felt, at the very least, peaceful (Moody 1975).

Naturally, this research had its skeptics. A few questioned Dr. Moody's protocols, which included patient selection and interview techniques. This gap was quickly filled by Kenneth Ring, Ph.D. In a well-received peer-reviewed book published in 1985, Dr. Ring randomly selected 101 patients who had experienced an NDE. Dr. Moody's patients were collected as their data were presented to him. This offered some but not complete randomness.

By contrast, the 101 patients studied by Dr. Ring were chosen randomly to eliminate any bias, imagination, hallucination, inconsistency, and other elements possibly affecting the objectivity of their after-death experience. Of the 101 subjects, a third reported out-of-body experiences, and a quarter reported entering the darkness or tunnel with the light at the end.

About 60% reported at least a positive, peaceful experience. Those NDE subjects whose death was the result of a suicide attempt experienced no tunnel with light. The suicide NDEs in this study experienced a "murky darkness," after feeling separated from their body, but they did not proceed any further (Ring 1985).

Ring's findings—though not in the exact same percentages—were substantiated by professor of medicine and cardiologist Michael Sabom, M.D. in a 1982 work called *Recollections of Death: A Medical Investigation.* There have been other investigations confirming these experiences (Blackmore 1996). Dr. Elisabeth Kubler-Ross documents researching some twenty thousand cases of near-death in her 1991 book *On Life After Death*, confirming the same primary conclusions of the research done by Sabom, Moody and Ring.

Upon review of the other various explanations, it appears unlikely any of the possible physical causes could suitably explain the NDE—except that the self is not the body. The sheer cross-section of people with this same experience provides too much variance to provide any other rational explanation. The common NDE experiences regardless of the level of religious reverence, expectation levels, drug-administration, knowledge of NDE and brain or biochemical stimulation certainly provides few alternatives.

Additionally, when both Moody and Sabom tested the observations of NDE out-of-body observations with hospital staff, they almost without exception confirmed the observations the NDE subjects made from outside of a body clinically unconscious.

While unconscious and with eyes closed, the patient could hardly be expected to observe those events—even if by subconscious hearing—due to the detail of the NDE subject descriptions. To this, skeptical researchers have suggested some sort of paranormal experience. We must ask those skeptics how rational it is to accept the notion of a paranormal experience but not accept an out-of-body observation?

Again by far the most logical and scientific approach to this topic is the self is truly a separate entity from the body and after the body dies, the self departs.

Therefore, since the self departs from the body at the time of death, we have to accept that the self can separate from the body during dreaming. This is further confirmed in remote viewing.

Remote Viewing

For twenty-three years, the Stanford University Research Institute studied *parapsychological phenomena* (commonly termed psi—after the Greek letter *psi*, or *psyche*) and *remote viewing* with a grant from the United States government.

Two physicists named Dr. Russel Targ and Dr. Harold Puthoff teamed up for much of this research, and they conducted controlled experiments under the watchful eye of the CIA. Much of this top-secret research was not released to the scientific community due to its sensitivity to international security. Part of the research consisted of sealing talented subjects into guarded rooms with observers. From the sealed rooms, the subjects remotely viewed and described in detail events and locations thousands of miles away.

Their viewing documented minute details of the locations, down to the current weather conditions. They described specific geographical facilities, the locations of specific buildings, and activities taking place—years before internet use was common. The locations and specifics of these observations were controlled and confirmed as being otherwise unavailable to the viewer.

Two particular viewers, Pat Price and Ingo Swann, were able to identify military installations around the world, including then-secret Soviet bases on the other side of the planet, including accurate weather conditions at the time of viewing. Other experiments included placing objects on a table in a room on the east coast. From a sealed room on the west coast, the psi observers were able to describe the objects in detail, including their positioning and orientation (Puthoff and Targ 1981; Puthoff *et al.* 1981).

Other remote viewing experiments over the years have since confirmed that many of us have this ability to "see" things not within our physical sensory range. Moreover, it seems this skill can be developed. Targ and Katra (1999) describe being able to develop that skill by attempting to "separate out the psychic signal from the mental noise of memory, analysis and imagination."

These controlled studies illustrate the existence of a seer existing outside of the realm of the physical senses and neurons of the brain. If seeing was merely a bio-chemical and physiological experience driven by a mixture of molecules and cells, then *who is it* that is able to *see* things that are beyond the physical range of the eyeballs? Who is it that can visualize and describe material objects half way around the world?

The limitations of our physical senses have been well established by science. As humankind has progressed technologically, we continue to gain new information about things we previously did not perceive through our gross sense organs.

This growing technical observational facility increas-ingly makes us aware that our physical senses can only perceive a small portion of the vast spectra of wavelengths bouncing around us. Quite simply, the spectral range of our senses and technology are still only a tiny portion of the complete spectrum surrounding us.

The seer—the self—is the seer of dreams as well as the seer of physical reality. What is the self watching while we dream?

Identity and the Mind

When we dream, we are watching the mind.

Many have confused the self with the mind. Further-more, many have proposed that the mind is an all-powerful entity, with the capacity to manipulate the physical world. This was proposed more than a century ago by William Walker Atkinson in the book *Thought Vi-bration or the Law of Attraction in the Thought World* (1906).

Atkinson's theory attracted many followers, including influential writers such as Mary Baker Eddy of *Christian Science* fame and Wallace Wattles, author of *The Science of Getting Rich* (1910). The *governing mind* philosophy of the late Mr. Atkinson and Mr. Wattles has influenced various other books, including *Think and Grow Rich* (1937) by Na-poleon Hill, *The Greatest Salesman in the World* (1968) by

Og Mandino, and the wildly popular recent book and movie *The Secret* (2006), by Rhonda Byrne among others.

These works have attracted the masses because of their promise of material successes such as wealth and admiration. These appeals to our selfish natures appear to be grounded in the idea seemingly first proposed by Atkinson: Each of us is the mind, and the mind ultimately drives and controls the physical world. This has led to the unfortunate proposition that nothing real exists but the mind, and the mind is the creator of the universe. Many go to the extent of saying that we are all part of one single mind.

The interesting part of this seductive proposal is that while the mind is theoretically the all-pervading controller, the intent of all these self-help writings is to theoretically help people by *changing their minds*. The techniques proposed may vary slightly, but the intent is generally to help the reader gain greater wealth, fame, success, attention and influence by *changing* their thinking.

The problem with this proposal is that if the person is the mind, then *who* is it that decides to *change the mind?* In order to change the mind there must be a driver and observer who can intend and initiate that change. Furthermore, as noted in these works, the process required in order to change the mind is quite difficult.

Who is the constant force making the determination to change the mind; despite all of its former thinking habits? And lastly, *who* remains to reap the rewards once the mind has been changed? If the self is the mind, and the mind has changed, that former self is gone once the mind changes. Therefore, no one remains to realize any reward, since the last mind—the one who initially read the book— is gone, replaced by the changed mind.

The reality is that the mind is simply another physical tool of the constant living self. Like the body, the mind is an instrument the self uses through intention. The mind is a subtle sorting, translating and recording device. The mind reflects and categorizes the waveform interference patterns onto its mapping system, giving the self the ability to observe a holographic image of the information. With that holographic image, the self can concoct particular desires and intentions for the mind to execute through the neural network.

We can observe how the mind records this information when a particular vision or music piece can be recalled minutes, days and even years after first being seen or heard. We can see it immediately by looking at an image, closing our eyes immediately afterward, and seeing that image imprinted onto our mind. Our mind can also associate and compare stored waveform data with incoming sensory images of tastes, sounds, tactile sensations and other images our senses collect over the years.

As the mind imprints these images, the self subtly directs the mind through intelligence to record these images, cataloging them according to priority. The mind is thus like a software program, designed to utilize the biochemical bonds within the neurons to resonate waveforms for storage and playback. This system might be compared to the recording capability of magnetic recording tape or diskettes, which store music, images, and data via magnetic arrangement.

The mind's operations transcend the body just as the operating system software of the computer transcends the actual hard disk or other hardware of the computer. Just as the operating system software provides an interfacing language between the various hardware devices of the computer, the mind interacts closely with the limbic system and neural networks of the body to execute commands, and feedback regarding the condition of the body.

The mind is a changeable, subtle mechanism, yet is distinct from the self. The separate existence of the mind can be easily shown in practical behavior: We can each observe the workings of our mind. We can watch images on the mind and see how sensory inputs become recorded and recalled. After watching a movie with special effects, we can close our eyes and watch a scene's mental imprint on the mind.

We can also replay music recorded by the mind. We

may hum or sing the words of a song we heard previously, with the tune replaying in our mind long after the song was heard. Like a television or a radio, we can also turn and change the mind's images.

Just as we can *change our mind* we can change the mind's images and watch those images. This is what dreaming is. Our mind has recorded various images throughout our daytime activities and these images can be manipulated and replayed onto the mindscreen. This is what we watch when we dream.

The Soul

Who is it that is watching the mindscreen when we dream?

Plato, Socrates and many other Greek philosophers have referred to the self as the *soul*. The translation is thought to originate with Aristotle who described the self with the Latin *telos*. Rather than a vague spirit-like organ, *telos* most specifically translates to a personality with purpose, will, and character. In this context, we would emphasize that each of us does not possess a soul: each of us *is* a soul. That being said, some refer to the soul as one's level of morality or even one's mission.

As we seek not to confuse, here we will refer to our identity as the *self* or the *living being*. We may also refer to the self as the transcendental living being to emphasize that the self is not within the physical or material plane. Rather, the living being accesses the physical plane via the vehicle of the physical body.

Empirical evidence reveals the existence of a transcendental living being operating the body. This is the "I" or the self of each of us. The self is the source of personality and life, which the body expresses through physical activity over its lifetime.

Since there is energy, personality and movement in a living body prior to death, followed by a lack of movement, personality and energy afterward, the source of the energy and personality must leave the body at death. Since each personality is unique and different from all other personalities, each living being is an independent entity.

When considering the living being outside of the body or after the death of the body, many will imagine the living being looks like the physical body somehow—with the same eyes, face, sex and stature as their physical body. Many media depictions will illustrate this with someone who has died appearing as a ghostly version of that person's aged body before they died. Although a departed self might still be able to project a mental image comparable to a gross physical body shortly after death, the nature of the living being is thoroughly distinct from the temporary physical body. As Aristotle and Socrates described to their students, the physical body is completely abandoned by the self at death.

Many philosophers have proposed that after death, the living being either fades into "nothingness," or expands into "everything." This philosophy proposes that the living being does not have an individual identity after death: Instead, the individual person or living being simply vanishes and evaporates into space. This is often described as merging into "nothingness"—also called the void—or merging into "everything"—sometimes referred to as the white light.

These two assumptions are basically the same proposition because either way there is no eventual individuality. There is no separate existence of the living being in these limited philosophies. To this, we can offer the simple observation of many ancient philosophers: Each individual is born with a unique and distinct personality.

This individuality is expressed by the special talents unique to each of us. These special talents point to an individual existence prior to birth. If a person existed as an individual prior to birth, is it logical that a person would lose that individuality after death?

The living being is the underlying source of our personality; our feelings; emotions; desires; the ability to love; and the desire to be loved. This personality is distinct from the mental programming taking place through the brainwaves and neural network of the physical body. Beyond the programming, each of us is an independent, active living being with a central objective of receiving love. Does it appear logical that this active being—continually seeking love and relationships—would want to suddenly abandon these propensities to permanently lose our existence within a void or nothingness?

Still others contend that after death we merge into a vast ocean of consciousness. The question this brings is; what is the purpose of existing within a body as an individual, if we evaporate into a vague ocean of consciousness? What should the purpose of temporary separate existence be then? Could a collective vague consciousness have a purpose?

Furthermore, the living self has maintained a steady active existence throughout many years of a changing physical body. Does it seem logical that the death of the body would affect a person's inherent will to survive and prosper? Should the death of our temporary body abruptly end our desire to love and exchange love? Should the active living being who is beyond the physical scope of our senses remand itself to the fate of the physical body?

Purpose and activity are the key distinctions between living and dead matter. Both of these elements (purpose and activity) indicate the existence of individuality. The very definition of *consciousness* requires individuality. Consciousness requires *awareness.* Awareness of something or someone requires a personality separate from that object or person being *aware* of. So an 'ocean of consciousness' would logically be an oxymoron.

Consistent with the ancient teachings of all major religions, the ancient philosophers and the vast majority of western scientists prior to the emergence of the concept of a chaotic accidental evolution of species; the existence of a unique individual entity transcendental to the gross physical plane is the only logical conclusion.

Of course, the word *spiritual* can also be misunderstood. Spirit can be confused with the subtle physical world of ghosts, which are living beings still embodied within the physical mind and subtle aethereal or plasma layer. They may be without the more gross physical body, but they still live within the confines of the physical dimension.

For clarity, we will utilize the word *transcendental* as indicating the dimension beyond these gross and subtle physical layers. To this end we might also refer to the transcendental living being as the *inner self*, identifying the transcendental self occupying the physical body.

Furthermore, the term *living organism* describes a physical body driven by and animated by an individual transcendental living being.

The Dreamscape

From the evidence laid out in this chapter, we can conclude that the person—each individual—is surrounded by a mind and a physical body. The mind is a subtle energy that transforms the desires of the self within into an orchestration of the physical world. It is like a converter, in other words. Utilizing the electromagnetic properties of the brain, the mind gains access to the physical senses and the brain's sorting abilities.

The mind is still physical, however. While it does reflect the self, the physical body also reflects the self, but on a more gross physical plane. The mind maintains the physical energy that drives the brain and thus the physical body. It maintains, in other words, memories, scenarios, thoughts and schemes. The mind provides us with a platform from which we can drive the brain and physical body.

Therefore, the mind provides a conduit for the self to express itself utilizing the brain and physical body.

The inner self is a nonphysical being temporarily encased within a physical body. Like the car driver, we have certain facilities we can use to direct the body. In a car, we have the steering wheel, the gas pedal, the brake, and a number of instruments we can adjust.

In the physical body, we steer through the frontal cortex, the motor cortices and the hippocampus. Through specialized neurons, we influence the body's direction, speed and braking ability. We can also observe sensual inputs of the body through the instrument panel of our frontal cortex and the windshields of our eyes. In the car, we use our hands to steer and our feet to push the gas and the brake. In the body, we use our mind to steer with.

The mind not only has the ability to drive the brain and mind through the physical world, however. The mind also has the ability to host the dreamscape. Because the mind contains so many plans, images and memories coming in from both the physical world and the senses, but the desires of the individual self, the mind can sort these in such a way as to formulate a creative dimension: the dreamscape. The mind utilizes sensual information to construct this region.

While it is considered the creative result of the mind, the dreamscape is also a real place in the sense that the self has the ability to operate within this region. A figment of the imagination it truly is, yet this figment still has reality.

This reality is in perception, however. During the dream, most of us feel that the dream is real. If we did not feel the dream was real, we would not become scared in our dreams. We would not become excited in our dreams. We would insert into our dreams no emotion if we were not being fooled that the dreamscape was real.

This also means that the dreamscape is not entirely our creation. We may be driving many of the components of, including the players, the background and some of the tactics, but we are not fully in control over our dreamscape. Even though who have perfected lucid dreaming do not claim to have full control. They can control certain events—just as we can in the physical world.

Just as we can to some degree, control whether we want to go to jail or not in the physical world by not committing a crime, we have limited control in our dreamscapes.

Our dreamscapes typically offer us the ability to determine our direction in the dream. They allow us to steer the dream.

This might be compared to driving a car. We can certainly hold the wheel of the car and steer it one direction or another. We can also put the brakes on and stop the car, and even get out.

But we cannot control how the car will run. The car can easily break down on us, leaving us stranded in the middle of nowhere.

We also cannot control other drivers. We cannot control whether we'll be hit from the side by another car or truck. We might try to avoid these by driving carefully, but we cannot completely control the situation.

It is the same with dreaming. Being able to steer our dreams does not guarantee that we can control the dream altogether. Like the car, we can steer the dream to where we want to go with our intentions and desires. But we had better buckle up and prepare for a few surprises.

Chapter Seven

Remembering Dreams

Each night we have multiple dreams. Some researchers have estimated that we have from five to eight different dreams each night. And most of those are permanently forgotten.

It is debatable whether a forced remembering of dreams will necessarily help resolve issues in our waking life. This is not to say that our dreams are not an important part of our existence and do help us resolve issues of our waking lives. But there is a very good reason that we do not to remember most of our dreams.

Furthermore, our waking consciousness does not have to be aware of how we came to the point of resolution from our dreaming. We may simply wake up the next morning, and realize the issue we were so upset about is really no bid deal. We may not know how we arrived at the conclusion, but who cares? Perhaps in our dream we faced up with a more serious issue to be concerned about, and the issue that upset us previously seemed a little trivial in comparison.

If we can accept that we forget most of our dreams by design, we can also accept that those dreams we remember are being recalled for a reason.

Our forgetfulness of dreams is precisely why we do not remember many traumatic events that happen in our lives. Deep within, the choice is made to forget those events (or dreams). They are too confusing, traumatic, weird, wild, outrageous or whatever. Perhaps we are ashamed of them.

Events and dreams we remember, on the other hand, are remembered because we feel there is an importance to the dream or event. We need to remember for a particular reason.

Consider our memory process during our waking hours. Some things we remember and other things we don't. Typically, we remember those things that are most important to us. As for those things we forget but strive to remember, there are other factors involved. Perhaps deep inside we don't see why that thing (say a name or date) is so important in the grand scheme of things.

Or perhaps we were not focused on them at the time and missed the opportunity to attach them. And what caused this lack of focus? Perhaps our focus on something we considered more important to us at the time.

Yes, this sounds a bit simplistic. Certainly, there are many complicating elements to this. We also have to coordinate our memory and recall with our tools—the hippocampus and various neuron storage locations. Assuming we have the tools, we ultimately decide which events take priority over others, given our focus at the time.

To this, we add that we are unlikely to even understand the meaning of most of our remembered dreams. They are extremely complicated. They might have some meaning if we are trying to analyze our underlying problems however. But remembering them might just prevent us from moving on and resolving those problems.

The question is whether our dreams are any more important or necessarily different in substance than the various schemes, plans, fantasies and reveries we have during our waking life. In our dreamscape, we can play out these scenarios, just as we can play them out during our waking hours.

Let's assume, however, that there is a good purpose for our forcing a remembering of our dreams. Perhaps we are trying to resolve a difficult matter and seeking some direction. Or perhaps we want to assure that we are having deep resolution REM dreams.

Remembering our dreams comes with practice and determination. The first step is to make a determination that we will remember our dreams. This can come at any time of the day or night, but must absolutely be steadfast and at the top of our priority list as we fall asleep. We must think to ourselves, *I will remember at least one dream tonight.* This will drive our deeper consciousness to lay out a plan for our mind to recall *something* when we awaken.

The other thing we must do is prepare for the remembering. The problem with dream memory is that it is so fleeting. Even if we remember what we were dreaming when we awaken, we will likely forget the dream within a few hours, or even minutes. The various priorities of our waking lives will surely take over the memory string and we'll lose the dream memory forever.

Probably the best way to prepare is to put a recording device next to our bed. Recording device could mean a pad and pencil, or, even better, a digital voice recorder. These are very inexpensive now, and many are available on smart phones (although it is not recommended that we keep the cell phone on next to the bed).

Assuming we know where the buttons are and can quickly turn on the recording button, this is by far the simplest strategy. Why?

Because we don't have to open our eyes to make a record of our dream. This will also allow us to record our dreams at any time of the night without disturbing our sleep quality to a great degree.

We do not need to record all the details of the dream, but just some vivid image or event that stands out and will help us remember more details later. We can simply click on the recorder, and say something like "dreamt about turtles swimming in the sky." This kind of detail is just enough to give us a string to recall. We can go back to it as we wake up. Hopefully (but don't count on it), we can record the rest of our dream later.

Pen and paper might be more practical and quieter, depending upon our mate and situation. In this case, it is probably better to try to write down our dream 'string' when we first wake up in the morning, rather than turning the lights on in the middle of the night and stimulating the wrong hormones.

It is best not to move out of bed before recording our dream. Best to stay in bed and write down or record the dream string before we rise out of bed. This will keep our mind focused on the dream for a minute. As soon as we rise, the day's priorities begin to take over and the dream will likely dissolve.

Dream Process Memory

Often it is not important to remember the specifics of a dream, but how the dream made us feel. The feeling that we get from our dream means a particular attitude or approach to something in particular in our waking life.

We might, for example, be hell-bent about confronting someone the day before, but in the morning we feel that we no longer have to confront them. In this case, our dreams helped resolve our issues about this particular thing. We may have worked through the various possible scenarios if we confronted them, and then the possible scenarios if we didn't. And deep within, we realized that our issues simply were not important in the grand scheme of things.

This may not seem like a dream memory, but it actually is more important than a dream memory. Dreams can get pretty scattered, as we work through all the various scenarios. This often becomes apparent if we are woken up during a dream. We will typically find that the particular situation we are in is absolutely odd, and not applicable to our waking lives. But this dream is likely just a segment of an entire dream process.

The dream process is an extended set of dreams that are related by a particular issue, fear or problem we face. While each dream segment may not obviously string together with others, there will often be some issue that is common among multiple dreams. This makes that dream process critical to the resolution of the entire issue.

Sometimes the dream process can string an issue between REM-stages. In other words, we may have a dream or multiple dreams within one REM-stage that consider a certain aspect of our issue. Then we pick up the issue again in another REM-stage. Each time we pick up the issue again, it will typically be approached differently. We'll have a different aspect or angle on the issue. These are very important.

This takes place in our waking life too. Let's say we write an important letter or email to someone. If we walked away before sending it, and then looked at it the next day, it is likely that we will have a different way of saying something, often better. Or we may delete sections, as we feel they aren't important.

We do the same thing as we dream about our issues. We approach an issue in one way during one dream, and another way during another. We may also dream of the same issue during multiple nights. Some people have dreams about the same issue(s) over and over. This often happens in nightmares, as we will face the same fears over and over, trying to resolve them.

Drugs and Dreamland

Statistics have shown that about one-fifth of all older adults in the U.S. take some form of medication for sleep, which includes prescription drugs, over-the-counter sleep drugs, and alcohol. We may be amazed at this number. Yes, it is astonishing how hard the pharmaceutical industry has worked over the past few decades to develop new pharmaceuticals that induce hypnotic and sedative effects.

The studies do illustrate, as do many testimonials, that many of these medications temporarily reduce insomnia. However, in many cases this comes at a cost. Some might say the cost is worth it, while others might say the cost has been too great.

As for costs, we are speaking, of course, about the side effects of pharmaceuticals in general. Then there are the environmental costs. The cost in dollars to purchase pharmaceuticals is another subject altogether. Before we review the pharmaceuticals themselves, let's examine some of the statistics regarding the medical application of pharmaceuticals by the health care (or better, sick care) industry.

In 1992, researchers from the University of Tasmania's School of Pharmacy (Rumble and Morgan 1992) followed 1,042 elderly adults over the age 65 for five years. There were 352 deaths during that period.

Of those, 208 were users of hypnotics: a significantly higher proportion of deaths compared with those who did not use hypnotics: The pharmaceutical hypnotic users were 2.5 times more likely to die than those not taking any pharmaceutical drugs.

Drugs and alcohol impede our REM-stage dreaming and thus will also disturb or inhibit any chance of lucid dreaming. We might compare this to waking activities that require focus and connectivity. Drugs and alcohol interrupt our neurotransmitter activity, distorting our ability to perceive and conduct ourselves with clarity and coordination.

This has been determined through polysomnographical sleep research. Cocaine decreases sleep in general. When sleep is attained for the cocaine user, less of it is spent in REM-stage sleep. In the same way, methylenedioxymethamphetamine, or MDMA (ecstasy) also reduces sleep quality, and REM-stage sleep. This would be expected, because like cocaine, MDMA is a stimulant. Marijuana, however, is not a stimulant. Yet marijuana also depresses REM-stage sleep, even if the user is getting adequate sleep time. Heavy marijuana use increases stage slow wave sleep while it depresses REM. This means that while the sleep might be deeper, the marijuana user is not adequately able to experience REM-stage dreaming. Alcohol is also a depressant, and depresses REM-stage sleep. Alcohol also causes rebound insomnia as we've mentioned earlier.

Withdrawal from drugs and alcohol often results in disturbing dreams and nightmares and a sustained inability to sleep restfully. This has been established in a number of studies on sleep and substance abuse (Schierenbeck *et al.* 2008).

What appears to be taking place here is that the former user suddenly must deal with a sustained period of time where there was inadequate REM-stage dreaming. Once giving up the drugs or alcohol, they must deal with an avalanche of impressions and conflicts to resolve within their rediscovered dreamscape.

Ironically, illicit drugs and alcohol are typically taken to escape from reality, yet they prevent us from the healthy escape of our REM-stage dreams. Because our dreamscapes allow us to resolve issues and come to terms with our dilemmas, the drug or alcohol abuser is missing out on nature's vital process that helps resolve those dilemmas they are trying to escape from with intoxication.

Dream Architecture

As we age, the architecture of our sleep changes. How it changes depends upon our external environment and how we deal with it. A life of constant stress and urgency will often create sleep cycles and dreamscapes of stress and urgency. A life of competition will result in a dreamscape where we are constantly competing with others.

People who tend to live spontaneous, carefree lives tend to have fantastic, even colorful dreams with lots of fantasy. A life of worry and concern about the future will likely lead to many dreams about the future, many of which may well be disconcerting.

In other words, we build the architecture of our dreams by the physical lives we lead. This also integrates with our diet, our exposure to the sun and other natural environments (or lack thereof), and so many other external factors. For example, a person whose high point in the day is a dark, dreary bar with drinks all around, will likely have not only diminished dreams as a result of a lack of REM-stage sleep, but those dreams that do emerge will likely also be dark and dreary. This type of external environment, also compounded by the depressant nature of alcohol, can easily translate to a dreamscape full of dark nightmares.

How we relate to reality and how we remember it are greatly dependent upon our sleeping and dreaming. When we dream, we recollect the events of our day and recent past. Within our dreams, we interpret those events. We translate them into graphic form, and we eventually consolidate them. We also integrate them and prioritize them with our other memories. This forms a constructive timeline and database for our later retrieval. This integration and consolidation allows us to also find meaning in the events of our past.

This process gives us the opportunity to learn from our past. Without this feature, we would not have the ability to learn from our mistakes and gain wisdom.

This also means that what we remember about events of the past is not simply what we experienced or observed physically. Our memories include how we recollected those events, how we interpreted the events, and how we consolidated the events with respect to other events (Stickgold 2005). This means that our memories, to some degree, are subject not only to our interpretation, but to the processes of sleep and dreaming.

This of course brings to bear the question of what happens should we not be sleeping adequately? What happens to our recollection of the past? Herein may lie not only some of the mysteries of dementia, but quite possibly some of the relationships between sleep and memory disorders such as Alzheimer's disease.

Memories that have not been properly consolidated are certainly subject to a misalignment, which can result in a loss of some of those memories. Should our consolidation processes be interrupted over a long period, a greater potential for dementia and memory loss exists.

This association is confirmed by the research mentioned earlier that shows that dementia risk is increased for those with REM-sleep disorders (Vecchierini 2010).

Are we saying that all Alzheimer's and dementia cases could be prevented with healthy sleep and dreaming? No, but it makes sense to submit that the risk of these diseases decreases with healthy REM-stage sleep.

What do our Dreams Mean?

Most of us wake up and realize that we've had a strange dream, and can't figure out what it means—if anything. This fact has made dream interpretation quite intriguing for most people, and there have been numerous books, articles and lectures on this topic.

This fact has also produced the theory that our dreams don't mean anything—they are simply mish-mashes of sensory information and imaginings that have no symbolism or allegory.

Many have issues with this, however, because they have experienced symbolism in a dream resulting in the symbolism or allegory being meaningful in one respect or another. Some have found that when they determined the symbolism of their dream, the event came true in the future. Some have also found that when they unfolded the allegory of the dream they learned something significant from the dream.

The supposition is that the symbolism or allegory was produced for the purpose of learning something. The other side of this is that the process of trying to elucidate a meaning from the dream could also *produce* the possible symbolism or allegory. In other words, in this case we may create the meaning from the dream rather than the dream having meaning in itself. Which is it? And does it matter?

Let's use an example. Say we have a dream where we see an airplane lose one of its wings and begin to fall from the sky. Then we dream that a fire engine pushes its ladders up and catches the plane before it hits the ground. We wake up and wonder what the dream means.

On one hand, we could say the dream itself must have had a meaning. Say if we were a baseball pitcher and we related the dream to us hurting our pitching arm and someone fixing our arm before we got hurt more. So we take it as a warning to be careful for our arm.

Or perhaps we go to a psychologist and they interpret our dream to mean that the falling airplane symbolizes a particular struggle or conflict we are facing, and because the plane does not hit the ground, we resolve the conflict (as falling is often related to struggling with a conflict).

Or let's say we recently watched a WWII movie, and the movie had lots of planes that had been shot down from the sky. Some of the planes crashed and local fire trucks and ambulances appeared on some of the scenes. Our mind simply put all these images together and presented a crazy scenario.

The first two scenarios present that the dream either

had an allegorical meaning or a symbolic meaning. The last scenario supposes that the dream was simply a permutation or combination of visual images, and had no meaning.

Now let's present a completely different perspective. Let's say that instead of the scene taking place with a dream, it was painted by an artist onto canvas. To render the painting, the artist had to specifically paint all the images onto one scene, including the plane and the fire truck below. What would we think about the scene in this case?

First, we would assume that the artist must have some kind of connection with planes and planes falling out of the sky, since he put so much time into creating a painting of the event. Maybe the artist's father died in a plane crash or something.

Then we would assume that the artist must have had some visual experience of airplanes falling from the sky somewhere. Perhaps he was a retired jet pilot. Whatever the input, we would assume that because how could the artist do a rendition of an airplane being hit and falling without some visual impression of it first?

So now, as we look at the artist's painting of this event, would we still assume the event is just an accidental combination of sensual experiences? No. We know that because the artist made an effort to paint it from scratch, the painting was no accident. The canvas didn't just mix a bunch of paints together, and the artist didn't simply throw paint onto the canvas: The painter specifically painted what he intended to paint.

We can also assume the artist had a purpose behind painting this image. Because it took significant effort, we know the artist had a connection with such an event. Should we eliminate the possibility that the artist was trying to make money from his painting, we would be left with the notion that the artist was perhaps reflecting on the event for some personal reason—since the event was not taking place in front of the artist at the time.

In other words, the painting had to mean something to the artist for the artist to make the effort to compile something so complex.

Is there a difference between creating a dreamscape in our mind and painting a painting? Certainly not. They both require a significant effort. In the case of a painting, this might require several hours of work. In the case of a dream, the dream might require only a few minutes of formulation, but there was an effort made to formulate the dreamscape nonetheless.

Just as the painter creates a painting using brushes and a canvas, every night we creating complex dreamscapes complete with perplexing situations using our mind as a paintbrush and canvas. Then we travel virtually through that dreamscape and experience it, and become intimately involved with it. Why would we spend so much effort creating a dreamscape with our mind if it did not mean something?

In other words, the dreamscape has a meaning *before it is created, as well as during its creation.* While we can certainly derive many interpretations from a particular dreamscape and the events that take place in that dreamscape, we still put a significant effort into creating the dreamscape.

This does not cancel the value of making interpretations about the dream. It does, however, mean that the interpretations may be altogether different than the purpose for the dreamscape.

In other words, we cannot disconnect the meaning of the dreamscape from our own desires, wishes, fears and tendencies. We also cannot disconnect our dreams from the environment and visual experiences that we surround ourselves with during our waking lives.

One last and important point about creating our dreamscape: While we are certainly involved in creating the dreamscape, because of the connection between the dreamscape and physical reality, the dreamscape is not completely our creation or the creation of our mind. The dreamscape is a *collaborative creation.*

We might compare this to an artist painting an oil painting of a beautiful seaside scene. The artist might be given lots of praise for their work of art—and justifiably so. But the artist will know that the painting is not completely their creation. They had lots of help.

First, the scene itself is beautiful, and the artist had to have the scene available to paint the image.

Second, the artist had lots of tools, such as oil paints, easel, good brushes and a good canvas.

Third, the artist was likely given lots of lessons in painting for many years. Over the years, the artist derived their skill from a variety of teachers who taught particular skills in making images flow or whatever.

Now with all of this assistance, what is left? The artist's interpretation of the scene and the resulting image this interpretation created within the painting.

In the same way, our dreams are driven by us, but our minds develop the images from elements derived from the images our senses obtained, together with a platform of REM-stage sleep and the ability to play out these dreams.

Since we share this facility amongst all humans and most animals, we know we did not create the facility. And since we did not create the visual images, those images did not come from us.

Thus we find that our dreams are collaborative efforts, driven by our own goals and desires. In this collaboration, the dreamscape and the various events within it are created.

Yet we drive them. Thus, we also drive the symbolism involved. If we are worried about our children, our minds may produce a dreamscape that puts some other child in danger because we don't want to imagine our own children being in danger. The symbolism was created by us because we didn't want to face the prospect directly.

We also do this in our waking lives. Say we are concerned about someone breaking into our house at night. What do we do? We create an environment around us that provides more protection against break-ins. We might put in a metal door screen. We might put a deadbolt on the front door, and security locks on the windows. Then we might have a security alarm installed in the house. In this way, the architecture of our physical environment reflects our fears.

In the same way, our fears are also reflected in our dream architecture.

Dream Interpretation

These understandings can now give us the tools to understand and interpret our dreams. We do not need to reach into some outside dream symbol reference to understand what our dream means. This in fact, is counterproductive, because the same symbol can mean two different things to two people.

For example, swimming in a dream might present a fearful situation for a person who hates the water and cannot swim, while it would relate to a fluidic situation—where nothing is concrete—to a person who enjoys the water.

Thus, we must look at our own fears and our own situations in order to judge our dreams.

The first clue as to our dream's meaning is how did we feel during the dream? Did it make us fearful, sad, unhappy, grateful or perhaps angry? This will tell us what we were trying to accomplish in the dream—what emotions we were trying to resolve or reflect upon.

The second clue is how clear is the dream? Did we see colors? The clearer the dream is, the more focus we gave it. More complexity also means more focus. More focus means the subject matter interested us, intrigued us, or overwhelmed us somehow. This is often why nightmares are often very clear: Our fear brought this subject into greater focus.

Do we remember the characters, the places or any other details of our dream? While it isn't absolute, dreams we remember are typically remembered for a reason. The less we can remember the dream, typically the less interesting it was to us.

This didn't mean it didn't teach some very good lessons, however. Sometimes even the dreams that we're not very focused upon and don't remember teach us more than others.

In other words, dreams we remember are the dreams that we wanted to remember while we were in the dream. We looked around our dream and realized that it was important for us to remember.

The exceptions to this are the dreams that we remember dreaming as we wake up, especially in the morning. We are remembering these dreams because we were still in the dream as we were waking up.

This topic has been studied intensely by researchers, as sleep science has been waking people up in the middle of night and asking them to recall their dreams. Many people will remember what they were dreaming in these instances.

But when we remember a dream from the middle of our night—and not as we are waking—these are typically memorable to us for some reason. They struck a chord with us for some reason.

What was it that made the dream so interesting? The answer to this question is often the key to the lesson that the dream taught us. Why? Because this is the element that we focused upon—the crux of the dream as it were.

The general theme of the dream will also indicate the lesson of the dream. Was the topic dealing with people? Or was it something strange that happened to us? Or perhaps we were sharing the event with someone close to us. Each of these general themes will often indicate more about the dream than symbolism.

For example, if we were in an argument in our dream, it doesn't necessarily matter what we were arguing about. If we remember what we were arguing about, then that might be important. But if we don't then the main issue is our arguing. Why were we so argumentative? Why were we so stubborn?

Why didn't we listen more to the other person? These are the lessons that can come from such a dream. It may not even matter who we were arguing with—but it can. If we remember who, this might tell us that we should be working harder to resolve an issue with that person.

If we don't, then perhaps the lesson should be directed to why we are so insistent that we are right about things? This assessment is often an internal one that we don't like to face consciously. We might internally feel that we are too self-righteous, but our dreams can confirm that we need to work on this aspect.

Someone else may hear about this dream or dream it, and feel that this means we will break up with someone, or have a terrible disruption in a relationship otherwise in the future.

As mentioned earlier, future dreaming may not actually indicate something that will happen in the future. It serves as a warning of "if I keep doing what I am doing this will happen."

Another issue we should be concerned about in our dreams is how it ended and whether we remember the ending. If the dream ended badly, this typically serves to warn us about some activity we are doing that can lead us downhill. Again, it is not necessarily a promotion as much as it is the obvious: We are playing out the scenarios of our activities, and this was one of them.

If we do not remember how the dream ends, then we likely simply got bored with the dream and left it. The dream no longer served us any useful purpose so we moved on.

This is often a good thing, as it often means we resolved our issue right there in the dream. Whatever we learned about the issue, we felt it needed to go no further.

Most people fail to realize that dreams are not much different than our waking lives, except that our waking lives are more structured and regimented. In both our waking and dream lives we move from place to place typically based upon either our perceived physical needs and our desires, combined with what we deserve from our past activities.

Let's say we move to a new city. What city will we move to? First we will likely move to a city because we landed a job there. Secondarily, we will go to the city because we like that place. If we had other job options, our desires to move there came to the forefront.

But then the move also related to our past activities. The type of job we got depended upon how hard we worked in school, including university. It also depended on how hard we worked in our last job. If we slacked off and got fired, we would likely not be able to get a job in the city we wanted to live in. Our past would dictate our choices.

Dreams are no different. Our dreams are the result of our perceived physical needs, our desires, and our past activities—both in our waking and dreaming lives.

For example, let's say that a rapist liked to watch horror movies. What would this person's dreams be like? They would be primarily nightmares. Or how about a person who just watched a lot of horror movies but was otherwise a nice person. They would also probably have lots of nightmares.

Why? Because their dreams were reflecting the fact that they liked to watch horror movies. They were attracted by them in their waking and dream lives.

But now a person who was violent and cruel to others, and hurt others who didn't like to watch horror movies would likely also experience many nightmares. These were related to his activities.

So all of these crossover—our perceived physical needs, our desires and our past activities. The result takes place in our dreams.

Chapter Eight

Steering Dreams

For thousands of years, humankind has speculated on the meaning of dreams. The mysteries regarding dream meaning and origin have continued to capture our attention to this day. In 1899, Sigmund Freud published his classic *Interpretation of Dreams.* This treatise proposed that dreams provided windows into the mind, and the "road to the unconscious."

Researchers have gained significant information over the past few decades about dreaming. Using advanced methods of brain analysis such as computed tomography (CT), magnetic resonance imaging (MRI), single photon emission computed tomography (SPECT) and positron emission tomography (PET), researchers have been able to monitor the location, movement and quality of neural activity.

This has allowed dream research to advance quickly, enabling a number of windows into our dreamscapes.

These advancements have led to a greater understanding of the relationship between dreaming and our waking lives. They have not given us, however, a full understanding about what our dreams mean and why we have them.

A lot remains unanswered, but we can combine recent science with thousands of years of documented dream study to arrive at some logical conclusions.

The Need for REM Dreaming

As we discussed earlier, researchers have established from sleep studies that that dreaming peaks during REM-stage sleep. REM-stage sleep has also been associated with higher quality sleep, and better health.

On the other hand, those lacking in REM-stage sleep have problems dealing with their waking lives. This indicates that REM dreaming is essential for not only getting sufficient rest: It is essential for a balanced outlook of our waking world.

As we've mentioned earlier, various nervous disorders can result without adequate REM-stage dreaming. Cognitive impairment and hallucinations have been associated with REM stage deficiency. Parkinson's disease and dementia have also been linked to a lack of REM-sleep. REM-stage deficiency often precedes Parkinson's and dementia occurrence by a number of years (Arnulf *et al.* 2008).

Non-REM sleep also will contain dreaming, but of a different sort. NREM sleep dreaming does not have the deep architecture, resolution quality and vividness that REM sleep dreaming has.

Some researchers have characterized NREM dreaming as more like hallucinations than dreams. Still, NREM sleep provides the important tasks of detail sorting and priority management. This is critical to the next sleep stages, because we need to sort through details and prioritize the things of the waking world before we can start consolidating memories and resolving issues.

Rapid eye movement sleep behavior disorder (RBD) has been seen increasingly among both adults and children. Children with RBD can have dramatic behavioral development problems. These include self-affliction, or the practice of hurting oneself by cutting. Depression, narcolepsy, epilepsy, and other nervous disorders have also been associated with RBD.

During our deepest REM-stage sleep, our cells become busy flushing toxins out and removing proteins that are no longer operable. During our REM-stage sleep, our probiotic activity also increases. Probiotics make up an important part of our immune system. They toss out microorganisms that threaten healthy metabolism and manage many epithelial areas.

During REM-stage dreaming, hippocampus stimulation regulates the body's production of critical neural hormones and neurotransmitters. These include cortisol, acetylcholine, dopamine, serotonin and norepinephrine.

When REM-stage sleep is inadequate, these critical biochemicals become imbalanced. This imbalance leads to a distortion of our moods and emotional responses to the waking world. This is one reason a lack of dreaming is associated with mood disorders such as mania, depression and anxiety.

Indeed, when REM-stage sleep is disturbed, a number of distortions can occur. In narcolepsy and sleep apnea, for example, dreams can become increasingly bizarre in their content. REM-stage interruption is also associated with negative and even haunting dreams.

In the case of Parkinson's disease sufferers, 15% to 60% will laugh, shout, and even fight dreamscape enemies in their sleep. They are often seen kicking, punching and writhing while they sleep (Cochen De Cock and Arnulf 2008).

Sleep research has more recently revealed that often the subjects of our REM-stage dreams are the more contradictory or stress-related areas of our waking life. This indicates the rationale for some of our more intense REM dreams. Those who subject themselves to stressful, complex and problematic situations during their waking life are also more prone to having intense dreamscapes.

When we dream, we are utilizing our body's REM facilities to produce the dreamscape. Sleep researchers have established that we utilize similar neuron firing mechanisms when we sleep as we do when we are awake—steering the physical body. What are we doing when we dream, then?

Through intention, the inner self is driving the neurons of the frontal and motor cortices, and utilizing the hypothalamus and other brain tissues to travel through a virtual fantasy world of the mind.

Just as a computer programmer can create a virtual fantasy world to play video games—creating virtual images of all sorts of figures and gaming identities—we can create a virtual fantasyland within our mind by the manipulation of electromagnetically charged neuron firings—amazingly similar to the on-off states of the digital computer code used by programmers.

Within this virtual fantasyland the self creates within the mind, we can take the various inputs from the physical world and reposition them to achieve our objectives, hidden desires and fears. In other words, we rearrange the various situations, people and images found in the physical world into our dreamscape in ways that can facilitate our desires.

This is actually no different from fantasizing during our waking life. Consider a person who wants to have a certain type of sports car but cannot afford it. Instead, he fantasizes about driving the car around—how he would feel behind the wheel and so on. Because of the rules of the physical world, he cannot accomplish his desires at the moment, but he can certainly take those away into his own fantasy within the mind.

Dreaming actually provides an extension to this fantasy making within the mind. The self provides the desire, the senses provide the imagery retained within the mind, and the mind provides the dreamscape within which the fantasy is played out.

Dream Resolution

As we dream, memories that normally circulate through the prefrontal cortex during our waking hours are processed through the hippocampus. Here they are sorted and filed away to different parts of the brain's temporal, amygdala and thalamus regions using synapse wave sequencing combined with the emotional direction of the self.

Contextual memories also become consolidated with episodic memories in the hippocampus. This allows us to release from some memories, and retain others we deem important to keep.

Essentially, dreaming allows us to work through and play out the various issues and problems of our waking life. This allows us to awaken with renewed expectations and a sorting of priorities, assuming we've had a restful sleep.

In other words, healthy dreams will allow us to work through both problems and traumatic events. Sigmund Freud called these types of dreams *biographical*.

Some researchers have underpinned biographical dreaming as an extraordinary state of awareness, where the brain creates a virtual reality version of the world around us. We might compare this to a computer game: Where virtual players represent waking associations and events are played out graphically and symbolically.

This explanation of REM dreaming fits with the scientific observations that those with defective REM dreaming tend to have more difficulties working through the issues of waking life. For this reason, this theory of dreaming has been gaining ground among researchers over the past few years. It is called the *continuity hypothesis* (Pesant and Zadra 2006)

There is agreement among many psychologists that dreams with traumatic experiences allow the dreamer to come to terms with and make sense of extraordinary events that have occurred during his or her waking life.

It is for this same reason that psychoanalysis has proved to be one of the more beneficial therapies among psychologists.

Emotional issues are frequently part of the dreamscape. Emotional complexities of relationships or problematic outcomes are often intermixed with goals and objects we aim for. This intermixing allows the person to find a pathway through the problems and issues (Giustino 2009).

For this same reason, people with post-traumatic stress also have a high incidence of nightmares—also called post-traumatic nightmares (PTNMs). Many of these nightmares are explicitly reflecting on the particular traumatic experience.

Some replay the experience with symbolic additions that present the dreamer with the ability to change the direction of the event and the ultimate result.

These considerations have led researchers to pinpoint a particular state of consciousness established during REM-stage dreaming, called *protoconsciousness.*

The protoconscious state is a state where the individual is involved in a virtual world driven by the mix of emotions, goals, and recent history. This protoconscious state allows a platform for problem solving and goal testing.

Here the personal conflicts with identity and self/non-self situations are presented in a bizarre array of complexity and visual imagery (Hobson 2009).

What is the purpose of this complexity? Learning. Dreams offer us the opportunity to learn and try to make sense of those things that occur around us.

Learning from Dreams

Research has established that we can learn significantly from our dreams. For example, researchers have given new tasks to human subjects to learn, and then allowed part of the group to REM-stage dream before resuming the task, while the other group rested quietly without falling asleep.

Those who were allowed to REM-stage dream were far better at learning the task than those who rested without REM-stage dreaming.

Other tests that measure brain impulses using magnetic resonance have determined that we often follow the same thought patterns during our REM-stage dreaming as we follow during our waking hours and focus on a particular task.

This means dreams allow us to rehearse what we are learning during our waking hours, in order to become more efficient and productive at the task.

Furthermore, the conclusion of much of the research we have investigated here along with others, is that our dreams allow us to investigate different aspects of an issue that we aren't able to investigate during our waking lives.

For example, our waking lives might offer us a particular decision to make with regard to doing something. In our waking life we have to quickly look at the choices and make a decision.

But in our dreamscape we can play out all the different choices. We can imagine ourselves playing out one side in one dream, and play out the other side in another dream. Or perhaps if there are two choices, we might just play out the more ridiculous choice.

Many of us can remember these sorts of dreams. We

might remember being in a very odd situation within our dream. What we likely will not remember, however, is that this odd situation is one of the options that would likely play out if we had taken—or will take—in one of our waking decisions.

The conclusion is that the areas we focus on and desire to accomplish are typically also areas we dream about.

Why? Because the inner self, who has certain desires, ultimately steers where we are going in life, whether it is within our dreamscape or our waking life. The inner self may not be able to control the outcome, but we can certainly alter our destiny by heading in a certain direction.

That direction is determined consciously. We do not need to get other-worldly here. It is a practical matter. Just as the driver of a car can steer a car, we can steer the direction of our physical lives, and this will also steer the direction of our dreams.

Taking the Wheel of our Dreams

The concept of steering our dreams might seem foreign simply because most of us can hardly even remember many of our dreams let alone steer them. Most people are lucky to remember one dream in a night, while we might have as many as ten dreams or more during the night.

Consider this point: Why can most of us—if we direct ourselves to awaken at a certain time—almost certainly awaken at that time? While many people do need an alarm clock to assure their awakening, this is simply a crutch we accept.

For those who do not realize that we can wake ourselves at a certain time, just try it. Before going to bed one night (say on a weekend), instruct yourself to awaken at say, sunrise, or some other time. Tell yourself that you need to wake up then, and then give yourself a reason to wake up then. It is best if this is a real thing, even if it is getting up to make breakfast for someone.

Then go to sleep, and see what time you wake up. Most likely it will be pretty close to the time pre-determined. If it is not, then there is a possibility that the attempt was sabotaged somehow. Consider whether you also told yourself that you didn't believe you could do it at the same time. Or perhaps went to bed late just to see if you could do it even when you were sleep-deprived.

In most cases, the result will be that you will wake at almost the exact time pre-determined. How did that happen? It happened because even though the body is sleeping and the mind has set up the dreamscape for you to travel within, you are still conscious. You are still aware of your goals. If waking up at a certain time was important to your goals, then you'll be sure to stimulate the mind and body to wake up at that time.

It is the same with dreams. If you tell yourself that you will resolve a particular problem before going to sleep, then your dreams will take you to areas where the problem will be run through numerous scenarios.

This may not occur in one particular dream. Rather, it will likely occur within several dreams. The problem will likely be presented within each dreamscape slightly differently, and played out differently.

In this case, we would likely not remember a particular resolution to our dream. Since the problem was reviewed among different scenarios, its resolution will not seem obvious to us. We won't wake up with an "alas" moment, and go about to change our situation.

Rather, the scenarios we played out in our dreams will resonate within our deep conscious self. We then simply have to reconsider the problem. As we do this, those deep conscious scenarios will come stirring back to us. And then we are likely to have our solution. We may or may not realize that the solution was produced at least in part through our dreams. But we'll have the solution nonetheless.

This is the illusion of dreaming. We think that dreaming is this magical secret activity we cannot readily access without some grand technique. Rather, our dreams are simply scenarios we play out, albeit graphically and vividly, within our minds while we sleep. And we are playing out scenarios 24/7, because we are always conscious, and always actively seeking happiness.

Most of the scenarios we play out in our waking lives are also quickly forgotten. Our mind runs through one scenario after another so quickly that we simply cannot remember all of them. What we can remember, however, are the scenarios we lock on to and reconsider, and then effect with action.

The trick is simply to apply our conscious mind towards our dreams: Just as we can do with the scenarios we play out during our waking lives, we can make our dreams work for us by consciously providing our mind with goals before we go to sleep: What do we want to accomplish during our sleep?

If this is difficult to get firm into the mind, we can simply write it down on a scratchpad by the bedside. We can write down our goal for the night. What do we want to resolve?

Or where do we want to go? Do we want to see someone we haven't seen in awhile? Or do we simply want to be happier and more productive with our life? Do we want to find the meaning of life? These objectives can be quite productive during our dreamscapes.

Steering Lucidly

The ability to direct our lucid dream state is a fascinating topic. It incorporates all of the facets of sleeping and dreaming. In order to have lucid dreaming, we must have sufficient sleep to allow a considerable amount of REM-stage sleep. Lucid dreaming typically comes at the end or during the depths of REM-stage sleep. So we must have good quality REM sleep just to arrive at the lucid dream state.

Stephen LeBerge, Ph.D. has been a pioneer of lucid dream research for over two decades. His research methods enabled the first evidence that lucid dreaming could in fact occur. To prove lucid dreaming, Dr. LeBerge's laboratory subjects—who were accomplished lucid dreamers—would arrange in advance to signal the sleep researchers when they were lucid dreaming. So they arranged to display particular eye movements indicating they were lucid dreaming at that moment.

This would act as sort of a code, so the sleep researchers could wake them up to record their experiences. For example, the sleeper and researcher might agree on a darting motion one way twice, then the other way once with the eyes. This would signal to the researcher (using an EOG) that the sleeper was having a lucid dream.

Once the signal was made, the researcher would awaken the subject, and the subject would proceed to tell the researcher what they were dreaming. This method has been performed and controlled enough times for the scientific community to accept that lucid dreaming indeed exists.

This research also discovered that many of us steer our dreams but we do not remember doing so. With a little practice, however, steering our dreams can become lucid—that is, we can consciously steer them and even control them.

Furthermore, we can steer each of the major dream-states. NREM dreaming, which are sorting and prioritizing, can be steered using simple commands prior to falling asleep. Our more fantasy REM-stage dreams and our lucid dreams require a bit more practice, clarity and discipline, however.

To steer our dreams, we must begin to see our dreams not as some sort of separate world, but as facilities to help us accomplish our goals and objectives. Like our waking life, our dreamscape is simply a world where we can express our desires and proclivities. It is also a place where our fears become manifest.

It is for this reason that we bring our problems and struggles into our dreams: We need to resolve the issues or fears we bring in. We need to find comfort and resolution with our waking lives, within our grand vision or life strategy.

For this reason, we will often play out situations that incorporate images we consider to be inconsistent with our picture of reality. For example, if our objective is sensual enjoyment, seeing the world as a place of pure enjoyment and pleasure, we will need to resolve events that disturb that overall vision.

This means if we were to see images of starving people, or people being imprisoned or tortured, we would be presented with a conflict. We would then likely need to work through these conflicts before we could take charge of our dreamscape.

If, for example, we were to realize that life was not sitting under and umbrella sipping lemonade, we might learn to see the world as a place of learning and development—like a school of sorts. In this picture, we would likely deal with events and our dreams quite differently: Certainly, our conflict resolution would become minimized.

The bottom line is that we bring our frustrations, conflicts, desires and fears into our dreamscape. These are mixed with the visual inputs derived from our waking life. As we observe this mix in a dream, we have a choice: we can emotionally wrestle with each conflict or we can observe and learn from life's seeming incongruities.

These are options we have in lucid dreaming. If we take the option of learning and observing, we can step back and realize the events in our dream are living reflections of our desires, goals, and waking lives. Once we make this connection, we can begin to manipulate the dreamscape.

This is no different from learning to drive. First, we must make a determination to do it. While awake, we should make a determination to become conscious that we are dreaming, and watch the dream unfolding.

Once we have accomplished this (may take some time), we may instruct ourselves before we go to bed that we are going to 'take the wheel' for a bit during our next lucid dream. Making this determination means we are already realizing we have some control over our dreams. It is a simple but powerful realization.

Once we connect our pre-sleep 'self-commands,' we can begin to instruct our self to take some control during our next night's dream. This confident instruction must be made with resolution, and it is best made right before we fall asleep.

Now we may or may not remember we had a lucid dream, or even that we began to steer it the night before. But this does not mean we didn't. Once we make a clear and confident command, we will likely follow through during the dream. The research supports this.

Once we instruct ourselves in this way over a period of time, if we are not remembering, we can take the next step to tell ourselves to remember the dream we steer.

This process can also be done if we are having nightmares. Before falling asleep, we can command our mind that should we have our nightmare, we will investigate the monster or villain in the dream, and find out why they are terrorizing me. This will prompt us to face the cause of our nightmares and find a resolution.

The only problem here is that we may not realize we have in fact done this once we wake up. We may soon realize we're not having the nightmare, however. This will reveal that we resolved the nightmare through conscious determination.

One of the few ways to can confirm our lucid dream control is by having someone wake us up during our deepest REM-stage sleep, and ask us what we were dreaming. Otherwise, we can hope (or even command) that we have a WILD type of lucid dream. Either way, our determination creates the opportunity.

Dream Reality

This can bring up the question: Which plane is real, the dreamscape or physical plane? To this we would volunteer that both planes are real to the inner self during the experience. Yet at the same time, both planes are temporary: The physical plane lasts a few decades, while the dreamscape lasts a few moments.

These points become very important, as we consider dreaming and insomnia. Anxiety comes from a position of identity: When we consider our physical body the end all be all, issues that concern our physical situation become big problems. They become more important than they actually are.

When we see our physical body as a temporary vehicle, we can step back from our physical issues and see their temporary nature.

In other words, the solutions brought forth to heal sleep issues should be balanced with a scientific understanding of our core identity:

Understanding that the same inner personality who observes life through the waking body also observes the dreamscape conjured by the mind. In other words, while sleep engages certain physiological processes critical to the health of the body and mind, it also allows the self to seek its desires and objectives, while learning critical lessons.

One might wonder: if our dreams are fantasy worlds created by our minds, then why do we sometimes have nightmares?

Again, it is not as if we always have full control of our dreamscapes. There are rules and consequences. Most of us have awakened in a cold sweat from a dream we didn't like.

We were relieved to find upon waking that it was only a dream. Our dreams get out of hand because these are the consequences of our desires, objectives and fears.

So what could be so fantasy-like about having a nightmare? To answer this, we must solve why a person will to go to a horror movie or watch a gruesome show on television. Some will even pay to see a traumatic horror movie on a huge movie screen. Why? Because the inner personality has developed a desire to experience the thrill of being frightened.

The problem with this desire is that it has its consequences. Our desires can get out of hand in our dreamscape. Our mind can rearrange sensual information in such a way as to *really* frighten us.

In other words, there are no props in our dreamscape. We can make our dreamscape as real as reality can get. Our mind may even take what we've seen in a horror movie and put us in a dreamscape that makes us experience that horror movie personally.

As for those who experience nightmares and detest any suggestion that their inner desires are causing their nightmares, we present another side of desire: fear. Because our mind and brain are simple machines, they cannot make a distinction between simple pleasures and frightening scenarios.

The mind can take any mix of input that the inner self has been focusing on during a combination of waking life, movies and computer games, and mix it up into a dreamscape.

In other words, our dreamscape is a reflection of a combination of our innermost desires, our innermost fears, the sensual inputs we receive, and the activities we participate in during our waking lives. These are all mixed into a virtual dreamscape automatically by the programming of our mind combined with the consequences of our activities and desires.

Yes: Just as we experience in our waking lives, there are still rules to the dreamscape. We cannot completely control this virtual reality. We also have to deal with the consequences of our decisions and activities.

In the waking world, if we slap someone for no reason, we will either be slapped back or arrested for abuse. In the dreamscape world, if we slap someone, they could turn into a monster and freak us out completely.

Our consequences can also cross over between the physical and virtual realities. Consider if we slapped someone during our waking life, and somehow got away with not being punished or slapped back. Such a situation unresolved could create a virtual dreamscape consequence where the person we slapped in the face came back in a dream and slapped us back. Or worse, they might throw acid on our dreamscape face.

It is for these very reasons that not remembering our dreams can be a good thing. If we remembered all of the traumatic things that took place during our dreams, we'd be traumatized during our waking lives. Still this does happen sometimes. For people who are awakened during a nightmare to remember it, going back to sleep can be terrorizing.

Again, those dreams we remember are those dreams that during the dream we—the inner self—realize are important enough to remember during our waking life. This might be because the dream is so curious we want to figure it out. It could also be the dream relates to something we have been concerned about during our waking life, so the inner self pushes the mind to remember such a dream.

The bottom line here is there is no mystery involved in sleep or dreaming. We create the concept of a mystery because we like to keep our fantasy world separated from our waking world. Our dreams are our private fantasy worlds, and we—the inner self—doesn't want to wreck it with reality.

This is also healthy. It is healthy for us to escape into this world because we not only are able to play out our innermost fantasies with little effect upon our waking lives: It is healthy because during that escape we can learn.

We can learn some of the same lessons our waking life teaches us: We can learn that honesty is the best policy. We can learn that when we hurt others we only hurt ourselves. We can learn that when we care for others we are happier.

And we can learn perhaps one of the greatest lessons of both our waking and dream states: that the world does not—despite our best attempts—actually revolve around us.

The Teacher

Any dream expert will convey that our dreams teach us lessons about ourselves and the world around us. Some warn us about our current behavior. Some simply warn us about some future event out of our control—as 9/11 dreams warned thousands of people within their dreams months before the event.

What or who provides these teachings?

There are two levels of this answer. The first depends largely upon the influences we choose in our lives. If our influences are our family members, our friends, peers or others, then our dreams will reach out for these influences for teaching as well.

The facility works in three possible ways:

First, we may simply draw upon what they taught us during our waking lives, and apply those lessons during a dream.

Second, we may reach out to them intuitively. This will allow our mind to connect with them in a broader manner. We may be able to hear their thoughts or intentions in our dream.

The third is that we may allow our dreamscape entry to them. We may allow them to enter our dreamscape via their own dreaming, or we may be drawn into their dreamscape.

These three facilities allow those who influence us to keep influencing us when we dream. Note that the party may have good or bad intentions. They may be wanting to take advantage of us for some reason. We should be wary of this, and consciously shut them down.

We can do this simply by instructing our mind before we go to sleep that we do not want anything to do with this person. This will reverberate into our dreams, helping us prevent their influence.

We can typically tell whether these influences are positive or negative by the emotions within dreams they appeared in. If they were in a dream that scared us, we should consider their influence negative—even if they seemingly protected us.

If they did protect us, then we can keep an open mind. Best to err on the side of caution if we find that someone we know or knew is appearing in multiple dreams with us.

Then there is another level of teacher we might consider. The physical and dream worlds are both arranged in such a way to provide us with the ability to steer and forge our direction, but they are also arranged to provide specific results and consequences from our decisions.

When we look around us at events taking place within our lives and the lives of those around us, we can see clearly that the world is a place of consequence. There is a consequence for every action we take. While this is often termed scientifically as being that there is a reaction for every action, when we talk about events that take place in our personal lives, we are talking consequence.

This is simple to prove scientifically. We can easily connect one event to previous events. Each event takes place following preceding events.

For example, if we go to bed late, we wake up tired or oversleep. If we wake up tired and rushed we might make a mistake and forget our wallet or purse at home when we go to work.

When we want to go to lunch, we won't have any money so we ask to borrow money from our workmate. They say no, because we forgot to pay them back for last time. On and on it goes. One event—actually a combination of events—leads to another event. Thus, each decision we make will have an array of consequences.

Many feel that life is chaotic and random. Does this make sense, however?

We might want to consider chance research. The subject of chance has undergone increasing research by modern scientists over the past few centuries.

Early modern scientists studied the possibilities and the mathematics of chance using coin-tosses, dice throws, and card games.

Because larger tosses do not consistently close the variance between 50% as would be expected, most researchers assumed the dice or coins themselves had some sort of inborn bias towards landing on one side or another. Perhaps a slight weight differential on one side or one edge of that coin existed. Perhaps other gravitational effects or wind resistance were preventing an unbiased coin toss.

Over the last few decades, these tools have been replaced by computer-controlled devices to more closely study theoretically random events. Some very interesting observations have resulted from these experiments.

In 1969, a machine called the Random number generator was invented by Dr. Helmut Schmidt, a physicist at
Boeing. This device utilized a mechanical basis to produce
a theoretically random flashing of one of four lights.

An observer could predict the result by pressing a button under one of the lights, indicating which light would
be lit up next. Because the lights are tied to decay emissions from the strontium-90 isotope, they achieve a theoretically natural randomness.

With a choice of four selections, the statistical average
over a large number of guesses should be no more than
25%. However, large trial numbers resulted in levels closer
to 27%, indicating some sort of ability to predict the result
(Schmidt 1969, Palmer 1997).

Following these studies, questions arose (Wagenaar
1972) as to whether the effect was kinetic or precognition.
In other words, were the observers predicting the results
or affecting the results?

In an attempt to isolate this, Dr. Schmidt refined the
methodology and instrumentation of the RNG (or REG for
random event generator), which performed randomized
calculations resulting in either an even or an odd result.
This machine was set up to duplicate the theoretically
random result of a coin-toss: heads or tails. With this sort
of programming, large volumes of results could be compiled quickly and accurately.

As mentioned, over its history of research, coin-tosses
traditionally resulted in a decreasing variance between a
50/50 result when the number of tosses increased—up to
a point. As the toss numbers get higher, the variances do
not decrease as expected. This notion perplexed researchers, because a seemingly accidental series of results
should continue to trend towards the unbiased 50% level
as the number of tosses increased.

Dr. Schmidt's series of studies with the RNG confirmed
this problem. As the number of results increased, significant variances remained, staying above 1-4% higher than
the unbiased 50/50 level. What could be preventing the

expected and gradual descent to 50/50?

In the early 1970s, Princeton Professor Dr. Robert Jahn refined random number generator research. Dr. Jahn improved upon the machine, increased the number of controls in the protocol, and expanded the range of its study. Like Dr. Schmidt's, Dr. Jahn's machines would randomly produce either a one or a zero in a random sequence, but with any possible source of bias removed.

As hundreds of these RNG studies were compiled by Dr. Jahn and others, the same results emerged. RNG variances from 50/50 continued with larger runs, with substantial differences.

After investigating all the potentially related causes, Dr. Jahn began investigating various unrelated outside events in an attempt to correlate the variances. The first of Dr. Jahn's discovered variances related to the attendants monitoring the RNG run.

Amazingly, variances trended differently for females than for male observers. Investigating the human even further, his trials began asking observers to wish for one result or another.

These resulted in larger variances. While some observers tended to "wish" the result towards the wish, results for other observers resulted trends away from their wishes.

In other words, some observers could affect the RNG results more than other observers could, while still others might produce still opposite results.

Note these observers were not physically able to affect the results, and most were not considered gifted in psi. They were merely observing the results (Jahn and Dunne 1987; Jahn et al. 1985; Jahn et al. 1987).

Dr. Roger Nelson, an emeritus researcher and professor at Princeton, took over the research from Professor Jahn. Dr. Nelson began taking the RNG machines to group events and discovered that group intentions could influence the RNG results in an even greater way.

Everything changed on September 6, 1997. On this day, billions of people throughout the world watched the funeral of the once Princess of Wales Diana. On this day, the RNG machine also made a massive spike, illustrating some kind of relationship to population consciousness (Radin 1997; Jahn *et al.* 1997).

Shortly after, Dr. Nelson brought together a team of seventy-five researchers from around the world and connected forty RNGs through the internet—naming these linked RNG satellites "EGGs." The EGGs essentially brought RNG data from all over the world into a central computer for analysis. At first, the data did not seem to reveal anything of great significance (Radin 1997; Jahn and Dunne 1997).

The first events to stimulate the EGGs around the world were the bombing of American embassies in Nairobi and Tanzania in August of 1998. After these extraordinary results, the *Global Consciousness Project* was in full swing. Dr. Nelson and his associates began watching other mass events. Events like the Super Bowl, the Olympics, O.J. Simpson verdict, and the Academy Awards produced spikes in the RNG graphs.

Major catastrophes such as earthquakes and even major sporting events would move the RNG results significantly one way or another. In other words, events involving greater levels of consciousness among large populations affect RNG results significantly. It became clear that globally relevant events are followed by leanings of mass consciousness, which somehow affect random events (Radin 1997).

A stirring RNG result took place on September 11, 2001. Of course, the RNG charts were spiking significantly after the bombing, associated with the world's reaction to the bombing and the death toll count. However, something even more mysterious happened: *The shift in RNG results began four hours before the first plane hit.*

While the RNG research initially focused on the ability of humans to influence events, another relationship began to emerge. A theoretically random event—supposedly isolated and thus unattached to any other event—appears to be connected to various unrelated events after isolating all known forms of bias.

Since the RNG machine is the ultimate test of isolated, seemingly random and controlled events, it is the perfect vehicle to test modern science's notion of a chaotic universe of randomness. These test results, performed by researchers with integrity and impeccable credentials, reveals a universe of design and programming.

We must therefore ask what is behind this level of programming. Why do we face bad consequences when we act in ways that harm others, and face good consequences when we act in ways that help others? What are we learning?

The only scientific conclusion is that we are learning about love. We are learning about how to treat others and how to care for others.

Let's say that we are a small child, and we did something mean to our pet and hurt the pet. Our mother or father would likely punish us. Why? Did they punish us when we petted the pet? No, only when we hurt the pet. What are they trying to teach us?

Isn't it obvious? They are trying to teach us to treat the pet—and anyone else for that matter—kindly. Don't be hurtful.

The consequences pervading our waking lives and our dreaming lives teach us the same kind of lessons. When we hurt someone, we get hurt. When we mistreat someone, eventually we get mistreated. This is the law of nature.

Now we should ask whether this is a random thing or not. Is our suffering a particular consequence for our past behavior chance?

Was the punishment by our parents for our hurting our pet also by chance? No, it wasn't. And neither are the consequences of our dreams and waking lives.

The empirical evidence shows us that our waking and dream lives are structured in such a way as to teach us to care for others. This illustrates that there is a design put in place to teach us.

Did this design appear by accident? By chance? If it

did, why are all of us learning the same lessons through different consequences? Why is it set up so that regardless of what we did, we still suffer consequences that ultimately teach us the same thing—that we should care for each other?

We might consider that many of us—seen by the nature of this world and the suffering committed upon others by some—are engaged in a self-centered manner and do not care for each other.

Why do these actions have consequences? Because we are being rehabilitated. We are being schooled. We are being taught how to become more giving and caring for others.

Since we cannot control it, like the punishment by parents of the child who hurt the pet, this design must come from a Superior Consciousness: One greater than us. It must also come from Someone who cares for us.

Dr. John Harvey Kellogg wrote:

"The heart is a muscle. The heart beats. My arm will contract and cause the fist to beat; but it beats only when my will commands. But here is a muscle in the body that beats when I am asleep. It beats when my will is inactive and I am utterly unconscious. It keeps on beating all the time. What will is it that causes this heart to beat? The heart can not beat once without a command. To me it is a most wonderful thing that a man's heart goes on beating. It does not beat by means of my will; for I can not stop the heart's beating, or make it beat faster or slower by commanding it by my will.

But there is a will that controls the heart. It is the divine will that causes it to beat, and in the beating of that heart that you can feel, as you put your hand upon the breast, or as you put your finger against the pulse, an evidence of the divine presence that we have within us, that God is within, that there is an intelligence, a power, a will within, that is commanding the functions of our bodies and controlling them..."

This logic extends to the dream world as well. Furthermore, Gustavus Hindman Miller wrote:

"Dream life is fuller of meaning and teaching of the inner, or God life, than is the exterior life of man."

References and Bibliography

Abeysena C, Jayawardana P, DE A Seneviratne R. Maternal sleep deprivation is a risk factor for small for gestational age: a cohort study. *Aust N Z J Obstet Gynaecol.* 2009 Aug;49(4):382-7.

Abourashed EA, Koetter U, Brattström A. In vitro binding experiments with a Valerian, hops and their fixed combination extract (Ze91019) to selected central nervous system receptors. *Phytomedicine.* 2004 Nov;11(7-8):633-8.

Ackerman D. *A Natural History of the Senses.* New York: Vintage, 1991.

Adams C. *Healthy Sun: Healing with Sunshine and the Myths About Skin Cancer.* Wilmington, DE: Sacred Earth Publ. 2009.

Adams C. *The Conscious Anatomy: Healing the Real You.* Wilmington, DE: Sacred Earth Publ., 2009.

Aeschbach D, Matthews JR, Postolache TT, Jackson MA, Giesen HA, Wehr TA. Dynamics of the human EEG during prolonged wakefulness: evidence for frequency-specific circadian and homeostatic influences. *Neurosci Lett.* 1997 Dec 19;239(2-3):121-4.

Aeschbach D, Postolache TT, Sher L, Matthews JR, Jackson MA, Wehr TA. Evidence from the waking electroencephalogram that short sleepers live under higher homeostatic sleep pressure than long sleepers. *Neuroscience.* 2001;102(3):493-502.

Aeschbach D, Sher L, Postolache TT, Matthews JR, Jackson MA, Wehr TA. A longer biological night in long sleepers than in short sleepers. *J Clin Endocrinol Metab.* 2003 Jan;88(1):26-30.

Agarwal SK, Singh SS, Verma S. Antifungal principle of sesquiterpene lactones from Anamirta cocculus. *Indian Drugs.* 1999;36:754-5.

Airola P. *How to Get Well.* Phoenix, AZ: Health Plus, 1974.

Albrechtsen O. The influence of small atmospheric ions on human well-being and mental performance. *Intern. J. of Biometeorology.* 1978;22(4): 249-262.

Alien, SR, Oswald J, Lewis S, Tagney, J. The effect of distort visual input on sleep. Psychophysiology. 1972;9:498-504.

Alonso Osorio MJ. States of nervousness. Useful medicinal plants. *Rev Enferm.* 2004 Mar;27(3):8-12.

Altan L, Bingöl U, Aykaç M, Koç Z, Yurtkuran M. Investigation of the effects of pool-based exercise on fibromyalgia syndrome. *Rheumatol Int.* 2004 Sep;24(5):272-7.

An L, Zhang YZ, Yu NJ, Liu XM, Zhao N, Yuan L, Li YF. Role for serotonin in the antidepressant-like effect of a flavonoid extract of Xiaobuxin-Tang. *Pharmacol Biochem Behav.* 2008 Jun;89(4):572-80.

Ancolu-Isreal S. Insomnia in the elderly: a review for the primary care practitioner. *Sleep* 2000;23 Suppl 1: S23–38.

Anderson JL, Rosen LN, Mendelson WB, Jacobsen FM, Skwerer RG, Joseph-Vanderpool JR, Duncan CC, Wehr TA, Rosenthal NE. Sleep in fall/winter seasonal affective disorder: effects of light and changing seasons. *J Psychosom Res.* 1994 May;38(4):323-37.

Anderson RC, Anderson JH. Respiratory toxicity of mattress emissions in mice. *Arch Environ Health.* 2000 Jan-Feb;55(1):38-43.

Anderson RC, Anderson JH. Toxic effects of air freshener emissions. *Arch Environ Health.* 1997 Nov-Dec;52(6):433-41.

Andreatini R, Sartori VA, Seabra ML, Leite JR. Effect of valepotriates (valerian extract) in generalized anxiety disorder: a randomized lacebo-controlled pilot study. *Phytother Res.* 2002;16(7): 650–54.

Andreucci VE, Russo D, Cianciaruso B, Andreucci M. Some sodium, potassium and water changes in the elderly and their treatment. *Nephrol Dial Transplant.* 1996;11 Suppl 9:9-17.

Anund A, Kecklund G, Peters B, Forsman A, Lowden A, Akerstedt T. Driver impairment at night and its relation to physiological sleepiness. *Scand J Work Environ Health.* 2008 Apr;34(2):142-50.

Apuya NR, Park JH, Zhang L, Ahyow M, Davidow P, Van Fleet J, Rarang JC, Hippley M, Johnson TW, Yoo HD, Trieu A, Krueger S, Wu CY, Lu YP, Flavell RB, Bobzin SC. Enhancement of alkaloid production in opium and California poppy by transactivation using heterologous regulatory factors. *Plant Biotechnol J.* 2008 Feb;6(2):160-75.

Arai H, Suzuki T, Sasaki H, Hanawa T, Toriizuka K, Yamada H. A new interventional strategy for Alzheimer's disease by Japanese herbal medicine. *Nippon Ronen Igakkai Zasshi.* 2000 Mar;37(3):212-5.

Argash O, Caspi O. Touching cancer: shiatsu as complementary treatment to support cancer patients. *Harefuah.* 2008 Aug-Sep;147(8-9):707-11, 750, 749.

Aritake-Okada S, Kaneita Y, Uchiyama M, Mishima K, Ohida T. Non-pharmacological self-management of sleep among the Japanese general population. *J Clin Sleep Med.* 2009 Oct 15;5(5):464-9.

Armstrong D. How the New England Journal Missed Warning Signs on Vioxx. *Wall Street J.* 2006 May 15, A1. http://online.wsj.com/article/SB114765430315252591.html.

Arnulf I, Leu S, Oudiette D. Abnormal sleep and sleepiness in Parkinson's disease. *Curr Opin Neurol.* 2008 Aug;21(4):472-7.

Arnulf I, Quintin P, Alvarez JC, Vigil L, Touitou Y, Lebre AS, Bellenger A, Varoquaux O, Derenne JP, Allilaire JF, Benkelfat C, Leboyer M. Mid-morning tryptophan depletion delays REM sleep onset in healthy subjects. *Neuropsychopharmacology.* 2002 Nov;27(5):843-51.

Arterburn LM, Oken HA, Bailey Hall E, Hamersley J, Kuratko CN, Hoffman JP. Algal-oil capsules and cooked salmon: nutritionally equivalent sources of docosahexaenoic acid. *J Am Diet Assoc.* 2008 Jul;108(7):1204-9.

Arterburn LM, Oken HA, Hoffman JP, Bailey-Hall E, Chung G, Rom D, Hamersley J, McCarthy D. Bioequivalence of Docosahexaenoic acid from different algal oils in capsules and in a DHA-fortified food. *Lipids.* 2007 Nov;42(11):1011-24.

Asplund R, Aberg HE. Oral dryness, nocturia and the menopause. *Maturitas.* 2005 Feb 14;50(2):86-90.

Associated Press. Merck to Pay $4.85B Vioxx Settlement. *Newsvine.com.* 2007 Nov 9. 6:57 AM EST . http://www.newsvine.com/news/2007/ 11/09/ 1084627-merck-to-pay-485b-vioxx-settlement. Accessed August 19, 2009.

Aton SJ, Colwell CS, Harmar AJ, Waschek J, Herzog ED. Vasoactive intestinal polypeptide mediates circadian rhythmicity and synchrony in mammalian clock neurons. *Nat Neurosci.* 2005 Apr;8(4):476-83.

Atsumi T, Tonosaki K. Smelling lavender and rosemary increases free radical scavenging activity and decreases cortisol level in saliva. *Psychiatry Res.* 2007 Feb 28;150(1):89-96.

Attele AS, Xie JT, Yuan CS. Treatment of insomnia: an alternative approach. *Altern Med Rev.* 2000 Jun;5(3):249-59.

Avanzini G, Lopez L, Koelsch S, Majno M. The Neurosciences and Music II: From Perception to Performance. *Annals of the New York Academy of Sciences.* 2006 Mar;1060.

Awad R, Arnason JT, Trudeau V, Bergeron C, Budzinski JW, Foster BC, Merali Z. Phytochemical and biological analysis of skullcap (Scutellaria lateriflora L.): a medicinal plant with anxiolytic properties. *Phytomedicine.* 2003 Nov;10(8):640-9.

Awad R, Levac D, Cybulska P, Merali Z, Trudeau VL, Arnason JT. Effects of traditionally used anxiolytic botanicals on enzymes of the gamma-aminobutyric acid (GABA) system. *Can J Physiol Pharmacol.* 2007 Sep;85(9):933-42.

Bach E. *Heal Thyself.* Walden: Saffron CW Daniel, 1931-2003.

Bader K, Schäfer V, Schenkel M, Nissen L, Kuhl HC, Schwander J. Increased nocturnal activity associated with adverse childhood experiences in patients with primary insomnia. *J Nerv Ment Dis.* 2007 Jul;195(7):588-95.

Baker SM. *Detoxification and Healing.* Chicago: Contemporary Books, 2004.

Balch P, Balch J. *Prescription for Nutritional Healing.* New York: Avery, 2000.

Balderer G, Borbely AA. Effect of valerian on human sleep. *Psychopharmacology* . 1985;87: 406–9.

Ballentine R. *Diet & Nutrition: A holistic approach.* Honesdale, PA: Himalayan Int., 1978.

Ballentine RM. *Radical Healing.* New York: Harmony Books, 1999.

Baran D, Apostol I. Signification of biorhythms for human performance assessment. *Rev Med Chir Soc Med Nat Iasi.* 2007 Jan-Mar;111(1):295-302.

Barbato G, Barker C, Bender C, Giesen HA, Wehr TA. Extended sleep in humans in 14 hour nights (LD 10:14): relationship between REM density and spontaneous awakening. *Electroencephalogr Clin Neurophysiol.* 1994 Apr;90(4):291-7.

Barbato G, Barker C, Bender C, Wehr TA. Spontaneous sleep interruptions during extended nights. Relationships with NREM and REM sleep phases and effects on REM sleep regulation. *Clin Neurophysiol.* 2002 Jun;113(6):892-900.

Barbato G, Wehr TA. Homeostatic regulation of REM sleep in humans during extended sleep. *Sleep.* 1998 May 1;21(3):267-76.

Barber CF. The use of music and colour theory as a behaviour modifier. *Br J Nurs.* 1999 Apr 8-21;8(7):443-8.

Bardia A, Nisly NL, Zimmerman MB, Gryzlak BM, Wallace RB. Use of herbs among adults based on evidence-based indications: findings from the National Health Interview Survey. *Mayo Clin Proc.* 2007 May;82(5):561-6.

Barker A. *Scientific Method in Ptolemy's Harmonics.* Cambridge: Cambridge University Press, 2000.

Baron RA. Effects of negative ions on interpersonal attraction: evidence for intensification. *J Pers Soc Psychol.* 1987 Mar;52(3):547-53.

Barrel TR, Ekstrand BR. Effect of sleep on memory. III. Controlling for time of day effect. J. Exp. Psychol. 1972;96:321-327.

Barron M. Light exposure, melatonin secretion, and menstrual cycle parameters: an integrative review. *Biol Res Nurs.* 2007 Jul;9(1):49-69.

Bastidas Ramírez BE, Navarro Ruíz N, Quezada Arellano JD, Ruíz Madrigal B, Villanueva Michel MT, Garzón P. Anticonvulsant effects of Magnolia grandiflora L. in the rat. *J Ethnopharmacol.* 1998 Jun;61(2):143-52.

Bates DW, Cullen DJ, Laird N, Petersen LA, Small SD, Servi D, Laffel G, Sweitzer BJ, Shea BF, Hallisey R, et al. Incidence of adverse drug events and potential adverse drug events. Implications for prevention. ADE Prevention Study Group. *JAMA.* 1995 Jul 5;274(1):29-34.

Batmanghelidj F. *Your Body's Many Cries for Water.* 2nd Ed. Vienna, VA: Global Health, 1997.

Bazil CW, Battista J, Basner RC. Gabapentinimproves sleep in the presence of alcohol. *J Clin Sleep Med.* 2005;1: 284–87.

Beecher GR. Phytonutrients' role in metabolism: effects on resistance to degenerative processes. *Nutr Rev.* 1999 Sep;57(9 Pt 2):S3-6.

Beeson, C. The moon and plant growth. *Nature.* 1946;158:572–3.

Bell B, Defouw R. Concerning a lunar modulation of geomagnetic activity. *J Geophys Res.* 1964;69:3169-3174.

Bell IR, Baldwin CM, Schwartz GE, Illness from low levels of environmental chemicals: relevance to chronic fatigue syndrome and fibromyalgia. *Am J Med.* 1998;105 (suppl 3A).:74-82. S.

Benedetti F, Radaelli D, Bernasconi A, Dallaspezia S, Falini A, Scotti G, Lorenzi C, Colombo C, Smeraldi E. Clock genes beyond the clock: CLOCK genotype biases neural correlates of moral valence decision in depressed patients. *Genes Brain Behav.* 2007 Mar 26.

Benke D, Barberis A, Kopp S, Altmann KH, Schubiger M, Vogt KE, Rudolph U, Möhler H. GABA A receptors as in vivo substrate for the anxiolytic action of valerenic acid, a major constituent of valerian root extracts. *Neuropharmacology.* 2009 Jan;56(1):174-81.

Bennet LW, Cardone S, Jarczyk J. Effects of therapeutic camping program on addiction recovery. *Journal of Substance Abuse Treatment.* 1998;15(5):469-474.

Bennett JA. Dehydration: hazards and benefits. *Geriatr Nurs.* 2000 Mar-Apr;21(2):84-8.

Benor D. Healing Research. Volume 1. Munich, Germany: Helix Verlag, 1992.

Bensky D, Gable A, Kaptchuk T (transl.). *Chinese Herbal Medicine Materia Medica.* Seattle: Eastland Press, 1986.

Benson K, Feinberg J. The beneficial effect of sleep on extended Jenkins and Dallenback paradigm. Psychophysiology. 1977; 14:375-383.

Bentley E. *Awareness: Biorhythms, Sleep and Dreaming.* London: Routledge, 2000.

Berger M, Gray JA, Roth BL. The expanded biology of serotonin. *Ann Rev Med.* 2009;60: 355–66.

Bergeron C, Gafner S, Clausen E, Carrier DJ. Comparison of the chemical composition of extracts from Scutellaria lateriflora using accelerated solvent extraction and supercritical fluid extraction versus standard hot water or 70% ethanol extraction. *J Agric Food* Chem. 2005 Apr 20;53(8):3076-80.

Berkow R., (Ed.) *The Merck Manual of Diagnosis and Therapy.* 16th Edition. Rahway, N.J.: Merck Research Labs, 1992.

Berman S, Fein G, Jewett D, Ashford F. Luminance-controlled pupil size affects Landolt C task performance. *J Illumin Engng Soc.* 1993;22:150-165.

Berman S, Jewett D, Fein G, Saika G, Ashford F. Photopic luminance does not always predict perceived room brightness. *Light Resch and Techn.* 1990;22:37-41.

Berry J. Work efficiency and mood states of electronic assembly workers exposed to full-spectrum and conventional fluorescent illumination. *Diss Abstr Internl.* 1983;44:635B.

Bhattacharjee C, Bradley P, Smith M, Scally A, Wilson B. Do animals bite more during a full moon? *BMJ.* 2000 December 23; 321(7276): 1559-1561.

Bhattacharyya D, Jana U, Debnath PK, Sur TK. Initial exploratory observational pharmacology of Valeriana wallichii on stress management: a clinical report. *Nepal Med Coll J.* 2007;9(1): 36–39.

Birdsall TC. 5-Hydroxytryptophan: a clinically-effective serotonin precursor. *Altern Med Rev.* 1998;3(4): 271–80

Bittman BB, Berk LS, Felten DL, Westengard J, Simonton OC, Pappas J, Ninehouser M. Composite effects of group drumming music therapy on modulation of neuroendocrine-immune parameters in normal subjects. *Altern Ther Health Med.* 2001 Jan;7(1):38-47.

Bixler E. Sleep and society: an epidemiological perspective. *Sleep Med.* 2009 Sep;10 Suppl 1:S3-6.

Bjerregaard C. Plato and the Greeks on Music as an Element in Education. *The Word.* 1913 Feb.

Bjorvatn B, Grønli J, Pallesen S. Parasomnias. *Tidsskr Nor Laegeforen.* 2009 Sep 24;129(18):1892-4.

Block KI, Gyllenhaal C, Mead MN. Safety and efficacy of herbal sedatives in cancer care. *Integr Cancer Ther.* 2004 Jun;3(2):128-48.

Bloomfield HM, Nordfors M, McWilliams P. *Hypericum (St. John's Wort).* Prelude Press: Los Angeles. 1998.

Blumenthal M, Goldberg A, Brinckmann J. *Herbal Medicine: Expanded Commission E Monographs.* Newton, MA: Integrative Med Comm, 2000.

Bockemühl, J. *Towards a Phenomenology of the Etheric World.* New York: Anthroposophical Press, 1985.

Bodnar L, Simhan H. The prevalence of preterm birth varies by season of last menstrual period. *Am J Obst and Gyn.* 2003;195(6):S211-S211.

Boericke W. *Materia Medica with Repertory.* Santa Rosa, CA: Boericke & Tafel, 1927.

Boivin DB, Czeisler CA. Resetting of circadian melatonin and cortisol rhythms in humans by ordinary room light. Neuroreport. 1998 Mar 30;9(5):779-82.

Boivin DB, Duffy JF, Kronauer RE, Czeisler CA. Dose-response relationships for resetting of human circadian clock by light. *Nature.* 1996 Feb 8;379(6565):540-2.

Boivin DB, Duffy JF, Kronauer RE, Czeisler CA. Sensitivity of the human circadian pacemaker to moderately bright light. *J Biol Rhythms.* 1994 Winter;9(3-4):315-31.

Bollani L, Dolci C, Gerola O, Montaruli A, Rondini G, Carandente F. The early maturation of the circadian system in newborns. *Chronobiologia.* 1994 Jan-Jun;21(1-2):105-8.

Bonaccorsi A. How to correctly use herbs. *Assist Inferm Ric.* 2007 Oct-Dec;26(4):219-26.

Boscoe FP, Schymura MJ. Solar ultraviolet-B exposure and cancer incidence and mortality in the United States, 1993-2002. BMC Cancer. 2006 Nov 10;6:264.

Bose J. *Response in the Living and Non-Living.* New York: Longmans, Green & Co., 1902.

Boyce P. Investigations of the subjective balance between illuminance and lamp colour properties. *Light Resch and Technol.* 1977;9:11-24.

Boyd B, Zungoli P, Benson E. 2006. *Dust Mites.* HGIC 2551; Clemson University. http://hgic.clemson.edu.

Brody J. *Jane Brody's Nutrition Book.* New York: WW Norton, 1981.

Brown JS, Marcy SA. The use of botanicals for health purposes by members of a prepaid health plan. *Res Nurs Health.* 1991 Oct;14(5):339-50.

Brown RP, Gerbarg PL. Herbs and nutrients in the treatment of depression, anxiety, insomnia, migraine, and obesity. *J Psychiatr Pract.* 2001 Mar;7(2):75-91.

Brown, F. & Chow, C.S. Lunar-correlated variations in water uptake by bean seeds. *Biolog Bull.* 1973;145:265-278.

Brown, F. The rhythmic nature of animals and plants. *Cycles.* 1960 Apr:81-92.

Brown, J. Stimulation-produced analgesia: acupuncture, TENS and alternative techniques. *Anaesthesia &intensive care medicine.* 2005 Feb;6(2):45-47.

Brownstein D. *Salt: Your Way to Health.* West Bloomfield, MI: Medical Alternatives, 2006.

Bruseth S, Tveiten D. Homeopathy—the past or a part of future medicine? *Tidsskr Nor Laegeforen.* 1991 Dec 10;111(30):3692-4.

Buck L, Axel R. A novel multigene family may encode odorant receptors: A molecule basis for odor recognition. *Cell.* 1991;65(April 5):175-187.

Buckley NA, Whyte IM, Dawson AH. There are days ... and moons. Self-poisoning is not lunacy. *Med J Aust.* 1993 Dec 6-20;159(11-12):786-9.

Buijs RM, Scheer FA, Kreier F, Yi C, Bos N, Goncharuk VD, Kalsbeek A. Organization of circadian functions: interaction with the body. *Prog Brain Res.* 2006;153:341-60.

Bulkeley K, Kahan TL. The impact of September 11 on dreaming. *Conscious Cogn.* 2008 Dec;17(4):1248-56.

Burdge GC, Wootton SA. Conversion of alpha-linolenic acid to eicosapentaenoic, docosapentaenoic and docosahexaenoic acids in young women. *B J Nutr.* 2002 Oct;88(4):411-20.

Burikov AA, Bereshpolova YuI. The activity of thalamus and cerebral cortex neurons in rabbits during "slow wave-spindle" EEG complexes. *Neurosci Behav Physiol.* 1999 Mar-Apr;29(2):143-9.

Burkhardt S, Tan DX, Manchester LC, Hardeland R, Reiter RJ. Detection and quantification of the antioxidant melatonin in Montmorency and Balaton tart cherries (Prunus cerasus). *J Agric Food Chem.* 2001 Oct;49(10):4898-902.

Burkhart K, Phelps JR. Amber lenses to block blue light and improve sleep: a randomized trial. *Chronobiol Int.* 2009 Dec;26(8):1602-12.

Burr H. *The Fields of Life.* New York: Ballantine, 1972.

Buscemi N, Vandermeer B, Pandya R, Hooton N, Tjosvold L, Hartling L, Baker G, Vohra S, Klassen T. Melatonin for treatment of sleep disorders. *Evid Rep Technol Assess.* 2004 Nov;(108):1-7.

Buscemi N, Vandermeer B, Pandya R, Hooton N, Tjosvold L, Hartling L, Baker G, Vohra S, Klassen T. Melatonin for treatment of sleep disorders. *Evid Rep Technol Assess.* 2004 Nov;(108):1-7.

Butterweck V, Brattstroem A, Grundmann O, Koetter U. Hypothermic effects of hops are antagonized with the competitive melatonin receptor antagonist luzindole in mice. *J Pharm Pharmacol.* 2007 Apr;59(4):549-52.

Buzsaki G. Theta rhythm of navigation: link between path integration and landmark navigation, episodic and semantic memory. *Hippocampus.* 2005;15(7):827-40.

Cajochen C, Jewett ME, Dijk DJ. Human circadian melatonin rhythm phase delay during a fixed sleep-wake schedule interspersed with nights of sleep deprivation. *J Pineal Res.* 2003 Oct;35(3):149-57.

Cajochen C, Zeitzer JM, Czeisler CA, Dijk DJ. Dose-response relationship for light intensity and ocular and electroencephalographic correlates of human alertness. *Behav Brain Res.* 2000 Oct;115(1):75-83.

Caldwell MM, Bornman JF, Ballare CL, Flint SD, Kulandaivelu G. Terrestrial ecosystems, increased solar ultraviolet radiation, and interactions with other climate change factors. *Photochem Photobiol Sci.* 2007 Mar;6(3):252-66.

Campbell A. The role of aluminum and copper on neuroinflammation and Alzheimer's disease. *J Alzheimers Dis.* 2006 Nov;10(2-3):165-72.

Cao G, Shukitt-Hale B, Bickford PC, Joseph JA, McEwen J, Prior RL. Hyperoxia-induced changes in antioxidant capacity and the effect of dietary antioxidants. *J Appl Physiol.* 1999 Jun;86(6):1817-22.

Cao H, Pan X, Li H, Liu J. Acupuncture for treatment of insomnia: a systematic review of randomized controlled trials. *J Altern Complement Med.* 2009 Nov;15(11):1171-86.

Carlsen E, Olsson C, Petersen JH, Andersson AM, Skakkebaek NE. Diurnal rhythm in serum levels of inhibin B in normal men: relation to testicular steroids and gonadotropins. *J Clin Endocrinol Metab.* 1999 May;84(5):1664-9.

Carroll D. *The Complete Book of Natural Medicines.* New York: Summit, 1980.

Cartwright RD, Lloid, S, Butters, E, Wcmcr, L, McCarthy L, Hancock, J. Effects of REM time on what is recalled. Psycho-physiology. 1975; 12:561-568.

Cartwright RD. Problem solving: Waking and dreaming. J. Abnorm. Psychol. 1974;83:451-455.

Cauffield JS, Forbes HJ. Dietary supplements used in the treatment of depression, anxiety, and sleep disorders. Lippincotts Prim Care Pract. 1999 May-Jun;3(3):290-304.

Celec P, Behuliak M. Behavioural and endocrine effects of chronic cola intake. J Psychopharmacol. 2009 May 7.

Celec P, Ostanikova D, Skoknová M, Hodosy J, Putz Z, Kúdela M. Salivary sex hormones during the menstrual cycle. Endocr J. 2009 Jun;56(3):521-3.

Celec P, Ostatníková D, Hodosy J, Putz Z, Kúdela M. Increased one week soybean consumption affects spatial abilities but not sex hormone status in men. Int J Food Sci Nutr. 2007 Sep;58(6):424-8.

Celec P, Ostatníková D, Hodosy J, Skoknová M, Putz Z, Kúdela M. Infradian rhythmic variations of salivary estradioland progesterone in healthy men. Biol Res. 2006;37(1): 37-44.

Celec P, Ostatnikova D, Putz Z, Kudela M. The circalunar cycle of salivary testosterone and the visual-spatial performance. Bratisl Lek Listy. 2002;103(2):59-69.

Celec P. Analysis of rhythmic variance - ANORVA. A new simple method for detecting rhythms in biological time series. Biol Res. 2004;37:777-782.

Cengel YA, Heat Transfer: A Practical Approach. Boston: McGraw-Hill, 1998.

Chaitow L, Trenev N. ProBiotics. New York: Thorsons, 1990.

Chaitow L. Conquer Pain. San Francisco: Chronicle Books, 2002.

Chakúrski I, Matev M, Koïchev A, Angelova I, Stefanov G. Treatment of chronic colitis with an herbal combination of Taraxacum officinale, Hipericum perforatum, Melissa officinaliss, Calendula officinalis and Foeniculum vulgare. Vutr Boles. 1981;20(6):51-4.

Chapman S, Morrell S. Barking mad? another lunatic hypothesis bites the dust. BMJ. 2000 Dec 23-30;321(7276):1561-3.

Chase JE, Gidal BE. Melatonin: therapeutic use in sleep disorders. Ann Pharmacother. 1997;31(10): 1218–26.

Chatterjee SS, Biber A, Weibezahn C. Stimulation of glutamate, aspartate and gamma-aminobutyric acid release from synaptosomes by hyperforin. Pharmacopsychiatry. 2001;34(Suppl.1): S11–19.

Chavez C. Prickly business. The finer points of acupuncture. Posit Aware. 1995 Jan-Feb:14-5.

Cheek RE, Shaver JL, Lentz MJ. Lifestyle practices and nocturnal sleep in midlife women with and without insomnia. Biol Res Nurs. 2004 Jul;6(1):46-58.

Chen LC, Chen IC, Wang BR, Shao CH. Drug-use pattern of Chinese herbal medicines in insomnia: a 4-year survey in Taiwan. J Clin Pharm Ther. 2009 Oct;34(5):555-60.

Chen LC, Wang BR, Chou YC, Tien JH. Drug utilization pattern of Chinese herbal medicines in a general hospital in Taiwan. Pharmacoepidemiol Drug Saf. 2005 Sep;14(9):651-7.

Chen Z, Yang J, Tobak A. Designing new treatments for depression and anxiety. Drugs. 2008;11(3): 189–97.

Chen-Goodspeed M, Cheng Chi Lee. Tumor suppression and circadian function. J Biol Rhythms. 2007 Aug;22(4):291-8.

Chernik DN. Effect of REM sleep deprivation on learning and recall by humans. Percept. Mot. Skills. 1972;34:283-294.

Chien KL, Chen PC, Hsu HC, Su TC, Sung FC, Chen MF, Lee YT. Habitual sleep duration and insomnia and the risk of cardiovascular events and all-cause death: report from a community-based cohort. *Sleep.* 2010 Feb 1;33(2):177-84.

Chilton F, Tucker L. *Win the War Within.* New York: Rodale, 2006.

Chirkova E. Mathematical methods of detection of biological and heliogeophysical rhythms in the light of developments in modern heliobiology: A platform for discussion. *Cybernet Sys.* 2000;31(6):903-918.

Chirkova EN, Suslov LS, Avramenko MM, Krivoruchko GE. Monthly and daily biorhythms of amylase in the blood of healthy men and their relation with the rhythms in the external environment. *Lab Delo.* 1990;(4):40-4.

Chirkova EN, Suslov LS, Avramenko MM, Krivoruchko GE. Monthly and daily biorhythms of amylase in the blood of healthy men and their relation with the rhythms in the external environment. *Lab Delo.* 1990;(4):40-4.

Chiu YH, Chen CH, Shen WW. Somnambulism secondary to olanzapine treatment in one patient with bipolar disorder. *Prog Neuropsychopharmacol Biol Psychiatry.* 2008 Feb 15;32(2):581-2.

Cho HY, Rhee HS, Yoon SY, Park JM. Differential induction of protein expression and benzophenanthridine alkaloid accumulation in Eschscholtzia californica suspension cultures by methyl jasmonate and yeast extract. *J Microbiol Biotechnol.* 2008 Feb;18(2):255-62.

Chong NW, Codd V, Chan D, Samani NJ. Circadian clock genes cause activation of the human PAI-1 gene promoter with 4G/5G allelic preference. *FEBS Lett.* 2006 Aug 7;580(18):4469-72.

Christopher J. *School of Natural Healing.* Springville UT: Christopher Publ, 1976.

Chung KF, Lee CK. Over-the-counter sleeping pills: a survey of use in Hong Kong and a review of their constituents. *Gen Hosp Psychiatry.* 2002 Nov-Dec;24(6):430-5.

Chwirot WB, Popp F. White-light-induced luminescence and mitotic activity of yeast cells. *Folia Histochemica et Cytobiologica.* 1991;29(4):155.

Cicogna P, Cavallero C, Bosinelli M. Cognitive aspects of mental activity during sleep. *Am J Psychol.* 1991 Fall;104(3):413-25.

Cicogna P. Dreaming during sleep onset and awakening. *Percept Mot Skills.* 1994 Jun;78(3 Pt 1):1041-2.

Cipolli C, Baroncini P, Fagioli I, Fumai A, Salzarulo P. The thematic continuity of mental sleep experience in the same night. *Sleep.* 1987 Oct;10(5):473-9.

Cochen De Cock V, Arnulf I. REM sleep behavior disorders and their characteristics in Parkinson's disease. *Rev Neurol.* 2008 Aug-Sep;164(8-9):683-91.

Cocilovo A. Colored light therapy: overview of its history, theory, recent developments and clinical applications combined with acupuncture. *Am J Acupunct.* 1999;27(1-2):71-83.

Cohrs S. Sleep disturbances in patients with schizophrenia : impact and effect of antipsychotics. *CNS Drugs.* 2008;22(11):939-62.

Coles JA, Yamane S. Effects of adapting lights on the time course of the receptor potential of the anuran retinal rod. *J Physiol.* 1975 May;247(1):189-207.

Coll AP, Farooqi IS, O'Rahilly S. The hormonal control of food intake. *Cell.* 2007 Apr 20;129(2):251-62.

Conely J. Music and the Military. *Air University Review.* 1972 Mar-Ap.

Conquer JA, Holub BJ. Dietary docosahexaenoic acid as a source of eicosapentaenoic acid in vegetarians and omnivores. *Lipids.* 1997 Mar;32(3):341-5.

Contreras D, Steriade M. Cellular basis of EEG slow rhythms: a study of dynamic corticothalamic relationships. *J Neurosci.* 1995 Jan;15(1 Pt 2):604-22.

Cook J, The Therapeutic Use of Music. *Nursing Forum.* 1981;20:3:253-66.

Cooper K. *The Aerobics Program for Total Well-Being.* New York: Evans, 1980.

Costa G. The impact of shift and night work on health. Appl Ergon. 1996

Feb;27(1):9-16.

Couzy F, Kastenmayer P, Vigo M, Clough J, Munoz-Box R, Barclay DV. Calcium bioavailability from a calcium- and sulfate-rich mineral water, compared with milk, in young adult women. *Am J Clin Nutr.* 1995 Dec;62(6):1239-44.

Coxeter PD, Schluter PJ, Eastwood HL, Nikles CJ, Glasziou PP. Valerian does not appear to reduce symptoms for patients with chronic insomnia in general practice using a series of randomised n-of-1 trials. *Complement Ther Med.* 2003 Dec;11(4):215-22.

Crawley J. *The Biorhythm Book.* Boston: Journey Editions, 1996.

Creinin MD, Keverline S, Meyn LA. How regular is regular? An analysis of menstrual cycle regularity. *Contraception.* 2004 Oct;70(4):289-92.

Cuellar N. Gand Ratcliffe SJ. Does valerian improve sleepiness and symptom severity in people with restless legs syndrome? *Altern Ther Health Med.* 2009;15(2): 22–28

Curtis LH, Østbye T, Sendersky V, Hutchison S, Dans PE, Wright A, Woosley RL, Schulman KA. Inappropriate prescribing for elderly Americans in a large outpatient population. *Arch Intern Med.* 2004 Aug 9-23;164(15):1621-5.

Cutolo M, Straub RH. Circadian rhythms in arthritis: hormonal effects on the immune/inflammatory reaction. *Autoimmun Rev.* 2008 Jan;7(3):223-8.

Czeisler CA, Kronauer RE, Allan JS, Duffy JF, Jewett ME, Brown EN, Ronda JM. Bright light induction of strong (type 0) resetting of the human circadian pacemaker. *Science.* 1989 Jun 16;244(4910):1328-33.

Darby S, Hill D, Auvinen A, Barros-Dios JM, Baysson H, Bochicchio F, *et al.* Radon in homes and risk of lung cancer: collaborative analysis of individual data from 13 European case-control studies. *BMJ.* 2005 Jan 29;330(7485):223.

Davies G. *Timetables of Medicine.* New York: Black Dog & Leventhal, 2000.

DaVinci L. (Dickens E. ed.) *The Da Vinci Notebooks.* London: Profile, 2005.

Davis GE Jr, Lowell WE. Chaotic solar cycles modulate the incidence and severity of mental illness. *Med Hypotheses.* 2004;62(2):207-14.

Davis GE Jr, Lowell WE. The Sun determines human longevity: teratogenic effects of chaotic solar radiation. *Med Hypotheses.* 2004;63(4):574-81.

Davis S, Kaune WT, Mirick DK, Chen C, Stevens RG. Residential magnetic fields, light-at-night, and nocturnal urinary 6-sulfatoxymelatonin concentration in women. *Am J Epidemiol.* 2001 Oct 1;154(7):591-600.

de Castro Toledo Guimaraes LH, de Carvalho LB, Yanaguibashi G, do Prado GF. Physically active elderly women sleep more and better than sedentary women. *Sleep Med.* 2008 Jul;9(5):488-93.

De Leo V, Lanzetta D, Cazzavacca R, Morgante G. Treatment of neurovegetative menopausal symptoms with a phytotherapeutic agent. *Minerva Ginecol.* 1998 May;50(5):207-11.

Dean C. *Death by Modern Medicine.* Belleville, ON: Matrix Verite-Media, 2005.

Delcomyn F. *Foundations of Neurobiology.* New York: W.H. Freeman and Co., 1998.

Dement W, Vaughan C. *The Promise of Sleep.* New York: Dell, 1999.

Deng S, Chen SN, Lu J, Wang ZJ, Nikolic D, van Breemen RB, Santarsiero BD, Mesecar A, Fong HH, Farnsworth NR, Pauli GF. GABAergic phthalide dimers from Angelica sinensis (Oliv.) *Diels. Phytochem Anal.* 2006 Nov;17(6):398-405.

Deng S, Chen SN, Yao P, Nikolic D, van Breemen RB, Bolton JL, Fong HH, Farnsworth NR, Pauli GF. Serotonergic activity-guided phytochemical investigation of the roots of Angelica sinensis. *J Nat Prod.* 2006 Apr;69(4):536-41.

Deng S, West BJ, Palu AK, Zhou BN, Jensen CJ. Noni as an anxiolytic and sedative: a mechanism involving its gamma-aminobutyric acidergic effects. *Phy-*

tomedicine. 2007 Aug;14(7-8):517-22.

Depue BE, Banich MT, Curran T. Suppression of emotional and nonemotional content in memory: effects of repetition on cognitive control. *Psychol Sci.* 2006 May;17(5):441-7.

Devaraj TL. *Speaking of Ayurvedic Remedies for Common Diseases.* New Delhi: Sterling, 1985.

Devirian TA, Volpe SL. The physiological effects of dietary boron. *Crit Rev Food Sci Nutr.* 2003;43(2):219-31

Dhawan K, Kumar S, Sharma A. Anti-anxiety studies on extracts of Passiflora incarnata Linneaus. *J Ethnopharmacol.* 2001 Dec;78(2-3):165-70.

Dhond RP, Kettner N, Napadow V. Neuroimaging acupuncture effects in the human brain. *J Altern Complement Med.* 2007 Jul-Aug;13(6):603-16.

Di Carlo G, Borrelli F, Ernst E, Izzo AA. *Trends Pharmacol Sci.* 2001;22(11): 557–59.

Dimitriadis GD, Raptis SA. Thyroid hormone excess and glucose intolerance. *Exp Clin Endocrinol Diabetes.* 2001;109 Suppl 2:S225-39.

Dimpfel W, Pischel I, Lehnfeld R. Effects of lozenge containing lavender oil, extracts from hops, lemon balm and oat on electrical brain activity of volunteers. *Eur J Med Res.* 2004;9(9): 423–31.

Dimpfel W, Suter A. Sleep improving effects of a single dose administration of a valerian/hops fluid extract – a double blind, randomized, placebo-controlled sleep-EEG study in a parallel design using electrohypnograms. *Eur J Med Res.* 2008;13(5): 200–4.

Dinges DF, Carskadon MA, Dahl RE, Haulcy VP, Monk TH, Roehrs TA, Walsh JK, Wehr TA. Report by the Working Group on Problem Sleepiness. *Natl Inst Health.* 1997 August.

Dockrell TR, Leever JS. An overview of herbal medications with implications for the school nurse. *J Sch Nurs.* 2000 Aug;16(3):53-8.

Dolcos F, LaBar KS, Cabeza R. Interaction between the amygdala and the medial temporal lobe memory system predicts better memory for emotional events. *Neuron.* 2004 Jun 10;42(5):855-63.

Dole EJ, Rhyne RL, Zeilmann CA, Skipper BJ, McCabe ML, Low Dog T. The influence of ethnicity on use of herbal remedies in elderly Hispanics and non-Hispanic whites. *J Am Pharm Assoc* (Wash). 2000 May-Jun;40(3):359-65.

Donath F, Quispe S, Diefenbach K, Maurer A, Fietze I, Roots I. Critical evaluation of the effect of valerian extract on sleep structure and sleep quality. *Pharmacopsychiatry.* 2000 Mar;33(2):47-53.

Duke J. *The Green Pharmacy.* New York: St. Martins, 1997.

Duke M. *Acupuncture.* New York: Pyramid, 1973.

Duncan WC Jr, Johnson KA, Wehr TA. Decreased sensitivity to light of the photic entrainment pathway during chronic clorgyline and lithium treatments. *J Biol Rhythms.* 1998 Aug;13(4):330-46.

Duncan WC, Barbato G, Fagioli I, Garcia-Borreguero D, Wehr TA. A biphasic daily pattern of slow wave activity during a two-day 90-minute sleep wake schedule. Arch Ital Biol. 2009 Dec;147(4):117-30.

Dunlop KA, Carson DJ, Shields MD. Hypoglycemia due to adrenal suppression secondary to high-dose nebulized corticosteroid. *Pediatr Pulmonol.* 2002 Jul;34(1):85-6.

Dunne BJ, Jahn RG. Consciousness, information, and living systems. *Cell Mol Biol* 2005 Dec 14;51(7):703-14.

Ebbesen F, Agati G, Pratesi R. Phototherapy with turquoise versus blue light. *Arch Dis Child Fetal Neonatal Ed.* 2003 Sep;88(5):F430-1.

Edinger J, Wohlgemuth W, Radtke R, Marsh G, Quillian R. Cognitive Behavioral

Therapy for Treatment of Chronic Primary Insomnia:A Randomized Controlled Trial. *JAMA.* 2001;285:1856-1864.

Edinger JD, Wohlgemuth WK, Radtke RA, Marsh GR, Quillian RE. Cognitive Behavioral Therapy for Treatment of Chronic Primary Insomnia, A Randomized Controlled Trial. *JAMA.* 2001;285:1856-1864.

Edmonds CJ, Burford D. Should children drink more water?: the effects of drinking water on cognition in children. *Appetite.* 2009 Jun;52(3):776-9.

Edris AE. Pharmaceutical and therapeutic potentials of essential oils and their individual volatile constituents: a review. *Phytother Res.* 2007 Apr;21(4):308-23.

Edwards B. *Drawing on the Right Side of the Brain.* Los Angeles, CA: Tarcher, 1979.

Egan KM, Sosman JA, Blot WJ. Sunlight and reduced risk of cancer: is the real story vitamin D? *J Natl Cancer Inst.* 2005 Feb 2;97(3):161-3.

Eggermont S, Van den Bulck J. Nodding off or switching off? The use of popular media as a sleep aid in secondary-school children. *J Paediatr Child Health.* 2006 Jul-Aug;42(7-8):428-33.

Eisenberg MJ. Magnesium deficiency and sudden death. *Am. Heart J.* 1992;124:544-549.

Eiser AS. Physiology and psychology of dreams. *Semin Neurol.* 2005 Mar;25(1):97-105.

Ellingwood F, Lloyd JU. *American Materia Medica, Therapeutics and Pharmacognosy.* Portland, OR: Eclectic Medical Publications, 1989-1983.

elSohly HN, elSohly MA, Stanford DF. Poppy seed ingestion and opiates urinalysis: a closer look. *J Anal Toxicol.* 1990 Sep-Oct;14(5):308-10.

Elwood PC. Epidemiology and trace elements. *Clin Endocrinol Metab.* 1985 Aug;14(3):617-28.

Empson JA, Clarke PR. Rapid eye movements and remembering. Nature. 1970; 227:287-288.

EPA. *A Brief Guide to Mold, Moisture and Your Home.* Environmental Protection Agency, Office of Air and Radiation/Indoor Environments Division. EPA 2002;402-K-02-003.

Ernst E. A systematic review of systematic reviews of homeopathy. *Br J Clin Pharmacol.* 2002 Dec;54(6):577-82.

Ernst E. Frankincense: systematic review. *BMJ.* 2008 Dec 17;337:a2813.

Ernst E. Herbal remedies for anxiety - a systematic review of controlled clinical trials. *Phytomedicine.* 2006 Feb;13(3):205-8.

Evans P, Forte D, Jacobs C, Fredhoi C, Aitchison E, Hucklebridge F, Clow A. Cortisol secretory activity in older people in relation to positive and negative well-being. Psychoneuroendocrinology. 2007 Aug 7

FAO/WHO Expert Committee. Fats and Oils in Human Nutrition. Food and Nutrition Paper. 1994;(57).

FC&A (ed.). *801 Prescription Drugs: Good Effects, Side Effects and Natural Healing Alternatives.* Peachtree City, GA: FC&A Publ., 1996.

Fehring RJ, Schneider M, Raviele K. Variability in the phases of the menstrual cycle. *J Obstet Gynecol Neonatal Nurs.* 2006 May-Jun;35(3):376-84.

Felter HW. *The Eclectic Materia Medica, Pharmacology and Therapeutics.* Cincinnati: Eclectic Medical Publications, 1922-1983).

Ferentinos P, Paparrigopoulos T. Zopiclone and sleepwalking. *Int J Neuropsychopharmacol.* 2009 Feb;12(1):141-2.

Ferini-Strambi L, Manconi M. Treatment of restless legs syndrome. *Parkinsonism Relat Disord.* 2009 Dec;15 Suppl 4:S65-70.

Ferini-Strambi L. Treatment options for restless legs syndrome. *Expert Opin Pharmacother.* 2009 Mar;10(4):545-54.

Fioravanti A, Bellisai B, Capitani S, Manica P, Paolazzi G, Galeazzi M. Phyto-thermotherapy: a possible complementary therapy for fibromyalgia patients. *Clin Exp Rheumatol.* 2009 Sep-Oct;27(5 Suppl 56):S29-32.

Foer J, Siffre M. Caveman: An Interview with Michel Siffre. *Cabinet.* 2008 Summer (30).

Foster S, Hobbs C. *Medicinal Plants and Herbs.* Boston: Houghton Mifflin, 2002.

Fowler MJ. Sullivan, M. J, Ekstrand, B. R. Sleep and memory. Science. 1973; 179:302-304.

Frawley D, Lad V. *The Yoga of Herbs.* Sante Fe: Lotus Press, 1986.

Friede M, Henneicke von Zepelin HH, Freudenstein J. Differential therapy of mild to moderate depressive episodes (ICD-10 F 32.0; F 32.1) with St. John's wort. *Pharmacopsychiatry.* 2001 Jul;34 Suppl 1:S38-41.

Fritschi G, Prescott WR Jr. Morphine levels in urine subsequent to poppy seed consumption. *Forensic Sci Int.* 1985 Feb;27(2):111-7.

Fugh-Berman A, Cott JM. Dietary supplements and natural products as psycho-therapeutic agents. *Psychosom Med.* 1999 Sep-Oct;61(5):712-28.

Fukada Y, Okano T. Circadian clock system in the pineal gland. *Mol Neurobiol.* 2002 Feb;25(1):19-30.

Fukuma E, Umczava Y, Kobayashi K, Moioikc M. Polygraphic study of the nocturnal sleep of children with Down syndrome and endogenous mental retardation. Folia Psychiatr. Ncu-rol. 1974; 28:333-345.

Füssel A, Wolf A, Brattström A. Effect of a fixed valerian-Hop extract combination (Ze 91019) on sleep polygraphy in patients with non-organic insomnia: a pilot study. *Eur J Med Res.* 2000 Sep 18;5(9):385-90.

Gafner S, Bergeron C, Batcha LL, Angerhofer CK, Sudberg S, Sudberg EM, Guinaudeau H, Gauthier R. Analysis of Scutellaria lateriflora and its adulterants Teucrium canadense and Teucrium chamaedrys by LC-UV/MS, TLC, and digital photomicroscopy. *J AOAC Int.* 2003 May-Jun;86(3):453-60.

Gafner S, Bergeron C, Batcha LL, Reich J, Arnason JT, Burdette JE, Pezzuto JM, Angerhofer CK. Inhibition of [3H]-LSD binding to 5-HT7 receptors by flavonoids from Scutellaria lateriflora. *J Nat Prod.* 2003 Apr;66(4):535-7.

Gagnier JJ, DeMelo J, Boon H, Rochon P, Bombardier C. Quality of reporting of randomized controlled trials of herbal medicine interventions. *Am J Med.* 2006;119:1–11.

Gallagher RS, Ananth R, Granger K, Bradley B, Anderson JV, Fuerst EP. Phenolic and short-chained aliphatic organic acid constituents of wild oat (Avena fatua L.) seeds. *J Agric Food Chem.* 2010 Jan 13;58(1):218-25.

Gallicchio L, Kalesan B. Sleep duration and mortality: a systematic review and meta-analysis. *J Sleep Res.* 2009 Jun;18(2):148-58.

Gambini JP, Velluti RA, Pedemonte M. Hippocampal theta rhythm synchronizes visual neurons in sleep and waking. *Brain Res.* 2002 Feb 1;926(1-2):137-41.

Gammack JK, Burke JM. Natural light exposure improves subjective sleep quality in nursing home residents. *J Am Med Dir Assoc.* 2009 Jul;10(6):440-1.

Gandhi T, Weingart S, Borus J, Seger A, Peterson J, Burdick E, Seger D, Shu K, Federico F, Leape L, Bates D. Adverse drug events in ambulatory care. *N Engl J Med.* 2003 Apr 17;348(16):1556-64.

Gange R. UVA sunbeds - are there longterm hazards. In Cronley-Dillon J, Rosen E, Marshall J (Eds.):*Hazards of Light, Myths and Realities.* Oxford, U.K.: Pergamon Press, 1986.

Garcia-Lazaro JA, Ahmed B, Schnupp JW. Tuning to natural stimulus dynamics in primary auditory cortex. *Curr Biol.* 2006 Feb 7;16(3):264-71.

Gau SS, Soong WT, Merikangas KR. Correlates of sleep-wake patterns among children and young adolescents in Taiwan. Sleep. 2004 May 1;27(3):512-9.

Gerber R. *Vibrational Healing.* Sante Fe: Bear, 1988.

Ghadioungui P. (transl.) *The Ebers Papyrus.* Academy of Scientific Research. Cairo, 1987.

Ghayur MN, Gilani AH. Ginger lowers blood pressure through blockade of voltage-dependent calcium Channels acting as a cardiotonic pump activator in mice, rabbit and dogs. *J Cardiovasc Pharmacol.* 2005 Jan;45(1):74-80.

Gibbons E. *Stalking the Healthful Herbs.* New York: David McKay, 1966.

Gibson RA. Docosa-hexaenoic acid (DHA) accumulation is regulated by the polyunsaturated fat content of the diet: Is it synthesis or is it incorporation? *Asia Pac J Clin Nutr.* 2004;13(Suppl):S78.

Giedke H, Breyer-Pfaff U. Critical evaluation of the effect of valerian extract on sleep structure and sleep quality. *Pharmacopsychiatry.* 2000 Nov;33(6):239.

Giustino G. Memory in dreams. *Int J Psychoanal.* 2009 Oct;90(5):1057-73.

Glover J. *The Philosophy of Mind.* Oxford University Press, 1976.

Gohil K, Packer L. Bioflavonoid-Rich Botanical Extracts Show Antioxidant and Gene Regulatory Activity. *Ann N Y Acad Sci.* 2002:957:70-7.

Golub E. *The Limits of Medicine.* New York: Times Books, 1994.

Gottesmann C. GABA mechanisms and sleep. *Neuroscience,* 2002;111:.231–39.

Gounder R. Kava consumption and its health effects. *Pac Health Dialog.* .2006;13(2): 131–35.

Grandner MA, Hale L, Moore M, Patel NP. Mortality associated with short sleep duration: The evidence, the possible mechanisms, and the future. *Sleep Med Rev.* 2009 Nov 23.

Grandner MA, Patel NP, Gehrman PR, Perlis ML, Pack AI. Problems associated with short sleep: Bridging the gap between laboratory and epidemiological studies. *Sleep Med Rev.* 2009 Nov 5.

Grasmuller S, Irnich D. Acupuncture in pain therapy. *MMW Fortschr Med.* 2007 Jun 21;149(25-26):37-9.

Gray-Davison F. *Ayurvedic Healing.* New York: Keats, 2002.

Green ML, Green RG, Santoro W. Daily relaxationmodifies serum and salivary immunoglobulins and psychophysiologic symptom severity. *Biofeedback SelfRegul.* 1988;13: 187–99.

Grenell G. Affect integration in dreams and dreaming. *J Am Psychoanal Assoc.* 2008 Mar;56(1):223-51.

Grenell G. Affect integration in dreams and dreaming. *J Am Psychoanal Assoc.* 2008 Mar;56(1):223-51.

Grieser C, Greenberg R, Harrison R. The adaptive function of sleep. The differential effects of sleep and dreaming on recall. *J. Abnorm. Psychol.* 1972;80:280-286.

Grimmett A, Sillence MN. Calmatives for the excitable horse: a review of L-tryptophan. *Vet J.* 2005;170(1): 24–32.

Groggy Workforce, Sleepy "Generation Y" Among Key Poll Findings. *National Sleep Foundation.* 2000;Mar 28.

Gronfier C, Wright KP Jr, Kronauer RE, Czeisler CA. Entrainment of the human circadian pacemaker to longer-than-24-h days. *Proc Natl Acad Sci U S A.* 2007 May 22;104(21):9081-6.

Grønli J, Fiske E, Murison R, Bjorvatn B, Sørensen E, Ursin R, Portas CM. Extracellular levels of serotonin and GABA in the hippocampus after chronic mild stress in rats. A microdialysis study in an animal model of depression. *Behav Brain Res.* 2007 Jul 19;181(1):42-51.

Grundmann O, Nakajima J, Seo S, Butterweck V. Anti-anxiety effects of Apocynum venetum L. in the elevated plus maze test. *J Ethnopharmacol.* 2007;110(3): 406–11.

Grundmann O, Wang J, McGregor GP, Butterweck V. Anxiolytic activity of a phytochemically characterized Passifl ora incarnata extract is mediated via the GABAergic system. *Planta Med.* 2008;74(15): 1769–73.

Grzanna R, Lindmark L, Frondoza CG. Ginger—an herbal medicinal product with broad anti-inflammatory actions. *J Med Food.* 2005 Summer;8(2):125-32.

Gupta YK, Gupta M, Kohli K. Neuroprotective role of melatonin in oxidative stress vulnerable brain. *Indian J Physiol Pharmacol.* 2003 Oct;47(4):373-86.

Gutmanis J. *Hawaiian Herbal Medicine.* Waipahu, HI: Island Heritage, 2001.

Gyllenhaal C, Merritt SL, Peterson SD, Block KI, Gochenour T. Efficacy and safety of herbal stimulants and sedatives in sleep disorders. Sleep Med Rev. 2000 Jun;4(3):229-251.

Hadjikhani R. Anxiolytic-like Effects of Dichloromethane Extracts of Valerian (DEV) in Adult Male Wistar Rats. *World Acad Sci, Eng Tech.* 2009;(55): 532–36.

Hadley S, Petry JJ. Valerian. *Am Fam Physician.* 2003 Apr 15;67(8):1755-8.

Hafeez ZH, Kalinowski CM. Somnambulism induced by quetiapine: two case reports and a review of the literature. *CNS Spectr.* 2007 Dec;12(12):910-2.

Hagins WA, Yoshikami S. Ionic mechanisms in excitation of photoreceptors. *Ann N Y Acad Sci.* 1975 Dec 30;264:314-25.

Hagins WA, Yoshikami S. Proceedings: A role for Ca2+ in excitation of retinal rods and cones. *Exp Eye Res.* 1974 Mar;18(3):299-305.

Hahnemann S. *Oreganon of Homeopathic Medicine.* New York: W. Radde, 1843.

Halpern G, Miller A. *Medicinal Mushrooms.* New York: M. Evans, 2002.

Halpern S. *Tuning the Human Instrument.* Palo Alto, CA: Spectrum Research Institute, 1978.

Hamel P. *Through Music to the Self: How to Appreciate and Experience Music.* Boulder: Shambala, 1979.

Hameroff SR, Penrose R. Conscious events as orchestrated spacetime selections. *J Consc Studies.* 1996;3(1):36-53.

Hammond BG, Mayhew DA, Kier LD, Mast RW, Sander WJ. Safety assessment of DHA-rich microalgae from Schizochytrium sp. *Regul Toxicol Pharmacol.* 2002 Apr;35(2 Pt 1):255-65.

Hannoun AB, Nassar AH, Usta IM, Zreik TG, Abu Musa AA. Effect of war on the menstrual cycle. *Obstet Gynecol.* 2007 Apr;109(4):929-32.

Happe S, Klösch G, Zeitlhofer J. Perception of dreams and subjective sleep quality in patients with myasthenia gravis. *Neuropsychobiology.* 2004;50(1):21-7.

Hardin P. Transcription regulation within the circadian clock: the E-box and beyond. *J Biol Rhythms.* 2004 Oct;19(5):348-60.

Harney JW, Barofsky IM, Leary JD. Behavioral and toxicological studies of cyclopentanoid monoterpenes from Nepeta cataria. *Lloydia.* 1978 Jul-Aug;41(4):367-74.

Hartmann E. Functions of sleep. In: Jovanovic, U, ed. Nature of sleep. Stuttgart: Fisher Vcrlag. 1975:238-252.

Hashimoto S. Anxiolytic effects of serotonin reuptake inhibitors and their mechanism of action. *Hokkaido Igaku Zasshi.* 2000;75(6): 421–36.

Hattesohl M, Feistel B, Sievers H, Lehnfeld R, Hegger M, Winterhoff H. Extracts of Valeriana officinalis L. s.l. show anxiolytic and antidepressant effects but neither sedative nor myorelaxant properties. *Phytomedicine.* 2008 Jan;15(1-2):2-15.

Heaney RP. Absorbability and utility of calcium in mineral waters. *Am J Clin Nutr.* 2006 Aug;84(2):371-4.

Hendel B, Ferreira P. *Water & Salt: The Essence of Life.* Gaithersburg: Natural Resources, 2003.

Henih HIa, Ladna LIa. Phytochemical study of the dropworts, Filipendula ulmaria and F. hexapetala, from the flora of Lvov Province. *Farm Zh.* 1980;(1):50-2.

Hensel J, Pillmann F. Late-life somnambulism after therapy with metoprolol. *Clin Neuropharmacol.* 2008 Jul-Aug;31(4):248-50.

Herrera-Arellano A, Luna-Villegas G, Cuevas-Uriostegui ML, Alvarez L, Vargas-Pineda G, Zamilpa-Alvarez A, Tortoriello J. Polysomnographic evaluation of the hypnotic effect of Valeriana edulis standardized extract in patients suffering from insomnia. *Planta Med.* 2001 Nov;67(8):695-9.

Hillecke T, Nickel A, Bolay HV. Scientific perspectives on music therapy. *Ann N Y Acad Sci.* 2005 Dec;1060:271-82.

Hirayama J, Sahar S, Grimaldi B, Tamaru T, Takamatsu K, Nakahata Y, Sassone-Corsi P. CLOCK-mediated acetylation of BMAL1 controls circadian function. *Nature.* 2007 Dec 13;450(7172):1086-90.

Hirayama J, Sahar S, Grimaldi B, Tamaru T, Takamatsu K, Nakahata Y, Sassone-Corsi P. CLOCK-mediated acetylation of BMAL1 controls circadian function. *Nature* 450, 1086-1090 (13 December 2007)

Hisamitsu T, Seto A, Nakazato S, Yamamoto T, Aung SK. Emission of extremely strong magnetic fields from the head and whole body during oriental breathing exercises. *Acupunct Electrother Res.* 1996 Jul-Dec;21(3-4):219-27.

Hobbs C. *Medicinal Mushrooms.* Summertown, TN: Botanica Press, 1986.

Hobbs C. *Stress & Natural Healing.* Loveland, CO: Interweave Press, 1997.

Hobbs. C. *Herbal Remedies for Dummies.* New York: Wiley Publ., 1998.

Hobson JA. REM sleep and dreaming: towards a theory of protoconsciousness. *Nat Rev Neurosci.* 2009 Nov;10(11):803-13.

Hodoba D, Hrabrić K, Krmpotić P, Brecić P, Kujundzić-Tiljak M, Majdaneić Z. Dream recall after night awakenings from tonic/phasic REM sleep. *Coll Antropol.* 2008 Jan;32 Suppl 1:69-73.

Hoffmann D. *Holistic Herbal.* London: Thorsons, 1983-2002.

Holick MF. Sunlight and vitamin D for bone health and prevention of autoimmune diseases, cancers, and cardiovascular disease. *Am J Clin Nutr.* 2004 Dec;80(6 Suppl):1678S-88S.

Holick MF. Vitamin D: importance in the prevention of cancers, type 1 diabetes, heart disease, and osteoporosis. *Am J Clin Nutr.* 2004 Mar;79(3):362-71.

Holladay, S.D. Prenatal Immunotoxicant Exposure and Postnatal Autoimmune Disease. *Environ Health Perspect.* 1999; 107(suppl 5):687-691.

Hollfoth K. Effect of color therapy on health and wellbeing: colors are more than just physics. *Pflege.Z* 2000;53(2):111-112.

Hollwich F, Dieckhues B. Effect of light on the eye on metabolism and hormones. *Klinische Monatsblatter fur Augenheilkunde.* 1989;195(5):284-90.

Hollwich F. Hartmann C. Influence of light through the eyes on metabolism and hormones. *Ophtalmologie.* 1990;4(4):385-9.

Hollwich F. *The influence of ocular light perception on metabolism in man and in animal.* New York: Springer-Verlag, 1979.

Holmes A, Yang RJ, Murphy DL, Crawley JN. Evaluation of antidepressant-related behavioral responses in mice lacking the serotonin transporter. *Neuropsychopharmacology.* 2002;27(6): 914–23

Holsboer-Trachsler E. Phytotherapeutic drugs and sleep. *Praxis.* 2000 Dec 21;89(51-52):2178-82.

Holst L, Wright D, Haavik S, Nordeng H. The use and the user of herbal remedies during pregnancy. *J Altern Complement Med.* 2009 Jul;15(7):787-92.

Home JA, Walmslcy B. Day-time visual load and the effects upon human sleep. Psychophysiology. 1976; 13:115-120.

Hope M. *The Psychology of Healing.* Longmead UK: Element Books, 1989.

Hoskin M.(ed.). *The Cambridge Illustrated History of Astronomy.* Cambridge: Cambridge Press, 1997.

Huber R, Schuderer J, Graf T, Jütz K, Borbély AA, Kuster N, Achermann P. Radio frequency electromagnetic field exposure in humans: Estimation of SAR distribution in the brain, effects on sleep and heart rate. *Bioelectromagnetics.* 2003 May;24(4):262-76.

Huber R, Treyer V, Borbély AA, Schuderer J, Gottselig JM, Landolt HP, Werth E, Berthold T, Kuster N, Buck A, Achermann P. Electromagnetic fields, such as those from mobile phones, alter regional cerebral blood flow and sleep and waking EEG. *J Sleep Res.* 2002 Dec;11(4):289-95.

Hübner WD, Lande S, Podzuweit H. Hypericum treatment of mild depressions with somatic symptoms. *J Geriatr Psychiatry Neurol.* 1994 Oct;7 Suppl 1:S12-4.

Huen MS, Hui KM, Leung JW, Sigel E, Baur R, Wong JT, Xue H. Naturally occurring 2'-hydroxyl-substituted flavonoids as high-affinity benzodiazepine site ligands. *Biochem Pharmacol.* 2003 Dec 15;66(12):2397-407.

Hui KM, Huen MS, Wang HY, Zheng H, Sigel E, Baur R, Ren H, Li ZW, Wong JT, Xue H. Anxiolytic effect of wogonin, a benzodiazepine receptor ligand isolated from Scutellaria baicalensis Georgi. *Biochem Pharmacol.* 2002 Nov 1;64(9):1415-24.

Hui KM, Huen MS, Wang HY, Zheng H, Sigel E, Baur R, Ren H, Li ZW, Wong JT, Xue H. Anxiolytic effect of wogonin, a benzodiazepine receptor ligand isolated from Scutellaria baicalensis Georgi. *Biochem Pharmacol.* 2002 Nov 1;64(9):1415-24.

Igarashi T, Izumi H, Uchiumi T, Nishio K, Arao T, Tanabe M, Uramoto H, Sugio K, Yasumoto K, Sasaguri Y, Wang KY, Otsuji Y, Kohno K. Clock and ATF4 transcription system regulates drug resistance in human cancer cell lines. *Oncogene.* 2007 Jul 19;26(33):4749-60.

Ikeda M, Toyoshima R, Inoue Y, Yamada N, Mishima K, Nomura M, Ozaki N, Okawa M, Takahashi K, Yamauchi T. Mutation screening of the human Clock gene in circadian rhythm sleep disorders. *Psychiatry Res.* 2002 Mar 15;109(2):121-8.

Ikehara S, Iso H, Date C, Kikuchi S, Watanabe Y, Wada Y, Inaba Y, Tamakoshi A; JACC Study Group. Association of sleep duration with mortality from cardiovascular disease and other causes for Japanese men and women: the JACC study. *Sleep.* 2009 Mar 1;32(3):295-301.

Ikonomov OC, Stoynev AG. Gene expression in suprachiasmatic nucleus and circadian rhythms. *Neurosci Biobehav Rev.* 1994 Fall;18(3):305-12.

Iliffe S, Curran HV, Collins R, Yuen Kee SC, Fletcher S, Woods B. Attitudes to long-term use of benzodiazepine hypnotics by older people in general practice: findings from interviews with service users and providers. *Aging Ment Health.* 2004 May;8(3):242-8.

Innis SM, Hansen JW. Plasma fatty acid responses, metabolic effects, and safety of microalgal and fungal oils rich in arachidonic and docosahexaenoic acids in adults. *Am J Clin Nutr.* 1996 Aug;64(2):159-67.

Iowa State University. Food and Nutrition: Choices for Health. http://www.extension.iastate.edu/nutrition /supplements/melatonin.php

Is it true that the scent of lavender can calm you and help you sleep? *Mayo Clin Womens Healthsource.* 2003 Aug;7(8):8.

Ivanovic-Zuvic F, de la Vega R, Ivanovic-Zuvic N, Renteria P. Affective disorders and solar activity. *Actas Esp Psiquiatr.* 2005 Jan-Feb;33(1):7-12.

Ivry GB, Ogle CA, Shim EK. Role of sun exposure in melanoma. *Dermatol Surg.* 2006 Apr;32(4):481-92.

Iwase T, Kajimura N, Uchiyama M, Ebisawa T, Yoshimura K, Kamei Y, Shibui K,

Kim K, Kudo Y, Katoh M, Watanabe T, Nakajima T, Ozeki Y, Sugishita M, Hori T, Ikeda M, Toyoshima R, Inoue Y, Yamada N, Mishima K, Nomura M, Ozaki N, Okawa M, Takahashi K, Yamauchi T. Mutation screening of the human Clock gene in circadian rhythm sleep disorders. *Psychiatry Res.* 2002 Mar 15;109(2):121-8.

Jacob TC, Moss SJ, Jurd R. GABA(A) receptor trafficking and its role in the dynamic modulation of neuronal inhibition. *Nat Rev Neurosci.* 2008;9(5): 331–43.

Jahn R, Dunne, B. *Margins of Reality: the Role of Consciousness in the Physical World.* New York: Harcourt Brace Jovanovich, 1987.

Janson C, Norback D, Omenaas E, Gislason T, Nystrom L, Jogi R, Lindberg E, Gunnbjornsdottir M, Norrman E, Wentzel-Larsen T, Svanes C, Jensen EJ, Toren K. Insomnia is more common among subjects living in damp buildings. *Occup Environ Med.* 2005 Feb;62(2):113-8.

Jarvis DC. *Folk Medicine.* Greenwich, CN: Fawcett, 1958.

Jennings KA, Loder MK, Sheward WJ, Pei Q, Deacon RM, Benson MA, Olverman HJ, Hastie ND, Harmar AJ, Shen S, Sharp T. Increased expression of the 5-HT transporter confers a low-anxiety phenotype linked to decreased 5-HT transmission. *J Neurosci.* 2006 Aug 30;26(35):8955-64.

Jensen B. *Foods that Heal.* Garden City Park, NY: Avery Publ, 1988, 1993.

Jensen B. *Nature Has a Remedy.* Los Angeles: Keats, 2001.

Jensen R, Lammi-Keefe C, Henderson R, Bush V, Ferris A.M. Effect of dietary intake of n-6 and n-3 fatty acids on the fatty acid composition of human milk in North America. J Pediatr. 1992;120:S87-92.

Jiang JG, Huang XJ, Chen J, Lin QS. Comparison of the sedative and hypnotic effects of flavonoids, saponins, and polysaccharides extracted from Semen Ziziphus jujube. *Nat Prod Res.* 2007 Apr;21(4):310-20.

Jiang JG, Huang XJ, Chen J. Separation and purification of saponins from Semen Ziziphus jujuba and their sedative and hypnotic effects. *J Pharm Pharmacol.* 2007 Aug;59(8):1175-80.

Johari H. *Ayurvedic Massage: Traditional Indian Techniques for Balancing Body and Mind.* Rochester, VT: Healing Arts, 1996.

Johnson LM. Gitksan medicinal plants—cultural choice and efficacy. *J Ethnobiol Ethnomed.* 2006 Jun 21;2:29.

Johnston RE. Pheromones, the vomeronasal system, and communication. From hormonal responses to individual recognition. *Ann N Y Acad Sci.* 1998 Nov 30;855:333-48.

Jorgenson J. Therapeutic use of companion animals in health care. *Image J Nurs Sch.* 1997;29(3):249-54.

Jung JW, Yoon BH, Oh HR, Ahn JH, Kim SY, Park SY, Ryu JH. Anxiolytic-like effects of Gastrodia elata and its phenolic constituents in mice. *Biol Pharm Bull.* 2006 Feb;29(2):261-5.

Jurkovicová I, Celec P. Sleep apnea syndrome and its complications. *Acta Med Austr.* 2004 May;31(2):45-50.

Jutte R, Riley D. A review of the use and role of low potencies in homeopathy. *Complement Ther Med.* 2005 Dec;13(4):291-6.

Kagawa D, Jokura H, Ochiai R, Tokimitsu I, Tsubone H. The sedative effects and mechanism of action of cedrol inhalation with behavioral pharmacological evaluation. *Planta Med.* 2003 Jul;69(7):637-41.

Kähkönen MP, Hopia AI, Vuorela HJ, Rauha JP, Pihlaja K, Kujala TS, Heinonen M. Antioxidant activity of plant extracts containing phenolic compounds. *J Agric Food Chem.* 1999 Oct;47(10):3954-62.

Kalman DS, Feldman S, Feldman R, Schwartz HI, Krieger DR, Garrison R. Effect of a proprietary Magnolia and Phellodendron extract on stress levels in healthy women: a pilot, double-blind, placebo-controlled clinical trial. *Nutr J*. 2008 Apr 21;7:11.

Kalmijn S, Launer LJ, Ott A, Witteman JC, Hofman A, Breteler MM. Dietary fat intake and the risk of incident dementia in the Rotterdam Study. *Ann Neurol*. 1997 Nov;42(5):776-82.

Kalsbeek A, Perreau-Lenz S, Buijs RM. A network of (autonomic) clock outputs. *Chronobiol Int*. 2006;23(1-2):201-15.

Kamide Y. We reside in the sun's atmosphere. *Biomed Pharmacother*. 2005 Oct;59 Suppl 1:S1-4.

Kammerer E. Phytogenic sedatives-hypnotics—does a combination of valerian and hops have a value in the modern drug repertoire? *Z Arztl Fortbild*. 1993 Apr 12;87(5):401-6.

Kandel E, Siegelbaum S, Schwartz J. *Synaptic transmission. Principles of Neural Science*. New York: Elsevier, 1991.

Kaneko M, Kumashiro H, Takahashi Y, Hoshino Y. L-5HTP treatment and serum 5-HT level after L-5-HTP loading on depressed patients. *Neuropsychobiology* 1979;5(4):232-40.

Kaplan R. The psychological benefits of nearby nature. In: Relf, D. (ed) *The Role of Horticulture in Human Well-Being and Social Development: A National Symposium*. Portland: Timber Press. 1992:125-133.

Kaplan S. A model of person - environment compatibility. *Environment and Behaviour* 1983;15:311-332.

Kaplan S. The restorative environment: nature and human experience. In: Relf, D. (ed) *The Role of Horticulture in Human Well-Being and Social Development: A National Symposium*. Portland: Timber Press. 1992:134-142.

Karnstedt J. Ions and Consciousness. *Whole Self*. 1991 Spring.

Kasper S, Wehr TA. The role of sleep and wakefulness in the genesis of depression and mania. *Encephale*. 1992 Jan;18 Spec No 1:45-50.

Kato Y, Kawamoto T, Honda KK. Circadian rhythms in cartilage. *Clin Calcium*. 2006 May;16(5):838-45.

Kelder P. *Ancient Secret of the Fountain of Youth: Book 1*. New York: Doubleday, 1998.

Kelechi TJ, McNeil RB. A prospective, descriptive study of hour-to-hour and day-to-day temperature variability of skin affected by chronic venous disorders. *Ostomy Wound Manage*. 2008 Apr;54(4):18-34.

Kelly SP, Gomez-Ramirez M, Montesi JL, Foxe JJ. L-theanine and caffeine in combination affect human cognition as evidenced by oscillatory alpha-band activity and attention task performance. *J Nutr*. 2008;138(8): 1572S–77S.

Kemper KJ, Wornham WL. Consultations for holistic pediatric services for inpatients and outpatient oncology patients at a children's hospital. *Arch Pediatr Adolesc Med*. 2001 Apr;155(4):449-54.

Kennedy DO, Little W, Haskell CF, Scholey AB. Anxiolytic effects of a combination of Melissa offi cinalis and Valeriana offi cinalis during laboratory induced stress. *Phytother Res*. 2006;20(2): 96–102.

Kennedy DO, Little W, Scholey AB. Attenuation of laboratory-induced stress in humans after acute administration of Melissa officinalis (Lemon Balm). *Psychosom Med*, 2004;66(4): 607–13.

Kennedy DO, Pace S, Haskell C, Okello EJ, Milne A, Scholey AB. Effects of cholinesterase inhibiting sage (Salvia officinalis) on mood, anxiety and performance on a psychological stressor battery. *Neuropsychopharmacology*. 2006 Apr;31(4):845-52.

Kennedy DO, Wake G, Savelev S, Tildesley NT, Perry EK, Wesnes KA, Scholey AB. Modulation of mood and cognitive performance following acute administration of single doses of Melissa officinalis (Lemon balm) with human CNS nicotinic and muscarinic receptor-binding properties. *Neuropsychopharmacology.* 2003 Oct;28(10):1871-81.

Keogh JB, Grieger JA, Noakes M, Clifton PM. Flow-Mediated Dilatation Is Impaired by a High-Saturated Fat Diet but Not by a High-Carbohydrate Diet. *Arterioscler Thromb Vasc Biol.* 2005 Mar 17

Kerr CC, Rennie CJ, Robinson PA. Physiology-based modeling of cortical auditory evoked potentials. *Biol Cybern.* 2008 Feb;98(2):171-84.

Keville K, Green M. *Aromatherapy: A Complete Guide to the Healing Art.* Freedom, CA: Crossing Press, 1995.

Khom S, Baburin I, Timin E, Hohaus A, Trauner G, Kopp B, Hering S. Valerenic acid potentiates and inhibits GABA(A) receptors: molecular mechanism and subunit specificity. *Neuropharmacology.* 2007 Jul;53(1):178-87.

Kiecolt-Glaser JK, Graham JE, Malarkey WB, Porter K, Lemeshow S, Glaser R. Olfactory influences on mood and autonomic, endocrine, and immune function. *Psychoneuroendocrinology.* 2008 Apr;33(3):328-39.

Kim JT, Ren CJ, Fielding GA, Pitti A, Kasumi T, Wajda M, Lebovits A, Bekker A. Treatment with lavender aromatherapy in the post-anesthesia care unit reduces opioid requirements of morbidly obese patients undergoing laparoscopic adjustable gastric banding. *Obes Surg.* 2007 Jul;17(7):920-5.

Kircheimer S. *The Doctors Book of Home Remedies II.* New York: Bantam, 1993.

Klein R, Armitage R. Rhythms in human performance: 1 1/2-hour oscillations in cognitive style. *Science.* 1979 Jun 22;204(4399):1326-8.

Klein R, Landau MG. *Healing: The Body Betrayed.* Minneapolis: DCI:Chronimed, 1992.

Kleitman N. *Sleep and Wakefulness.* Univ Chicago Press, 1963.

Klepser TB, Klepser ME. Unsafe and potentially safe herbal therapies. *Am J Health Syst Pharm.* 1999 Jan 15;56(2):125-38; quiz 139-41.

Kloss J. *Back to Eden.* Twin Oaks, WI: Lotus Press, 1939-1999.

Kniazeva TA, Kuznetsova LN, Otto MP, Nikiforova TI. Efficacy of chromotherapy in patients with hyper-tension. *Vopr Kurortol Fizioter Lech Fiz Kult.* 2006 Jan-Feb;(1):11-3.

Koetter U, Barrett M, Lacher S, Abdelrahman A, Dolnick D. Interactions of Magnolia and Ziziphus extracts with selected central nervous system receptors. *J Ethnopharmacol.* 2009 Jul 30;124(3):421-5.

Koetter U, Schrader E, Käufeler R, Brattström A. A randomized, double blind, placebo-controlled, prospective clinical study to demonstrate clinical efficacy of a fixed valerian hops extract combination (Ze 91019) in patients suffering from non-organic sleep disorder. *Phytother Res.* 2007 Sep;21(9):847-51.

Kollerstrom N, Staudenmaier G. Evidence for Lunar-Sidereal Rhythms in Crop Yield: A Review. *Biolog Agri & Hort.* 2001;19:247–259.

Kollerstrom N, Steffert B. Sex difference in response to stress by lunar month: a pilot study of four years' crisis-call frequency. *BMC Psychiatry.* 2003 Dec 10;3:20.

Komori T, Matsumoto T, Motomura E, Shiroyama T. The sleep-enhancing effect of valerian inhalation and sleep-shortening effect of lemon inhalation. *Chem Senses.* 2006 Oct;31(8):731-7.

Konmck JM, Proulx G, Hcaly T, Arsenauli R, Prcvost F. Intensive language learning and REM sleep. Sleep Res 1975;4:150-155.

Konno M, Uchiyama M. Update on the treatment of restless legs syndrome. *Brain Nerve.* 2009 May;61(5):549-57.

Koren D, Arnon I, Lavie P, Klein E. Sleep complaints as early predictors of post-traumatic stress disorder: a 1-year prospective study of injured survivors of motor vehicle accidents. *Am J Psychiatry.* 2002 May;159(5):855-7.

Kotagal S, Silber MH. Childhood-onset restless legs syndrome. *Ann Neurol.* 2004 Dec;56(6):803-7.

Kotaka S. Research on the original plants of Gou-wen and Ye-Ge—and the herbological thoughts of Jin. *Yakushigaku Zasshi.* 2007;42(2):97-102.

Kotani S, Sakaguchi E, Warashina S, Matsukawa N, Ishikura Y, Kiso Y, Sakakibara M, Yoshimoto T, Guo J, Yamashima T. Dietary supplementation of arachidonic and docosahexaenoic acids improves cognitive dysfunction. *Neurosci Res.* 2006 Oct;56(2):159-64.

Kowalchik C, Hylton W (eds). *Rodale's Illustrated Encyclopedia of Herbs.* Emmaus, PA: 1987.

Kowalczyk E, Krzesiński P, Kura M, Niedworok J, Kowalski J, Błaszczyk J. Pharmacological effects of flavonoids from Scutellaria baicalensis. *Przegl Lek.* 2006;63(2):95-6.

Krause R, Buhring M, Hopfenmuller W, Holick MF, Sharma AM. Ultraviolet B and blood pressure. *Lancet.* 1998 Aug 29;352(9129):709-10.

Kreig M. *Black Market Medicine.* New York: Bantam, 1968.

Krenn L. Passion Flower (Passiflora incarnata L.)—a reliable herbal sedative. *Wien Med Wochenschr.* 2002;152(15-16):404-6.

Kripke DF, Garfinkel L, Wingard DL, Klauber MR, Marler MR. Mortality associated with sleep duration and insomnia. *Arch Gen Psychiatry.* 2002 Feb;59(2):131-6.

Krsnich-Shriwise S. Fibromyalgia syndrome: an overview. *Phys Ther.* 1997;77:68-75.

Krueger AP, Reed EJ. Biological impact of small air ions. *Science.* 1976 Sep 24;193(4259):1209-13.

Krystal AD. Treating the health, quality of life, and functional impairments in insomnia. *J. Clin Sleep Med,* 2007;3(1): 63–72.

Krystal AD. Treating the health, quality of life, and functional impairments in insomnia. *J Clin Sleep Med.* 2007 Feb 15;3(1):63-72.

Krystal JH, Sanacora G, Blumberg H. Glutamate and GABA systems as targets for novel antidepressant and mood-stabilizing treatments. *Mol Psychiatry.* 2002;7: S71–80.

Kubler-Ross E. *On Life After Death.* Berkeley, CA: Celestial Arts, 1991.

Küller R, Laike T. The impact of flicker from fluorescent lighting on well-being, performance and physiological arousal. *Ergonomics.* 1998 Apr;41(4):433-47.

Kumar A, Singh A. Protective effect of St. John's wort (Hypericum perforatum) extract on 72-hour sleep deprivation-induced anxiety-like behavior and oxidative damage in mice. *Planta Med.* 2007 Oct;73(13):1358-64.

Kumari M, Badrick E, Sacker A, Kirschbaum C, Marmot M, Chandola T. Identifying patterns in cortisol secretion in an older population. Findings from the Whitehall II study. *Psychoneuroendocrinology.* 2010 Feb 17.

Kung HC, Hoyert DL, Xu J, Murphy SL. Deaths: Final Data for 2005. *National Vital Statistics Reports.* 2008;56(10). http://www.cdc.gov/nchs/data/nvsr/nvsr56/nvsr56_10.pdf. Accessed: 2008 Jun.

Kuo FF, Kuo JJ. *Recent Advances in Acupuncture Research, Institute for Advanced Research in Asian Science and Medicine.* Garden City, New York. 1979.

Kuribara H, Stavinoha WB, Maruyama Y. Honokiol, a putative anxiolytic agent extracted from magnolia bark, has no diazepam-like side-effects in mice. *J Pharm Pharmacol.* 1999 Jan;51(1):97-103.

Kuuler R, Ballal S, Laike T Mikellides B, Tonello G. The impact of light and colour on psychological mood: a cross-cultral study of indoor work environments. Ergonomics. 2006 Nov 15;49(14):1496.

Lad V. *Ayurveda: The Science of Self-Healing.* Twin Lakes, WI: Lotus Press.

Lakin-Thomas PL. Transcriptional feedback oscillators: maybe, maybe not. *J Biol Rhyth.* 2006 Ap;21(2):83-92.

Lam SP, Fong SY, Yu MW, Li SX, Wing YK. Sleepwalking in psychiatric patients: comparison of childhood and adult onset. *Aust N Z J Psychiatry.* 2009 May;43(5):426-30.

Lamarche LJ, De Koninck J. Sleep disturbance in adults with posttraumatic stress disorder: a review. *J Clin Psychiatry.* 2007 Aug;68(8):1257-70.

Lancee J, Spoormaker VI, Krakow B, van den Bout J. A systematic review of cognitive-behavioral treatment for nightmares: toward a well-established treatment. *J Clin Sleep Med.* 2008 Oct 15;4(5):475-80.

Landis CA, Moe KE. Sleep and menopause. *Nurs Clin North Am.* 2004 Mar;39(1):97-115.

Larzelere MM, Wiseman P. Anxiety, depression, and insomnia. *Prim Care.* 2002 Jun;29(2):339-60, vii.

Latash LP, Manov GA. The relationships between delta-sleep and REM sleep phasic components with the retention and reproduction of the verbal material learned before bleep. Fiziol. Cloveka 1975;1:262-270.

Lauderdale DS, Knutson KL, Yan LL, Liu K, Rathouz PJ. Self-reported and measured sleep duration: how similar are they? *Epidemiology.* 2008 Nov;19(6):838-45.

Laurance J. Scientists' financial conflicts of interest may skew drug debate. *The Independent.* 19 March 2010.

LaValle JB. *The Cox-2 Connection.* Rochester, VT: Healing Arts, 2001.

Laverty WH, Kelly IW. Cyclical calendar and lunar patterns in automobile property accidents and injury accidents. *Percept Mot Skills.* 1998 Feb;86(1):299-302.

Lazarou J, Pomeranz BH, Corey PN. Incidence of adverse drug reactions in hospitalized patients: a meta-analysis of prospective studies. *JAMA.* 1998 Apr 15;279(15):1200-5.

Lean G. US study links more than 200 diseases to pollution. London Independent. 2004 Nov 14.

Leape L. Lucian Leape on patient safety in U.S. hospitals. Interview by Peter I Buerhaus. *J Nurs Scholarsh.* 2004;36(4):366-70.

Leathwood PD, Chauffard F, Heck E, Munoz-Box R. Aqueous extract of valerian root (Valeriana officinalis L.) improves sleep quality in man. *Pharmacol Biochem Behav.* 1982;17:65-

Leathwood PD, Chauffard F. Aqueous extract of valerian reduces latency to fall asleep in man. *Planta Med.* 1985;2:144-148.

Lee IS, Lee GJ. Effects of lavender aromatherapy on insomnia and depression in women college students. *Taehan Kanho Hakhoe Chi.* 2006 Feb;36(1):136-43.

Lehmann B. The vitamin D3 pathway in human skin and its role for regulation of biological processes. *Photochem Photobiol.* 2005 Nov-Dec;81(6):1246-51.

Leibenluft E, Feldman-Naim S, Turner EH, Wehr TA, Rosenthal NE. Effects of exogenous melatonin administration and withdrawal in five patients with rapid-cycling bipolar disorder. *J Clin Psychiatry.* 1997 Sep;58(9):383-8.

Lenn NJ, Beebe B, Moore RY (1977) Postnatal development of the suprachiasmatic nucleus of the rat. Cell Tissue Res 178:463-475.

Lennihan B. Homeopathy: natural mind-body healing. *J Psychosoc Nurs Ment Health Serv.* 2004 Jul;42(7):30-40.

Leroux E, Ducros A. Cluster headache. *Orphanet J Rare Dis.* 2008 Jul 23;3:20.

Levin J, Glaubman H. The effect of REM deprivation: Is it detrimental, beneficial or neutral? Psychophysiology 1975;12:349-353.

Levitan L LaBerge S. How To Remember Your Dreams. *Nightlight.* 1989 1(1).

Levitan L LaBerge S. Other Worlds: Out-of-Body Experiences and Lucid Dreams. Nightlight 1991 3(2-3).

Lewis A. Rescue remedy. Nurs Times. 1999 May 26-Jun 1;95(21):27.

Lewis WH, Elvin-Lewis MPF. Medical Botany: Plants Affecting Man's Health. New York: Wiley, 1977.

Lewith GT, Godfrey AD, Prescott P. A single-blinded, randomized pilot study evaluating the aroma of Lavandula augustifolia as a treatment for mild insomnia. J Altern Comple Med. 2005 Aug;11(4):631-7.

Leyel CF. Culpeper's English Physician & Complete Herbal. Hollywood, CA: Wilshire, 1971.

Li J, Ding Y, Li XC, Ferreira D, Khan S, Smillie T, Khan IA. Scuteflorins A and B, dihydropyranocoumarins from Scutellaria lateriflora. J Nat Prod. 2009 Jun;72(6):983-7.

Li N, Wang DL, Wang CW, Wu B. Discussion on randomized controlled trials about clinical researches of acupuncture and moxibustion medicine. Zhongguo Zhen Jiu. 2007 Jul;27(7):529-32.

Li XZ, Ramzan I. Role of ethanol in kava hepatotoxicity. Phytother Res. 2010 Apr;24(4):475-80.

Li YS. The comparison of the treatment of insomnia in different Chinese Traditional Medicine formula. Zhejiang J Integr Trad Chi West Med. 2000;10: 169.

Li Z, Qian S, Pu S. Study on chemical constituents from Cicuta virosa var. latisecta. Zhongguo Zhong Yao Za Zhi. 2009 Mar;34(6):705-7.

Liao JF, Wang HH, Chen MC, Chen CC, Chen CF. Benzodiazepine binding site-interactive flavones from Scutellaria baicalensis root. Planta Med. 1998 Aug;64(6):571-2.

Liao WC, Chiu MJ, Landis CA. A warm footbath before bedtime and sleep in older Taiwanese with sleep disturbance. Res Nurs Health. 2008 Oct;31(5):514-28.

Liao WC, Landis CA, Lentz MJ, Chiu MJ. Effect of foot bathing on distal-proximal skin temperature gradient in elders. Int J Nurs Stud. 2005 Sep;42(7):717-22.

Liao WC. Effects of passive body heating on body temperature and sleep regulation in the elderly: a systematic review. Int J Nurs Stud. 2002 Nov;39(8):803-10.

Lieber AL. Human aggression and the lunar synodic cycle. J Clin Psychiatry. 1978 May;39(5):385-92.

Lin HQ, Ho MT, Lau LS, Wong KK, Shaw PC, Wan DC. Anti-acetylcholinesterase activities of traditional Chinese medicine for treating Alzheimer's disease. Chem Biol Interact. 2008 Sep 25;175(1-3):352-4.

Lin PW, Chan WC, Ng BF, Lam LC. Efficacy of aromatherapy (Lavandula angustifolia) as an intervention for agitated behaviours in Chinese older persons with dementia: a cross-over randomized trial. Int J Geriatr Psychiatry. 2007 May;22(5):405-10.

Lindahl O, Lindwall L. Double blind study of a valerian preparation. Pharm Biochem Behav. 1989;32: 1065–66.

Linden M, Bär T, Helmchen H. Prevalence and appropriateness of psychotropic drug use in old age: results from the Berlin Aging Study (BASE). Int Psychogeriatr. 2004 Dec;16(4):461-80.

Lininger S, Gaby A, Austin S, Brown D, Wright J, Duncan A. The Natural Pharmacy. NY: Three Rivers, 1999.

Linton SJ. Does work stress predict insomnia? A prosp study. Br J Health Psych. 2004 May;9(Pt 2):127-36.

Livanova L, Levshina I, Nozdracheva L, Elbakidze MG, Airapetiants MG. The protective action of negative air ions in acute stress in rats with different typological behavioral characteristics. *Zh Vyssh Nerv Deiat Im I P Pavlova.* 1998 May-Jun;48(3):554-7.

Lloyd D and Murray D. Redox rhythmicity: clocks at the core of temporal coherence. *BioEssays.* 2007;29(5):465-473.

Loftus EF, Davis D. Recovered memories. *Annu Rev Clin Psychol.* 2006;2:469-98.

Loizzo MR, Saab AM, Tundis R, Statti GA, Menichini F, Lampronti I, Gambari R, Cinatl J, Doerr HW. Phytochemical analysis and in vitro antiviral activities of the essential oils of seven Lebanon species. *Chem Biodivers.* 2008 Mar;5(3):461-70.

Lovejoy S, Pecknold S, Schertzer D. Stratified multifractal magnetization and surface geomagnetic fields—I. Spectral analysis and modeling. *Geophysical Journal International.* 2001;145(1);112-126.

Lu J, Cui Y, Shi R. *A Practical English-Chinese Library of Traditional Chinese Medicine: Chinese Acupuncture and Moxibustion.* Shanghai: Publ House of the Shanghai College of Traditional Chinese Medicine, 1988.

Lydic R, Schoene WC, Czeisler CA, Moore-Ede MC. Suprachiasmatic region of the human hypothalamus: homolog to the primate circadian pacemaker? *Sleep.* 1980;2(3):355-61.

Ma H, Jo YJ, Ma Y, Hong JT, Kwon BM, Oh KW. Obovatol isolated from Magnolia obovata enhances pentobarbital-induced sleeping time: Possible involvement of GABAA receptors/chloride channel activation. *Phytomedicine.* 2009 Apr;16(4):308-13.

Ma Y, Ma H, Eun JS, Nam SY, Kim YB, Hong JT, Lee MK, Oh KW. Methanol extract of Longanae Arillus augments pentobarbital-induced sleep behaviors through the modification of GABAergic systems. *J Ethnopharmacol.* 2009 Mar 18;122(2):245-50.

Maas J, Jayson, J. K.. & Kleiber, D. A. Effects of spectral differences in illumination on fatigue. *J Appl Psychol.* 1974;59:524-526.

Mabey R, (ed.). *The New Age Herbalist.* New York: Simon & Schuster, 1941.

Macdessi JS, Randell TL, Donaghue KC, Ambler GR, van Asperen PP, Mellis CM. Adrenal crises in children treated with high-dose inhaled corticosteroids for asthma. *Med J Aust.* 2003 Mar 3;178(5):214-6.

MacDougall D. The Soul: Hypothesis Concerning Soul Substance Together with Experimental Evidence of The Existence of Such Substance. *American Medicine.* 1907 April.

Magee CA, Iverson DC, Caputi P. Factors associated with short and long sleep. *Prev Med.* 2009 Dec;49(6):461-7.

Magni P, Motta M, Martini L. Leptin: a possible link between food intake, energy expenditure, and reproductive function. *Regul Pept.* 2000 Aug 25;92(1-3):51-6.

Magnussen I, Van Woert MH. Human pharmacokinetics of long term 5-hydroxytryptophan combined with decarboxylase inhibitors. *Eur J Clin Pharmacol* 1982;23(1):81-6.

Magnusson A, Stefansson JG. Prevalence of seasonal affective disorder in Iceland. *Arch Gen Psychiatry.* 1993 Dec;50(12):941-6.

Mahachoklertwattana P, Sudkronrayudh K, Direkwattanachai C, Choubtum L, Okascharoen C. Decreased cortisol response to insulin induced hypoglycaemia in asthmatics treated with inhaled luticasone propionate. *Arch Dis Child.* 2004 Nov;89(11):1055-8.

Makino T, Hishida A, Goda Y, Mizukami H. Comparison of the major flavonoid content of S. baicalensis, S. lateriflora, and their commercial products. *J Nat Med.* 2008 Jul;62(3):294-9.

Malva JO, Santos S, Macedo T. Neuroprotective properties of Valeriana officinalis extracts. *Neurotox Res.* 2004;6(2): 131–40.

Management of insomnia: a place for traditional herbal remedies. *Prescrire Int.* 2005 Jun;14(77):104-7.

Manni R. Rapid eye movement sleep, non-rapid eye movement sleep, dreams, and hallucinations. *Curr Psychiatry Rep.* 2005 Jun;7(3):196-200.

Mansour HA, Monk TH, Nimgaonkar VL. Circadian genes and bipolar disorder. *Ann Med.* 2005;37(3):196-205.

Manz F. Hydration and disease. *J Am Coll Nutr.* 2007 Oct;26(5 Suppl):535S-541S.

Marasanov SB, Matveev II. Correlation between protracted premedication and complication in cancer patients operated on during intense solar activity. *Vopr Onkol.* 2007;53(1):96-9.

Markov D, Goldman M. Normal sleep and circadian rhythms: neurobiologic mechanisms underlying sleep and wakefulness. *Psychiatr Clin North Am.* 2006 Dec;29(4):841-53.

Marks C. *Commissurotomy, Consciousness, and Unity of Mind.* Cambridge: MIT Press, 1981.

Marks L. *The Unity of the Senses: Interrelations among the Modalities.* New York: Academic Press, 1978.

Martínez AL, Domínguez F, Orozco S, Chávez M, Salgado H, González M, González-Trujano ME. Neuropharmacological effects of an ethanol extract of the Magnolia dealbata Zucc. leaves in mice. *J Ethnopharmacol.* 2006 Jun 30;106(2):250-5.

Martinez M. Docosahexaenoic acid therapy in docosahexaenoic acid-deficient patients with disorders of peroxisomal biogenesis. Versicherungsmedizin. 1996;31 Suppl:145-152

Mason D, Moore J, Green S, Liggett S. A gain-of-function polymorphism in a G-protein coupling domain of the human β1-adrenergic receptor. *J. Biol. Chem.* 1999;274:12670-12674.

Massoco CO, Silva MR, Gorniak SL, Spinosa MS, Bernardi MM. Behavioral effects of acute and long-term administration of catnip (Nepeta cataria) in mice. *Vet Hum Toxicol.* 1995 Dec;37(6):530-3.

Mastorakos G, Pavlatou M. Exercise as a stress model and the interplay between the hypothalamus-pituitary-adrenal and the hypothalamus-pituitary-thyroid axes. *Horm Metab Res.* 2005 Sep;37(9):577-84.

Masuda A, Kihara T, Fukudome T, Shinsato T, Minagoe S, Tei C. The effects of repeated thermal therapy for two patients with chronic fatigue syndrome. *J Psychosom Res.* 2005 Apr;58(4):383-7.

Matano S, Kinoshita H, Tanigawa K, Terahata S, Sugimoto T. Acute parvovirus B19 infection mimicking chronic fatigue syndrome. *Intern Med.* 2003 Sep;42(9):903-5.

Matutinovic Z, Galic M. Relative magnetic hearing threshold. *Laryngol Rhinol Otol.* 1982 Jan;61(1):38-41.

Mayron L, Ott J, Nations R, Mayron E. Light, radiation and academic behaviour: Initial studies on the effects of full-spectrum lighting and radiation shielding on behaviour and academic performance of school children. *Acad Ther.* 1974;10, 33-47.

Mayron L. Hyperactivity from fluorescent lighting - fact or fancy: A commentary on the report by O'Leary, Rosenbaum and Hughes. *J Abnorm Child Psychol.* 1978;6:291-294.

McClung CA. Role for the Clock gene in bipolar disorder. *Cold Spring Harb Symp Quant Biol.* 2007;72:637-44.

McColl SL, Veitch JA. Full-spectrum fluorescent lighting: a review of its effects on physiology and health. *Psychol Med.* 2001 Aug;31(6):949-64.

McLay RN, Daylo AA, Hammer PS. No effect of lunar cycle on psychiatric admissions or emergency evaluations. *Mil Med.* 2006 Dec;171(12):1239-42.

Meddis R. *The Sleep Instinct.* London: Routledge & K. Paul, 1977.

Meienberg P. The tonic aspects of human REM sleep during long-term intensive verbal learning. Physiol. Psychol. 1977; 5:250-256.

Melzack R, Coderre TJ, Katz J, Vaccarino AL. Central neuroplasticity and pathological pain. *Ann N Y Acad Sci.* 2001 Mar;933:157-74.

Mendoza J. Circadian clocks: setting time by food. *J Neuroendocrinol.* 2007 Feb;19(2):127-37.

Meolie AL, Rosen C, Kristo D, Kohrman M, Gooneratne N, Aguillard RN, Fayle R, Troell R, Townsend D, Claman D, Hoban T, Mahowald M. Oral nonprescription treatment for insomnia: an evaluation of products with limited evidence. *J Clin Sleep Med.* 2005 Apr 15;1(2):173-87.

Merchant RE and Andre CA. 2001. A review of recent clinical trials of the nutritional supplement Chlorella pyrenoidosa in the treatment of fibromyalgia, hypertension, and ulcerative colitis. *Altern Ther Health Med.* May-Jun;7(3):79-91.

Merrell WC, Shalts E. Homeopathy. *Med Clin North Am.* 2002 Jan;86(1):47-62.

Meyer A, Kirsch H, Domergue F, Abbadi A, Sperling P, Bauer J, Cirpus P, Zank TK, Moreau H, Roscoe TJ, Zahringer U, Heinz E. Novel fatty acid elongases and their use for the reconstitution of docosahexaenoic acid biosynthesis. *J Lipid Res.* 2004 Oct;45(10):1899-909.

Miles LE, Raynal DM, Wilson MA. Blind man living in normal society has circadian rhythms of 24.9 hours. *Science.* 1977 Oct 28;198(4315):421-3.

Milke Garcia Mdel P. Ghrelin: beyond hunger regulation. *Rev Gastroenterol Mex.* 2005 Oct-Dec;70(4):465-74.

Millen AE, Tucker MA, Hartge P, Halpern A, Elder DE, Guerry D 4th, Holly EA, Sagebiel RW, Potischman N. Diet and melanoma in a case-control study. *Cancer Epidem Biomarkers Prev.* 2004 Jun;13(6):1042-51.

Miller GT. *Living in the Environment.* Belmont, CA: Wadsworth, 1996.

Miller JD, Morin LP, Schwartz WJ, Moore RY. New insights into the mammalian circadian clock. *Sleep.* 1996 Oct;19(8):641-67.

Milligan SR, Kalita JC, Pocock V, Van De Kauter V, Stevens JF, Deinzer ML, Rong H, De Keukeleire D. 2000. The endocrine activities of 8-prenylnaringenin and related hop (Humulus lupulus L.) flavonoids. *J Clin Endocrinol Metab.* 2000 Dec; 85(12): 4912-5.

Minai OA, Malik N, Foldvary N, Bair N, Golish JA. Prevalence and characteristics of restless legs syndrome in patients with pulmonary hypertension. *J Heart Lung Transplant.* 2008 Mar;27(3):335-40.

Mindell E, Hopkins V. *Prescription Alternatives.* Keats: New Canaan CT, 1998.

Mitchell JL. *Out-of-Body Experiences: A Handbook.* New York: Ballantine Books, 1981.

Miu AC, Benga O. Aluminum and Alzheimer's disease: a new look. *J Alz Dis.* 2006 Nov;10(2-3):179-201.

Mizoguchi K, Tanaka Y, Tabira T. Anxiolytic effect of herbal medicine, yokukansan: involvement of serotonergic and dopaminergic transmissions in the prefrontal cortex. *J Ethnopharm.* 2009 Sep 29.

Mocchegiani E, Giacconi R, Cipriano C, Costarelli L, Muti E, Tesei S, Giuli C, Papa R, Marcellini F, Mariani E, Rink L, Herbein G, Varin A, Fulop T, Monti D, Jajte J, Dedoussis G, Gonos ES, Trougakos IP, Malavolta M. Zinc, metallothioneins, and longevity—effect of zinc supplementation: zincage study. Ann N Y Acad Sci. 2007 Nov;1119:129-46.

Monroe R. *Journeys Out of the Body.* Garden City, NY: Anchor Press, 1977.

Moody R. *Life After Life.* New York: Bantam, 1975.

Moody, R. *Reflections on Lfe After Life: More Important Discoveries In The Ongoing*

Investigation Of Survival Of Life After Bodily Death. New York: Bantam, 1977.

Moore R. Circadian Rhythms: A Clock for the Ages. Science 1999 June 25;284(5423):2102 – 2103.

Moore RY, Speh JC. Serotonin innervation of the primate suprachiasmatic nucleus. *Brain Res*. 2004 Jun 4;1010(1-2):169-73.

Moore RY. Neural control of the pineal gland. *Behav Brain Res*. 1996;73(1-2):125-30.

Moore RY. Organization and function of a central nervous system circadian oscillator: the suprachiasmatic hypothalamic nucleus. *Fed Proc*. 1983 Aug;42(11):2783-9.

Moorhead KJ, Morgan IIC. *Spirulina: Nature's Superfood*. Kailua-Kona, HI: Nutrex, 1995.

Morgan AJ, Jorm AF. Self-help interventions for depressive disorders and depressive symptoms: a systematic review. *Ann Gen Psychiatry*. 2008 Aug 19;7:13.

Morgan K, Dallosso H, Ebrahim S, Arie T, Fentem PH. Prevalence, frequency, and duration of hypnotic drug use among the elderly living at home. *Br Med J* (Clin Res Ed). 1988 Feb 27;296(6622):601-2.

Morgan K. Daytime activity and risk factors for late-life insomnia. *J Sleep Res*. 2003 Sep;12(3):231-8.

Morin CM, Belanger L, Bastien C, Vallieres A. Long-term outcome after discontinuation of benzodiazepines for insomnia: a survival analysis of relapse. *Behav Res Ther*. 2005 Jan;43(1):1-14.

Morin CM, Koetter U, Bastien C, Ware JC, Wooten V. Valerian-hops combination and diphenhydramine for treating insomnia: a randomized placebo-controlled clinical trial. *Sleep*. 2005 Nov 1;28(11):1465-71.

Morita T, Tokura H. The influence of different wavelengths of light on human biological rhythms. *Appl Human Sci*. 1998 May;17(3):91-6.

Movafegh A, Alizadeh R, Hajimohamadi F, Esfehani F, Nejatfar M. Preoperative oral Passiflora incarnata reduces anxiety in ambulatory surgery patients: a double-blind, placebo-controlled study. *Anesth Analg*. 2008 Jun;106(6):1728-32.

Muhlack S, Lemmer W, Klotz P, Muller T, Lehmann E, Klieser E. Anxiolytic effect of rescue remedy for psychiatric patients: a double-blind, placebo-controlled, randomized trial. *J Clin Psychopharmacol*. 2006 Oct;26(5):541-2.

Müller CE, Schumacher B, Brattström A, Abourashed EA, Koetter U. Interactions of valerian extracts and a fixed valerian-hop extract combination with adenosine receptors. *Life Sci*. 2002 Sep 6;71(16):1939-49.

Müller SF, Klement S. A combination of valerian and lemon balm is effective in the treatment of restlessness and dyssomnia in children. *Phytomedicine*. 2006;13(6): 383–87.

Müller-Limmroth W, Ehrenstein W. Experimental studies of the effects of Seda-Kneipp on the sleep of sleep disturbed subjects; implications for the treatment of different sleep disturbances. *Med Klin*. 1977 Jun 24;72(25):1119-25.

Murphy R. *Organon Philosophy Workbook*. Blacksburg, VA: HANA, 1994.

Murphy SE, Longhitano C, Ayres RE, Cowen PJ, Harmer CJ, Rogers RD. The role of serotonin in nonnormative risky choice: the effects of tryptophan supplements on the "reflection effect" in healthy adult volunteers. *J Cogn Neurosci*. 2009 Sep;21(9):1709-19.

Murray M, Pizzorno J. *Encyclopedia of Natural Medicine*. 2nd Edition. Roseville, CA: Prima Publishing, 1998.

Nadkarni AK, Nadkarni KM. *Indian Materia Medica*. (Vols 1 and 2). Bombay,

India: Popular Pradashan, 1908, 1976.

Naghii MR, Samman S. The role of boron in nutrition and metabolism. *Prog Food Nutr Sci.* 1993 Oct-Dec;17(4):331-49.

Nakamura MT, Nara TY. Structure, function, and dietary regulation of delta6, delta5, and delta9 desaturases. Annu Rev Nutr. 2004;24:345-76.

Nakatani K, Yau KW. Calcium and light adaptation in retinal rods and cones. *Nature.* 1988 Jul 7;334(6177):69-71.

Nemeroff CB. The role of GABA in thepathophysiology and treatment of anxiety disorders. *Psychopharmacol Bull,* 2003;37: 133–46

Nestor PJ, Graham KS, Bozeat S, Simons JS, Hodges JR. Memory consolidation and the hippocampus: further evidence from studies of autobiographical memory in semantic dementia and frontal variant frontotemporal dementia. *Neuropsychologia.* 2002;40(6):633-54.

Newmark T, Schulick P. *Beyond Aspirin.* Prescott, AZ: Holm, 2000.

Newton PE. The Effect of Sound on Plant Grwoth. *JAES.* 1971 Mar;19(3):202-205.

Nielsen T, Levin R. Nightmares: a new neurocognitive model. *Sleep Med Rev.* 2007 Aug;11(4):295-310.

Nielsen TA. Chronobiological features of dream production. *Sleep Med Rev.* 2004 Oct;8(5):403-24.

Nievergelt CM, Kripke DF, Remick RA, Sadovnick AD, McElroy SL, Keck PE Jr, Kelsoe JR. Examination of the clock gene Cryptochrome 1 in bipolar disorder: mutational analysis and absence of evidence for linkage or association. *Psychiatr Genet.* 2005 Mar;15(1):45-52.

Niggli H. Temperature dependence of ultraweak photon emission in fibroblastic differentiation after irradiation with artificial sunlight. Indian J Exp Biol. 2003 May;41:419-423.

Núñez S, Pérez Méndez L, Aguirre-Jaime A. Moon cycles and violent behaviours: myth or fact? *Eur J Emerg Med.* 2002 Jun;9(2):127-30.

Nusrat N, Nishat Z, Gulfareen H, Aftab M, Asia N. Knowledge, attitude and experience of menopause. *J Ayub Med Coll Abbottabad.* 2008 Jan-Mar;20(1):56-9.

O'Connor J., Bensky D. (ed). *Shanghai College of Traditional Chinese Medicine: Acupuncture: A Comprehensive Text.* Seattle: Eastland Press, 1981.

O'Connor MI. Warming strengthens an herbivore-plant interaction. *Ecology.* 2009 Feb;90(2):388-98.

Oh CK, Lücker PW, Wetzelsberger N, Kuhlmann F. The determination of magnesium, calcium, sodium and potassium in assorted foods with special attention to the loss of electrolytes after various forms of food preparations. *Mag.-Bull.* 1986;8:297-302.

Oh EY, Ansell C, Nawaz H, Yang CH, Wood PA, Hrushesky WJ. Global breast cancer seasonality. *Breast Cancer Res Treat.* 2010 Feb 4.

Okamura H. Clock genes in cell clocks: roles, actions, and mysteries. *J Biol Rhythms.* 2004 Oct;19(5):388-99.

O'Leary KD, Rosenbaum A, Hughes PC. Fluorescent lighting: a purported source of hyperactive behavior. *J Abnorm Child Psychol.* 1978 Sep;6(3):285-9.

Oliviero A, Della Marca G, Tonali PA, Pilato F, Saturno E, Dileone M, Rubino M, Di Lazzaro V. Functional involvement of cerebral cortex in adult sleepwalking. *J Neurol.* 2007 Aug;254(8):1066-72.

O'Malley P. The risks of pharmacological therapy for insomnia (part 1): update for the clinical nurse specialist. *Clin Nurse Spec.* 2007 Jul-Aug;21(4):188-90.

Onder G, Landi F, Volpato S, Fellin R, Carbonin P, Gambassi G, Bernabei R. Serum cholesterol levels and in-hospital mortality in the elderly. *Am J Med.*

2003 Sep;115(4):265-71.

One Hundred Million Americans See Medical Mistakes Directly Touching Them as Patients, Friends, Relatives. *National Patient Safety Foundation. Press Release.* 1997 Oct 9. http://npsf.org/pr/pressrel/ finalsur.htm. Accessed: 2007 Mar.

Oren DA, Turner EH, Wehr TA. Abnormal circadian rhythms of plasma melatonin and body temperature in the delayed sleep phase syndrome. *J Neurol Neurosurg Psychiatry.* 1995 Mar;58(3):379.

Ornstein RE. *The Psychology of Consciousness.* Harcourt Brace Joavonovich, Inc.: New York, 1977.

Ortiz JG, Nieves-Natal J, Chavez P. Effects of Valeriana officinalis extracts on [3H]fl unitrazcpam binding, synaptosomal [3H]GABA uptake, and hippocampal [3H]GABA release. *Neurochem Res.* 1999;24(11): 1373-78.

Ostrander S, Schroeder L, Ostrander N. *Super-Learning.* New York: Delta, 1979.

Otani S. Memory trace in prefrontal cortex: theory for the cognitive switch. *Biol Rev Camb Philos Soc.* 2002 Nov;77(4):563-77.

Otsu A, Chinami M, Morgenthale S, Kaneko Y, Fujita D, Shirakawa T. Correlations for number of sunspots, unemployment rate, and suicide mortality in Japan. *Percept Mot Skills.* 2006 Apr;102(2):603-8.

Ott J. Color and Light: Their Effects on Plants, Animals, and People (Series of seven articles in seven issues). *International Journal for Biosocial Research.* 1985-1991.

Ott J. *Health and Light: The Effects of Natural and Artificial Light on Man and Other Living Things.* Ott, 1973.

Otto SJ, van Houwelingen AC, Hornstra G. The effect of supplementation with docosahexaenoic and arachidonic acid derived from single cell oils on plasma and erythrocyte fatty acids of pregnant women in the second trimester. Prostaglandins *Leukot Essent Fatty Acids.* 2000 Nov;63(5):323-8.

Oudiette D, Leu S, Pottier M, Buzare MA, Brion A, Arnulf I. Dreamlike mentations during sleepwalking and sleep terrors in adults. *Sleep.* 2009 Dec 1;32(12):1621-7.

Owen C, Tarantello C, Jones M, Tennant C. Lunar cycles and violent behaviour. *Aust N Z J Psychiatry.* 1998 Aug;32(4):496-9.

Packard CC. *Pocket Guide to Ayurvedic Healing.* Freedom, CA: Crossing Press, 1996.

Pagel JF, Vann BH. Cross-cultural dream use in Hawaii. *Hawaii Med J.* 1993 Feb;52(2):44-6.

Paller KA, Voss JL. Memory reactivation and consolidation during sleep. *Learn Mem.* 2004 Nov-Dec;11(6):664-70.

Parcell S. Sulfur in human nutrition and applications in medicine. *Altern Med Rev.* 2002 Feb;7(1):22-44.

Parker D, Parker J. *Dreaming: Remembering, Interpreting, Benefiting.* New York: Fireside, 1985.

Parry BL, Mendelson WB, Duncan WC, Sack DA, Wehr TA. Longitudinal sleep EEG, temperature, and activity measurements across the menstrual cycle in patients with premenstrual depression and in age-matched controls. *Psychiatry Res.* 1989 Dec;30(3):285-303.

Parry BL, Wehr TA. Therapeutic effect of sleep deprivation in patients with premenstrual syndrome. *Am J Psychiatry.* 1987 Jun;144(6):808-10.

Patton JA, Townsend DW, Hutton BF. Hybrid imaging technology: from dreams and vision to clinical devices. *Semin Nucl Med.* 2009 Jul;39(4):247-63.

Payne JD, Nadel L. Sleep, dreams, and memory consolidation: the role of the stress hormone cortisol. *Learn Mem.* 2004 Nov-Dec;11(6):671-8.

Pedemonte M, Rodríguez-Alvez A, Velluti RA. Electroencephalographic frequencies associated with heart changes in RR interval variability during paradoxical sleep. *Auton Neurosci.* 2005 Dec 30;123(1-2):82-6.

Pelders MG, Ros JJ. Poppy seeds: differences in morphine and codeine content and variation in inter- and intra-individual excretion. *J Forensic Sci.* 1996 Mar;41(2):209-12.

Pendell D. *Plant Powers, Poisons, and Herbcraft.* San Francisco: Mercury House, 1995.

Penev PD. Association between sleep and morning testosterone levels in older men. *Sleep.* 2007 Apr 1;30(4):427-32.

Peredery O, Persinger MA. Herbal treatment following post-seizure induction in rat by lithium pilocarpine: Scutellaria lateriflora (Skullcap), Gelsemium sempervirens (Gelsemium) and Datura stramonium (Jimson Weed) may prevent development of spontaneous seizures. *Phytother Res.* 2004 Sep;18(9):700-5.

Perreau-Lenz S, Kalsbeek A, Van Der Vliet J, Pevet P, Buijs RM. In vivo evidence for a controlled offset of melatonin synthesis at dawn by the suprachiasmatic nucleus in the rat. *Neurosci.* 2005;130(3):797-803.

Perrin RN. Lymphatic drainage of the neuraxis in chronic fatigue syndrome: a hypothetical model for the cranial rhythmic impulse. *J Am Osteopath Assoc.* 2007 Jun;107(6):218-24.

Perry J. *A Dialogue on Personal Identity and Immortality.* Indianapolis, IN: Hackett, 1978.

Perry J. *Personal Identity.* Berkeley: University of California Press, 1975.

Persinger MA. Psi phenomena and temporal lobe activity: The geomagnetic factor. In L.A. Henkel & R.E. Berger (Eds.), *Research in parapsychology.* (121-156). Metuchen, NJ: Scarecrow Press, 1989.

Persinger MA., Krippner S. Dream ESP experiments and geomagnetic activity. *Journal of the American Society of Psychical Research.* 1989;83:101- 106.

Persson R, Orbaek P, Kecklund G, Akerstedt T. Impact of an 84-hour workweek on biomarkers for stress, metabolic processes and diurnal rhythm. *Scand J Work Environ Health.* 2006 Oct;32(5):349-58.

Pert C. *Molecules of Emotion.* New York: Scribner, 1997.

Pesant N, Zadra A. Dream content and psychological well-being: a longitudinal study of the continuity hypothesis. *J Clin Psychol.* 2006 Jan;62(1):111-21.

Phelps AJ, Forbes D, Creamer M. Understanding posttraumatic nightmares: an empirical and conceptual review. *Clin Psychol Rev.* 2008 Feb;28(2):338-55.

Physicians' Desk Reference. Montvale, NJ: Thomson, 2003-2008

Piggins HD. Human clock genes. *Ann Med.* 2002;34(5):394-400.

Pilkington K, Kirkwood G, Rampes H, Fisher P, Richardson J. Homeopathy for depression: a systematic review of the research evidence. *Homeopathy.* 2005 Jul;94(3):153-63.

Pillmann F. Complex dream-enacting behavior in sleepwalking. *Psychosom Med.* 2009 Feb;71(2):231-4.

Pilon M, Montplaisir J, Zadra A. Precipitating factors of somnambulism: Impact of sleep deprivation and forced arousals. *Neurology.* 2008 Jun 10;70(24):2284-90.

Pinckney C. *Callanetics.* New York: Avon, 1984.

Pinto JT, Sinha R, Papp K, Facompre ND, Desai D, El-Bayoumy K. Differential effects of naturally occurring and synthetic organoselenium compounds on biomarkers in androgen responsive and androgen independent human prostate carcinoma cells. *Int J Cancer.* 2007 Apr 1;120(7):1410-7.

Piolino P, Desgranges B, Belliard S, Matuszewski V, Lalevee C, De la Sayette V, Eustache F. Autobiographical memory and autonoetic consciousness: triple dissociation in neurodegenerative diseases. *Brain.* 2003 Oct;126(Pt

10):2203-19.

Pitt-Rivers R, Trotter WR. *The Thyroid Gland.* London: Butterworth Publisher, 1954.

Plaut T, Jones T. *Asthma Guide for People of All Ages.* Amherst MA: Pedipress, 1999.

Pływaczewski R, Stokłosa A, Bieleń P, Bednarek M, Czerniawska J, Jonczak L, Górecka D, Sliwiński P. Six-minute walk test in obstructive sleep apnoea. *Pneumonol Alergol Pol.* 2008;76(2):75-82.

Polkinghorne J. *Science and Providence.* Boston: Shambhala Publications, 1989.

Pope J. Surfing helps calm autistic children. *Las Vegas Sun.* 2009 June 20.

Popp F, Yan Y. Delayed luminescence of biological systems in terms of coherent states. *Phys.Lett.* 2000;293:91-97.

Popper KR, Eccles, JC. *The Self and Its Brain.* London: Routledge, 1983.

Portaluppi F, Cortelli P, Buonaura GC, Smolensky MH, Fabbian F. Do restless legs syndrome (RLS) and periodic limb movements of sleep (PLMS) play a role in nocturnal hypertension and increased cardiovascular risk of renally impaired patients? *Chronobiol Int.* 2009 Aug;26(6):1206-21.

Portaluppi F, Hermida RC. Circadian rhythms in cardiac arrhythmias and opportunities for their chronotherapy. *Adv Drug Deliv Rev.* 2007 Aug 31;59(9-10):940-51.

Poryazova R, Waldvogel D, Bassetti CL. Sleepwalking in patients with Parkinson disease. *Arch Neurol.* 2007 Oct;64(10):1524-7.

Potterton D. (Ed.) *Culpeper's Color Herbal.* New York: Sterling, 1983.

Poukens-Renwart P, Tits M, Wauters JN, Angenot L. Densitometric evaluation of spiraeoside after derivatization in flowers of Filipendula ulmaria (L.) Maxim. *J Pharm Biomed Anal.* 1992 Oct-Dec;10(10-12):1085-8.

Powell SL, Gödecke T, Nikolic D, Chen SN, Ahn S, Dietz B, Farnsworth NR, van Breemen RB, Lankin DC, Pauli GF, Bolton JL. In vitro serotonergic activity of black cohosh and identification of N(omega)-methylserotonin as a potential active constituent. *J Agric Food Chem.* 2008 Dec 24;56(24):11718-26.

Preisinger E, Quittan M. Thermo- and hydrotherapy. *Wien Med Wochenschr.* 1994;144(20-21):520-6.

Pressman MR, Mahowald MW, Schenck CH, Bornemann MC. Alcohol-induced sleepwalking or confusional arousal as a defense to criminal behavior: a review of scientific evidence, methods and forensic considerations. *J Sleep Res.* 2007 Jun;16(2):198-212.

Pressman MR. Why has sleepwalking research been "sleepwalking"? *Neurology.* 2008 Jun 10;70(24):2274-5.

Prevost F, Koninck de J, Proulx G. Stage REM rapid eye movements following visual inversion: further investigation and replication. Sleep Res. 1975;4:57.

Pronina TS. Circadian and infradian rhythms of testosterone and aldosterone excretion in children. *Probl Endokrinol.* 1992 Sep-Oct;38(5):38-42.

Protheroe WM, Captiotti ER, Newsom GH. *Exploring the Universe.* Columbus, OH: Merrill, 1989,

Provalova NV, Suslov NI, Skurikhin EG, Dygaï AM. Local mechanisms of the regulatory action of Scutellaria baicalensis and ginseng extracts on the erythropoiesis after paradoxical sleep deprivation. *Eksp Klin Farmakol.* 2006 Sep-Oct;69(5):31-5.

Quintana-Gallego E, Carmona-Bernal C, Capote F, Sanchez-Armengol A, Botebol-Benhamou G, Polo-Padillo J, Castillo-Gomez J. Gender differences in obstructive sleep apnea syndrome: a clinical study of 1166 patients. *Respir Med.* 2004 Oct;98(10):984-9.

Radin D. *The Conscious Universe.* San Francisco: HarperEdge, 1997.

Raison CL, Klein HM, Steckler M. The moon and madness reconsidered. *J Affect*

Disord. 1999;53(1):99-106.

Randløv C, Mehlsen J, Thomsen CF, Hedman C, von Fircks H, Winther K. The efficacy of St. John's Wort in patients with minor depressive symptoms or dysthymia—a double-blind placebo-controlled study. *Phytomedicine.* 2006 Mar;13(4):215-21.

Rappoport J. Both sides of the pharmaceutical death coin. *Townsend Letter for Doctors and Patients.* 2006 Oct.

Rawlings M. *Beyond Death's Door.* New York: Bantam, 1979.

Regel SJ, Negovetic S, Röösli M, Berdiñas V, Schuderer J, Huss A, Lott U, Kuster N, Achermann P. UMTS base station-like exposure, well-being, and cognitive performance. *Environ Health Perspect.* 2006 Aug;114(8):1270-5.

Regel SJ, Tinguely G, Schuderer J, Adam M, Kuster N, Landolt HP, Achermann P. Pulsed radio-frequency electromagnetic fields: dose-dependent effects on sleep, the sleep EEG and cognitive performance. *J Sleep Res.* 2007 Sep;16(3):253-8.

Reger D, Goode S, Mercer E. *Chemistry: Principles & Practice.* Fort Worth, TX: Harcourt Brace, 1993.

Reichrath J. The challenge resulting from positive and negative effects of sunlight: how much solar UV exposure is appropriate to balance between risks of vitamin D deficiency and skin cancer? *Prog Biophys Mol Biol.* 2006 Sep;92(1):9-16.

Reiffenberger DH, Amundson LH. Fibromyalgia syndrome: a review. *Am Fam Physician.* 1996;53:1698-704.

Reilly D. The puzzle of homeopathy. *J Altern Complement Med.* 2001;7 Suppl 1:S103-9.

Reilly T, Stevenson I. An investigation of the effects of negative air ions on responses to submaximal exercise at different times of day. *J Hum Ergol.* 1993 Jun;22(1):1-9.

Reiter RJ, Garcia JJ, Pie J. Oxidative toxicity in models of neurodegeneration: responses to melatonin. *Restor Neurol Neurosci.* 1998 Jun;12(2-3):135-42.

Reiter RJ, Tan DX, Korkmaz A, Erren TC, Piekarski C, Tamura H, Manchester LC. Light at night, chronodisruption, melatonin suppression, and cancer risk: a review. *Crit Rev Oncog.* 2007;13(4):303-28.

Reiter RJ, Tan DX, Manchester LC, Qi W. Biochemical reactivity of melatonin with reactive oxygen and nitrogen species: a review of the evidence. *Cell Biochem Biophys.* 2001;34(2):237-56.

Retallack D. *The Sound of Music and Plants.* Marina Del Rey, CA: Devorss, 1973.

Ribeiro S, Gervasoni D, Soares ES, Zhou Y, Lin SC, Pantoja J, Lavine M, Nicolelis MA. Long-lasting novelty-induced neuronal reverberation during slow-wave sleep in multiple forebrain areas. *PLoS Biol.* 2004 Jan;2(1):E24.

Richardson GS, Miner JD, Czeisler CA. Impaired driving performance in shiftworkers: the role of the circadian system in a multifactorial model. *Alcohol Drugs Driving.* 1989-1990;5-6(4-1):265-73.

Rieder M. *Mission to Millboro.* Nevada City, CA: Blue Dolphin, 1995.

Riemersma-van der Lek RF, Swaab DF, Twisk J, Hol EM, Hoogendijk WJ, Van Someren EJ. Effect of bright light and melatonin on cognitive and noncognitive function in elderly residents of group care facilities: a randomized controlled trial. *JAMA.* 2008 Jun 11;299(22):2642-55.

Ring K. *Life at Death: A Scientific Investigation of the Near-Death Experience.* New York: Quill, 1982.

Ringdahl E, Pereira S, Delzell J. Treatment of Primary Insomnia. *J Am Fam Pract.* 2004;17: 212-219.

Ringdahl EN, Pereira SL, Delzell JE Jr. Treatment of primary insomnia. *J Am Board Fam Pract.* 2004 May-Jun;17(3):212-9.

Roach M. *Stiff: The Curious Lives of Human Cadavers.* New York: W.W. Norton, 2003.

Robilliard DL, Archer SN, Arendt J, Lockley SW, Hack LM, English J, Leger D, Smits MG, Williams A, Skene DJ, Von Schantz M. The 3111 Clock gene polymorphism is not associated with sleep and circadian rhythmicity in phenotypically characterized human subjects. *J Sleep Res.* 2002 Dec;11(4):305-12.

Rodale R. *Our Next Frontier.* Emmaus, PA: Rodale, 1981.

Rodgers JT, Puigserver P. Fasting-dependent glucose and lipid metabolic response through hepatic sirtuin 1. *Proc Natl Acad Sci USA.* 2007 Jul 31;104(31):12861-6.

Romm A. Insomnia. *Jnl Am Herb Guild.* 2008;8(2):14-22.

Röösli M, Jüni P, Braun-Fahrländer C, Brinkhof MW, Low N, Egger M. Sleepless night, the moon is bright: longitudinal study of lunar phase and sleep. *J Sleep Res.* 2006 Jun;15(2):149-53.

Rosenthal N, Blehar M (Eds.). *Seasonal affective disorders and phototherapy.* New York: Guildford Press, 1989.

Ross SM. Sleep disorders: a single dose administration of valerian/hops fluid extract (dormeasan) is found to be effective in improving sleep. *Holist Nurs Pract.* 2009 Jul-Aug;23(4):253-6.

Rossner MJ, Oster H, Wichert SP, Reinecke L, Wehr MC, Reinecke J, Eichele G, Taneja R, Nave KA. Disturbed clockwork resetting in Sharp-1 and Sharp-2 single and double mutant mice. *PLoS One.* 2008 Jul 23;3(7):e2762.

Rostand SG. Ultraviolet light may contribute to geographic and racial blood pressure differences. *Hypertension.* 1997 Aug;30(2 Pt 1):150-6.

Routasalo P, Isola A. The right to touch and be touched. *Nurs Ethics.* 1996 Jun;3(2):165-76.

Rowland AS, Baird DD, Long S, Wegienka G, Harlow SD, Alavanja M, Sandler DP. Influence of medical conditions and lifestyle factors on the menstrual cycle. *Epidemiology.* 2002 Nov;13(6):668-74.

Roy M, Kirschbaum C, Steptoe A. Intraindividual variation in recent stress exposure as a moderator of cortisol and testosterone levels. *Ann Behav Med.* 2003 Dec;26(3):194-200.

Roybal K, Theobold D, Graham A, DiNieri JA, Russo SJ, Krishnan V, Chakravarty S, Peevey J, Oehrlein N, Birnbaum S, Vitaterna MH, Orsulak P, Takahashi JS, Nestler EJ, Carlezon WA Jr, McClung CA. Mania-like behavior induced by disruption of CLOCK. *Proc Natl Acad Sci USA* 2007;104(15):6406-6411.

Rozycki VR, Baigorria CM, Freyre MR, Bernard CM, Zannier MS, Charpentier M. Nutrient content in vegetable species from the Argentine Chaco. *Arch Latinoam Nutr.* 1997 Sep;47(3):265-70.

Rubenowitz E, Molin I, Axelsson G, Rylander R. (2000) Magnesium in drinking water in relation to morbidity and mortality from acute myocardial infarction. *Epidemiology.* 2000;11:416-421.

Rubin E., Farber JL. *Pathology.* 3rd Edition. Philadelphia: Lippincott-Raven, 1999.

Rumble R, Morgan K. Hypnotics, sleep, and mortality in elderly people. *J Am Geriatr Soc.* 1992 Aug;40(8):787-91.

Ryman D. *Aromatherapy: The Complete Guide to Plant and Flower Essences for Health and Beauty.* New York: Bantam, 1993.

Saarijarvi S, Lauerma H, Helenius H, Saarilehto S. Seasonal affective disorders among rural Finns and Lapps. *Acta Psychiatr Scand.* 1999 Feb;99(2):95-101.

Sabom M. *Light and Death: One Doctor's Fascinating Account of Near Death Ex-*

periences. Grand Rapids, MI: Zondervan Publishing, 1998.

Sabom M. *Recollection of Death - A Medical Investigation.* New York: Harper and Row, 1982.

Sack DA, Duncan W, Rosenthal NE, Mendelson WE, Wehr TA. The timing and duration of sleep in partial sleep deprivation therapy of depression. *Acta Psychiatr Scand.* 1988 Feb;77(2):219-24.

Sacks O. *The Man Who Mistook his Wife for a Hat and Other Clinical Tales.* New York: Simon & Schuster, 1998.

Sahar S, Sassone-Corsi P. Circadian clock and breast cancer: a molecular link. *Cell Cycle.* 2007 Jun 1;6(11):1329-31.

Sahlin C, Pettersson FE, Nilsson LN, Lannfelt L, Johansson AS. Docosahex-aenoic acid stimulates non-amyloidogenic APP processing resulting in re-duced Abeta levels in cellular models of Alzheimer's disease. *Eur J Neurosci.* 2007 Aug;26(4):882-9.

Saku M. The current clinical practice of herbal medicine in psychiatry in mainland China: a review of literature. *Jpn J Psychiatry Neurol.* 1991 Dec;45(4):825-32.

Salem N, Wegher B, Mena P, Uauy R. Arachidonic and docosahexaenoic acids are biosynthesized from their 18-carbon precursors in human infants. *Proc Natl Acad Sci.* 1996;93:49-54.

Sanders R. *Slow brain waves play key role in coordinating complex activity.* UC Berkeley News. 2006 Sep 14.

Sanfélix Genovés J, Palop Larrea V, Rubio Gomis E, Martínez-Mir I. Consump-tion of medicinal herbs and medicines. *Aten Primaria.* 2001 Sep 30;28(5):311-4.

Sanogo R, Vassallo A, Malafronte N, Imparato S, Russo A, Dal Piaz F. New phe-nolic glycosides from Securinega virosa and their antioxidant activity. *Nat Prod Commun.* 2009 Dec;4(12):1645-50.

Sarah Janssen S, Solomon G, Schettler T. *Chemical Contaminants and Human Disease: A Summary of Evidence.* The Collaborative on Health and the Envi-ronment. 2006. http://www.healthand-environment.org. Accessed: 2007 Jul.

Sarris J, Kavanagh DJ, Adams J, Bone K, Byrne G. Kava Anxiety Depression Spectrum Study (KADSS): a mixed methods RCT using an aqueous extract of Piper methysticum. *Complement Ther Med.* 2009 Jun;17(3):176-8.

Sarris J, Kavanagh DJ, Byrne G, Bone KM, Adams J, Deed G. The Kava Anxiety Depression Spectrum Study (KADSS): a randomized, placebo-controlled crossover trial using an aqueous extract of Piper methysticum. *Psy-chopharmacology.* 2009 Aug;205(3):399-407.

Sarris J. Herbal medicines in the treatment of psychiatric disorders: a system-atic review. *Phytother Res.* 2007 Aug;21(8):703-16.

Sato TK, Yamada RG, Ukai H, Baggs JE, Miraglia LJ, Kobayashi TJ, Welsh DK, Kay SA, Ueda HR, Hogenesch JB. Feedback repression is required for mammalian circadian clock function. *Nat Genet.* 2006 Mar;38(3):312-9.

Schauenberg P, Paris F. *Guide to Medicinal Plants.* New Canaan, CT: Keats Publ, 1977.

Schellenberg R, Sauer S, Abourashed EA, Koetter U, Brattström A. The fixed combination of valerian and hops (Ze91019) acts via a central adenosine mechanism. *Planta Med.* 2004 Jul;70(7):594-7.

Schierenbeck T, Riemann D, Berger M, Hornyak M. Effect of illicit recreational drugs upon sleep: cocaine, ecstasy and marijuana. *Sleep Med Rev.* 2008 Oct;12(5):381-9.

Schlebusch KP, Maric-Oehler W, Popp FA. Biophotonics in the infrared spectral range reveal acupuncture meridian structure of the body. *J Altern Comple-*

ment Med. 2005 Feb;11(1):171-3.

Schmidt C, Collette F, Cajochen C, Peigneux P. A time to think: circadian rhythms in human cognition. *Cogn Neuropsychol.* 2007 Oct;24(7):755-89.

Schmitt B, Frölich L. Creative therapy options for patients with dementia—a systematic review. *Fortschr Neurol Psychiatr.* 2007 Dec;75(12):699-707.

Schmitz M, Jäckel M. Comparative study for assessing quality of life of patients with exogenous sleep disorders (temporary sleep onset and sleep interruption disorders) treated with a hops-valarian preparation and a benzodiazepine drug. *Wien Med Wochenschr.* 1998;148(13):291-8.

Schredl M, Piel E. Prevalence of flying dreams. *Percept Mot Skills.* 2007 Oct;105(2):657-60.

Schredl M, Sartorius II. Dream recall and dream content in children with attention deficit/hyperactivity disorder. *Child Psychiatry Hum Dev.* 2010 Apr;41(2):230-8.

Schredl M. Dreams in patients with sleep disorders. Sleep Med Rev. 2009 Jun;13(3):215-21.

Schredl M. Dreams in patients with sleep disorders. *Sleep Med Rev.* 2009 Jun;13(3):215-21.

Schulick. *Ginger: Common Spice & Wonder Drug.* Brattleboro, VT: Herbal Free Press, 1996.

Schulz H, Jobert M. Effects of hypericum extract on the sleep EEG in older volunteers. *J Geriatr Psychiatry Neurol.* 1994 Oct;7 Suppl 1:S39-43.

Schwartz PJ, Rosenthal NE, Kajimura N, Han L, Turner EH, Bender C, Wehr TA. Ultradian oscillations in cranial thermoregulation and electroencephalographic slow-wave activity during sleep are abnormal in humans with annual winter depression. *Brain Res.* 2000 Jun 2;866(1-2):152-67.

Schwartz PJ, Rosenthal NE, Turner EH, Drake CL, Liberty V, Wehr TA. Seasonal variation in core temperature regulation during sleep in patients with winter seasonal affective disorder. *Biol Psychiatry.* 1997 Jul 15;42(2):122-31.

Schwartz PJ, Rosenthal NE, Wehr TA. Band-specific electroencephalogram and brain cooling abnormalities during NREM sleep in patients with winter depression. *Biol Psychiatry.* 2001 Oct 15;50(8):627-32.

Schwartz PJ, Rosenthal NE, Wehr TA. Serotonin 1A receptors, melatonin, and the proportional control thermostat in patients with winter depression. *Arch Gen Psychiatry.* 1998 Oct;55(10):897-903.

Schwartz S, De Mattei R, Brame E, Spottiswoode S. Infrared spectra alteration in water proximate to the palms of therapeutic practitioners. In: Wiener D, Nelson R (Eds.): *Research in parapsychology 1986.* Metuchen, NJ: Scarecrow Press, 1987:24-29.

Scott BO. The history of ultraviolet therapy. in Licht S. ed. *Therapeutic Electricity and Ultraviolet Radiation.* Phys Med Lib 4. Connecticut: Licht, 1967.

Scrima L. Isolated REM sleep facilitates recall of complex associative information. Psychophysiology. 1982;19.252-259.

Serway R. *Physicis For Scientists & Engineers.* Philadelphia: Harcourt Brace, 1992.

Shaffer D. *Developmental Psychology: Theory, Research and Applications.* Monterey, CA: Brooks/Cole, 1985.

Shafik A. Role of warm-water bath in anorectal conditions. The "thermosphincteric reflex". *J Clin Gastroenterol.* 1993 Jun;16(4):304-8.

Shankar A, Koh WP, Yuan JM, Lee HP, Yu MC. Sleep duration and coronary heart disease mortality among Chinese adults in Singapore: a population-based cohort study. *Am J Epidemiol.* 2008 Dec 15;168(12):1367-73.

Shankar R. *My Music, My Life.* New York: Simon & Schuster, 1968.

Shankaranarayan D, Gopalakrishnan C, Kameswaran L. Pharmacological profile of mangostin and its derivatives. *Arch Int Pharmacodyn Ther.* 1979 Jun;239(2):257-69.

Sharp KC. *After the Light.* New York: William Morrow & Co., 1995.

Shearman LP, Zylka MJ, Weaver DR, Kolakowski LF Jr, Reppert SM. Two period homologs: circadian expression and photic regulation in the suprachiasmatic nuclei. *Neuron.* 1997 Dec;19(6):1261-9.

Shen YF, Goddard G. The short-term effects of acupuncture on myofascial pain patients after clenching. *Pain Pract.* 2007 Sep;7(3):256-64.

Sherry CJ, Hunter PS. The effect of an ethanol extract of catnip (Nepeta cataria) on the behavior of the young chick. *Experientia.* 1979 Feb 15;35(2):237-8.

Shevelev IA, Kostelianetz NB, Kamenkovich VM, Sharaev GA. EEG alpha-wave in the visual cortex: check of the hypothesis of the scanning process. *Int J Psychophysiol.* 1991 Aug;11(2):195-201.

Shiah IS, Yatham LN. GABA function in mood disorders: an update and critical review. *Life Sci.* 1998;63: 1289–303.

Shub D, Darvishi R, Kunik ME. Non-pharmacologic treatment of insomnia in persons with dementia. *Geriatrics.* 2009 Feb;64(2):22-6.

Siddiqui F, Osuna E, Chokroverty S. Writing emails as part of sleepwalking after increase in *Zolpidem. Sleep Med.* 2009 Feb;10(2):262-4.

Sil'kis IG. Paradoxical sleep as a tool for understanding hippocampal mechanisms of contextual memory. *Zh Vyssh Nerv Deiat Im I P Pavlova.* 2008 Sep-Oct;58(5):521-39.

Singer P, Shapiro H, Theilla M, Anbar R, Singer J, Cohen J. Anti-inflammatory properties of omega-3 fatty acids in critical illness: novel mechanisms and an integrative perspective. Intensive Care Med. 2008 Sep;34(9):1580-92.

Sivertsen B, Omvik S, Pallesen S, Nordhus IH, Bjorvatn B. Sleep and sleep disorders in chronic users of zopiclone and drug-free insomniacs. *J Clin Sleep Med.* 2009 Aug 15;5(4):349-54.

Skoczylas A, Wiecek A. Ghrelin, a new hormone involved not only in the regulation of appetite. *Wiad Lek.* 2006;59(9-10):697-701.

Skwerer RG, Jacobsen FM, Duncan CC, Kelly KA, Sack DA, Tamarkin L, Gaist PA, Kasper S, Rosenthal NE. Neurobiology of Seasonal Affective Disorder and Phototherapy. *J Biolog Rhyth.* 1988;3(2):135-154.

Sleepy "Generation Y" Among Key Poll Findings. Press Release, *Groggy Workforce.* 2000 March 28.

Smith CW. Coherence in living biological systems. *Neural Network World.* 1994:4(3):379-388.

Smith MJ. Effect of Magnetic Fields on Enzyme Reactivity. In Barnothy M.(ed.). *Biological Effects of Magnetic Fields.* New York: Plenum Press, 1969.

Smith MJ. *The Influence on Enzyme Growth By the 'Laying on of Hands: Dimenensions of Healing.* Los Altos, California: Academy of Parapsychology and Medicine, 1973.

Smith T. *Homeopathic Medicine: A Doctor's Guide.* Rochester, VT: Healing Arts, 1989.

Smith-Sonneborn J. Age-correlated effects of caffeine on non-irradiated and UV-irradiated Paramecium Aurelia. *J Gerontol.* 1974 May;29(3):256-60.

Smith-Sonneborn J. DNA repair and longevity assurance in Paramecium tetraurelia. *Science.* 1979 Mar 16;203(4385):1115-7.

Smits MG, Williams A, Skene DJ, Von Schantz M. The 3111 Clock gene polymorphism is not associated with sleep and circadian rhythmicity in phenotypically characterized human subjects. *J Sleep Res.* 2002 Dec;11(4):305-12.

Sneader W. The discovery of aspirin: a reappraisal. *BMJ.* 2000 Dec 23:321;1591–1594.

Snow WB. *The Therapeutics of Radiant Light and Heat and Convective Heat.* New York: Scientific Authors Publishing Company. 1909.

Snyder K. Researchers Produce Firsts with Bursts of Light: Team generates most energetic terahertz pulses yet, observes useful optical phenomena. *Press Release: Brookhaven National Laboratory.* 2007 July 24.

Soden K, Vincent K, Craske S, Lucas C, Ashley S. A randomized controlled trial of aromatherapy massage in a hospice setting. *Palliat Med.* 2004 Mar;18(2):87-92.

Souetre E, Salvati E, Wehr TA, Sack DA, Krebs B, Darcourt G. Twenty-four-hour profiles of body temperature and plasma TSH in bipolar patients during depression and during remission and in normal control subjects. *Am J Psychiatry.* 1988 Sep;145(9):1133-7.

Soul Has Weight, Physician Thinks. *The New York Times.* 1907 March 11:5.

Spanagel R, Rosenwasser AM, Schumann G, Sarkar DK. Alcohol consumption and the body's biological clock. *Alcohol Clin Exp Res.* 2005 Aug;29(8):1550-7.

Spence A. *Basic Human Anatomy.* Menlo Park, CA: Benjamin/Commings, 1986.

Spillane M. Good Vibrations, A Sound 'Diet' for Plants. *The Growing Edge.* 1991 Spring.

Spiller G. *The Super Pyramid.* New York: HRS Press, 1993.

Spoormaker VI, Schredl M, van den Bout J. Nightmares: from anxiety symptom to sleep disorder. *Sleep Med Rev.* 2006 Feb;10(1):19-31.

Squire LR, Zola-Morgan S. The medial temporal lobe memory system. *Science.* 1991;253(5026):1380-1386.

St Hilaire MA, Gronfier C, Zeitzer JM, Klerman EB. A physiologically based mathematical model of melatonin including ocular light suppression and interactions with the circadian pacemaker. *J Pineal Res.* 2007 Oct;43(3):294-304.

Stampfer MJ, Willett WC, Colditz GA, Rosner B, Speizer FE, Hennekens CH. A prospective study of postmenopausal estrogen therapy and coronary heart disease. N Engl J Med. 1985 Oct 24;313(17):1044-9.

Steck B. Effects of optical radiation on man. *Light Resch Techn.* 1982;14:130-141.

Steiner R. *Agriculture.* Kimberton, PA: Bio-Dynamic Farming, 1924-1993.

Stengler M. *The Natural Physician's Healing Therapies.* Stamford, CT: Bottom Line Books, 2008.

Stenholm S, Kronholm E, Sainio P, Borodulin K, Era P, Fogelholm M, Partonen T, Porkka-Heiskanen T, Koskinen S. Sleep-Related Factors and Mobility in Older Men and Women. *J Gerontol A Biol Sci Med Sci.* 2010 Feb 16.

Stephenson R. Circadian rhythms and sleep-related breathing disorders. *Sleep Med.* 2007 Sep;8(6):681-7.

Stevenson I. *Children Who Remember Previous Lives: A Question of Reincarnation.* Charlottesville, VA: Univ Virginia Press, 1987.

Stickgold R. Sleep-dependent memory consolidation. *Nature.* 2005 Oct 27;437(7063):1272-8.

Stoebner-Delbarre A, Thezenas S, Kuntz C, Nguyen C, Giordanella JP, Sancho-Garnier H, Guillot B; Le Groupe EPI-CES. Sun exposure and sun protection behavior and attitudes among the French population. *Ann Dermatol Venereol.* 2005 Aug-Sep;132(8-9 Pt 1):652-7.

Stojakowska A, Malarz J, Kisiel W. Sesquiterpene Lactones in Tissue Culture of Lactuca virosa. *Planta Med.* 1994 Feb;60(1):93-4.

Stores G. Rapid eye movement sleep behaviour disorder in children and adolescents. *Dev Med Child Neurol.* 2008 Oct;50(10):728-32.

Stoupel E, Kalediene R, Petrauskiene J, Gaizauskiene A, Israelevich P, Abramson E, Sulkes J. Monthly number of newborns and environmental physical activity. *Medicina Kaunas.* 2006;42(3):238-41.

Stoupel E, Monselise Y, Lahav J. Changes in autoimmune markers of the anti-cardiolipin syndrome on days of extreme geomamagnetic activity. *J Basic Clin Physiol Pharmacol.* 2006;17(4):269-78.

Stoupel EG, Frimer H, Appelman Z, Ben-Neriah Z, Dar H, Fejgin MD, Gershoni-Baruch R, Manor E, Barkai G, Shalev S, Gelman-Kohan Z, Reish O, Lev D, Davidov B, Goldman B, Shohat M. Chromosome aberration and environmental physical activity: Down syndrome and solar and cosmic ray activity, Israel, 1990-2000. *Int J Biometeorol.* 2005 Sep;50(1):1-5.

Strange BA, Dolan RJ. Anterior medial temporal lobe in human cognition: memory for fear and the unexpected. *Cognit Neuropsychiatry.* 2006 May;11(3):198-218.

Strogatz SH, Kronauer RE, Czeisler CA. Circadian regulation dominates homeostatic control of sleep length and prior wake length in humans. *Sleep.* 1986 Jun;9(2):353-64.

Sugarman E. *Warning, The Electricity Around You May be Hazardous To Your Health.* New York: Simon & Schuster. 1992.

Sulman FG, Levy D, Lunkan L, Pfeifer Y, Tal E. New methods in the treatment of weather sensitivity. *Fortschr Med.* 1977 Mar 17;95(11):746-52.

Sulman FG. Migraine and headache due to weather and allied causes and its specific treatment. *Ups J Med Sci Suppl.* 1980;31:41-4.

Suppes P, Han B, Epelboim J, Lu ZL. Invariance of brain-wave representations of simple visual images and their names. Proceedings *Natl Acad Sci Psych-BS.* 1999;96(25):14658-14663.

Suzuki E, Yorifuji T, Ueshima K, Takao S, Sugiyama M, Ohta T, Ishikawa-Takata K, Doi H. Sleep duration, sleep quality and cardiovascular disease mortality among the elderly: a population-based cohort study. *Prev Med.* 2009 Aug-Sep;49(2-3):135-41.

Suzuki Y, Kondo K, Ichise H, Tsukamoto Y, Urano T, Umemura K. Dietary supplementation with fermented soybeans suppresses intimal thickening. *Nutrition.* 2003 Mar;19(3):261-4.

Svensson M, Holmstrom M, Broman JE, Lindberg E. Can anatomical and functional features in the upper airways predict sleep apnea? A population-based study in females. *Acta Otolaryngol.* 2006 Jun;126(6):613-20.

Tadros MG, Mohamed MR, Youssef AM, Sabry GM, Sabry NA, Khalifa AE. Involvement of serotoninergic 5-HT1A/2A, alpha-adrenergic and dopaminergic D1 receptors in St. John's wort-induced prepulse inhibition deficit: a possible role of hyperforin. *Behav Brain Res.* 2009 May 16;199(2):334-9.

Takasu NN, Hashimoto S, Yamanaka Y, Tanahashi Y, Yamazaki A, Honma S, Honma K. Repeated exposures to daytime bright light increase nocturnal melatonin rise and maintain circadian phase in young subjects under fixed sleep schedule. *Am J Physiol Regul Integr Comp Physiol.* 2006 Dec;291(6):R1799-807.

Tan DX, Manchester LC, Reiter RJ, Qi WB, Karbownik M, Calvo JR. Significance of melatonin in antioxidative defense system: reactions and products. *Biol Signals Recept.* 2000 May-Aug;9(3-4):137-59.

Tan LP. The effects of background music on quality of sleep in elementary school children. *J Music Ther.* 2004 Summer;41(2):128-50.

Tang G, Serfaty-Lacronsniere C, Camilo ME, Russell RM. Gastric acidity influences the blood response to a beta-carotene dose in humans. *Am J Clin Nutr.* 1996;64:622-6.

Tapiero, H., G. N. Ba. Polyunsaturated fatty acids (PUFA) and eicosanoids in human health and pathologies. *Biomed Pharmacother.* 2002;56(5): 215-22.

Tapsell LC, Hemphill I, Cobiac L, Patch CS, Sullivan DR, Fenech M, Roodenrys S, Keogh JB, Clifton PM, Williams PG, Fazio VA, Inge KE. Health benefits of herbs and spices: the past, the present, the future. *Med J Aust.* 2006 Aug 21;185(4 Suppl):S4-24.

Tassi P, Bonnefond A, Engasser O, Hoeft A, Eschenlauer R, Muzet A. EEG spectral power and cognitive performance during sleep inertia: the effect of normal sleep duration and partial sleep deprivation. *Physiol Behav.* 2006 Jan 30;87(1):177-84.

Tassone F, Broglio F, Gianotti L, Arvat E, Ghigo E, Maccario M. Ghrelin and other gastrointestinal peptides involved in the control of food intake. *Mini Rev Med Chem.* 2007 Jan;7(1):47-53.

Taylor A. *Soul Traveler: A Guide to Out-of-Body Experiences and the Wonders Beyond.* New York: Penguin, 2000.

Teitelbaum J. *From Fatigue to Fantastic.* New York: Avery, 2001.

Tender J, Kramer M. Dream recall. Am. J. Psychiat. 128:3-10; 1971.

Terawaki K, Ikarashi Y, Sekiguchi K, Nakai Y, Kase Y. Partial agonistic effect of yokukansan on human recombinant serotonin 1A receptors expressed in the membranes of Chinese hamster ovary cells. *J Ethnopharmacol.* 2010 Feb 3;127(2):306-12.

Tesch BJ. Herbs commonly used by women: an evidence-based review. *Am J Obstet Gynecol.* 2003 May;188(5 Suppl):S44-55.

Tesch BJ. Herbs commonly used by women: an evidence-based review. *Dis Mon.* 2002 Oct;48(10):671-96.

Teschke R, Schwarzenboeck A, Hennermann KH. Kava hepatotoxicity: a clinical survey and critical analysis of 26 suspected cases. *Eur J Gastroenterol Hepatol.* 2008;20(12): 1182–93.

Thakur CP, Sharma D. Full moon and crime. *Br Med J.* 1984 December 22; 289(6460): 1789-1791.

Thaut MH. The future of music in therapy and medicine. *Ann N Y Acad Sci.* 2005 Dec;1060:303-8.

The Mystery of Smell. Howard Hughes Medical Instit. http://www.hhmi.org/senses/d110.html. Acc. 2007 Jul.

The Timechart Company. *Timetables of Medicine.* New York: Black Dog & Leventhal, 2000.

Thie J. *Touch for Health.* Marina del Rey, CA: Devorss Publications, 1973-1994.

Thorne Research, Inc. Gamma-Aminobutyric Acid (GABA). *Altern Med Rev.* 2007;12(3).

Threlkeld DS, ed. Central Nervous System Drugs, Analeptics, Caffeine. *Facts and Comparisons Drug Information.* St. Louis, MO: Facts and Comparisons. 1998 Feb: 230-d.

Tierra L. *The Herbs of Life.* Freedom, CA: Crossing Press, 1992.

Tierra M. *The Way of Herbs.* New York: Pocket Books, 1990.

Timofeev I, Steriade M. Low-frequency rhythms in the thalamus of intact-cortex and decorticated cats. *J Neurophysiol.* 1996 Dec;76(6):4152-68.

Tisserand R. *The Art of Aromatherapy.* New York: Inner Traditions, 1979.

Tiwari M. *Ayurveda: A Life of Balance.* Rochester, VT: Healing Arts, 1995.

Todd GR, Acerini CL, Ross-Russell R, Zahra S, Warner JT, McCance D. Survey of adrenal crisis associated with inhaled corticosteroids in the United Kingdom. *Arch Dis Child.* 2002 Dec;87(6):457-61.

Tompkins, P, Bird C. *The Secret Life of Plants.* New York: Harper & Row, 1973.

Toomer G. "Ptolemy". *The Dictionary of Scientific Biography.* New York: Gale Cengage, 1970.

Towle A. *Modern Biology.* Austin: Harcourt Brace, 1993.

Trachte GJ, Uncini T, Hinz M. Both stimulatory and inhibitory effects of dietary

5-hydroxytryptophan and tyrosine are found on urinary excretion of serotonin and dopamine in a large human population. Neuropsychiatr Dis Treat. 2009;5: 227–35.

Trauner G, Khom S, Baburin I, Benedek B, Hering S, Kopp B. Modulation of GABAA receptors by valerian extracts is related to the content of valerenic acid. *Planta Med.* 2008 Jan;74(1):19-24.

Trevena L. Sleepless in Sydney - is valerian an effective alternative to benzodiazepines in the treatment of insomnia? *ACP J Club.* 2004;141:A14-A16.

Trivedi B. Magnetic Map Found to Guide Animal Migration. *National Geographic Today.* 2001 Oct 12.

Trojanowska A. Lettuce, lactuca sp., as a medicinal plant in polish publications of the 19th century. *Kwart Hist Nauki Tech.* 2005;50(3-4):123-34.

Trojanowska A. Lettuce, lactuca sp., as a medicinal plant in polish publications of the 19th century. *Kwart Hist Nauki Tech.* 2005;50(3-4):123-34.

Tsai JH, Yang P, Chen CC, Chung W, Tang TC, Wang SY, Liu JK. Zolpidem-induced amnesia and somnambulism: rare occurrences? *Eur Neuropsychopharmacol.* 2009 Jan;19(1):74-6.

Tsai SL. Audio-visual relaxation training for anxiety, sleep, and relaxation among Chinese adults with cardiac disease. *Res Nurs Health.* 2004 Dec;27(6):458-68.

Tsay SL, Cho YC, Chen ML. Acupressure and Transcutaneous Electrical Acupoint Stimulation in improving fatigue, sleep quality and depression in hemodialysis patients. *Am J Chin Med.* 2004;32(3):407-16.

Tsinkalovsky O, Smaaland R, Rosenlund B, Sothern RB, Hirt A, Steine S, Badiee A, Abrahamsen JF, Eiken HG, Laerum OD. Circadian variations in clock gene expression of human bone marrow CD34+ cells. *J Biol Rhythms.* 2007 Apr;22(2):140-50.

Tsong T. Deciphering the language of cells. *Trends in Biochem Sci.* 1989;14:89-92.

Tubek S. Role of trace elements in primary arterial hypertension: is mineral water style or prophylaxis? *Biol Trace Elem Res.* 2006 Winter;114(1-3):1-5.

Tucker J. *Life Before Life: A Scientific Investigation of Children's Memories of Previous Lives.* New York: St. Martin's Press, 2005.

Turner EH, Blackwell AD. 5-Hydroxytryptophan plus SSRIs for interferon-induced depression: synergistic mechanisms for normalizing synaptic serotonin. *Med Hypotheses.* 2005;65(1): 138–44.

Tweed K. Study: Conceiving in Summer Lowers Baby's Future Test Scores. *Fox.* 2007 May 9, 2007.

Ullman D. *Discovering Homeopathy.* Berkeley, CA: North Atlantic, 1991.

Ulrich RS. Aesthetic and affective response to natural environment. In Altman, I. and Wohlwill, J. F. (eds) *Human Behaviour and Environment: Advances in Theory and Research. Volume 6: Behaviour and the Natural Environment.* New York: Plenum Press: 1983:85-125.

Ulrich RS. Influences of passive experiences with plants on individual wellbeing and health. In Relf, D. (ed) *The Role of Horticulture in Human Well-Being and Social Development: A National Symposium.* Portland: Timber Press, Portland. 1992:93 -105.

Ulrich RS. Natural versus urban scenes: some psychophysiological effects. *Environment and Behaviour.* 1981:523-556.

Ulrich RS. Visual landscapes and psychological well being. *Landscape Research.* 1979;4:17-23.

Unger ER, Nisenbaum R, Moldofsky H, Cesta A, Sammut C, Reyes M, Reeves WC. Sleep assessment in a population-based study of chronic fatigue syndrome. *BMC Neurol.* 2004 Apr 19;4(1):6.

Unger M. Botanical sedatives. *Pharm Unserer Zeit.* 2007;36(3):206-12.

Unger RH. Leptin physiology: a second look. *Regul Pept.* 2000 Aug 25;92(1-3):87-95.

van Beelen VA, Roeleveld J, Mooibroek H, Sijtsma L, Bino RJ, Bosch D, Rietjens IM, Alink GM. A comparative study on the effect of algal and fish oil on viability and cell proliferation of Caco-2 cells. *Food Chem Toxicol.* 2007 May;45(5):716-24.

Van Cauter E, Leproult R, Plat L. Age-related changes in slow wave sleep and REM sleep and relationship with growth hormone and cortisol levels in healthy men. *JAMA.* 2000 Aug 16;284(7):861-8.

Van Cauter E. Slow wave sleep and release of growth hormone. *JAMA.* 2000 Dec 6;284(21):2717-8.

Van Someren EJ. Mechanisms and functions of coupling between sleep and temperature rhythms. *Prog Brain Res.* 2006;153:309-24.

Vaquero JM, Gallego MC. Sunspot numbers can detect pandemic influenza A: the use of different sunspot numbers. *Med Hypotheses.* 2007;68(5):1189-90.

Vargha-Khadem F, Polkey CE. A review of cognitive outcome after hemidecortication in humans. *Adv Exp Med Biol.* 1992;325:137-51.

Vecchierini MF. Sleep disturbances in Alzheimer's disease and other dementias. *Psychol Neuropsychiatr Vieil.* 2010 Mar;8(1):15-23.

Vera FM, Manzaneque JM, Maldonado EF, Carranque GA, Rodriguez FM, Blanca MJ, Morell M. Subjective Sleep Quality and hormonal modulation in long-term yoga practitioners. *Biol Psychol.* 2009 Jul;81(3):164-8.

Vermeeren A. Residual effects of hypnotics: epidemiology and clinical implications. *CNS Drugs.* 2004;18(5):297-328.

Vertes RP. Memory consolidation in sleep; dream or reality. *Neuron.* 2004 Sep 30;44(1):135-48.

Vescelius E. *Music and Health.* New York: Goodyear Book Shop, 1918.

Vgontzas AN, Bixler EO, Chrousos GP, Pejovic S. Obesity and sleep disturbances: meaningful sub-typing of obesity. *Arch Physiol Biochem.* 2008 Oct;114(4):224-36.

Vgontzas AN, Liao D, Bixler EO, Chrousos GP, Vela-Bueno A. Insomnia with objective short sleep duration is associated with a high risk for hypertension. *Sleep.* 2009 Apr 1;32(4):491-7.

Vgontzas AN. The diagnosis and treatment of chronic insomnia in adults. *Sleep.* 2005 Sep 1;28(9):1047-8.

Vialatte FB, Bakardjian H, Prasad R, Cichocki A. EEG paroxysmal gamma waves during Bhramari Pranayama: a yoga breathing technique. *Conscious Cogn.* 2009 Dec;18(4):977-88.

Vieno N, Tuhkanen T, Kronberg L. Elimination of pharmaceuticals in sewage treatment plants in Finland. Water Res. 2007 Mar;41(5):1001-12.

Vierling-Claassen D, Siekmeier P, Stufflebeam S, Kopell N. Modeling GABA alterations in schizophrenia: a link between impaired inhibition and altered gamma and beta range auditory entrainment. *J Neurophysiol.* 2008 May;99(5):2656-71.

Volz HP. Phytochemicals as means to induce sleep. *Z Arztl Fortbild Qualitatssich.* 2001 Jan;95(1):33-4.

von Schantz M, Archer SN. *Clocks, genes and sleep. J R Soc Med.* 2003 Oct;96(10):486-9.

Voss U, Holzmann R, Tuin I, Hobson JA. Lucid dreaming: a state of consciousness with features of both waking and non-lucid dreaming. *Sleep.* 2009 Sep 1;32(9):1191-200.

Wachiuli M, Koyama M, Utsuyama M, Bittman BB, Kitagawa M, Hirokawa K.

Recreational music-making modulates natural killer cell activity, cytokines, and mood states in corporate employees. *Med Sci Monit.* 2007 Feb;13(2):CR57-70.

Walach H, Jonas WB, Ives J, van Wijk R, Weingartner O. Research on homeopathy: state of the art. *J Altern Complement Med.* 2005 Oct;11(5):813-29.

Walch JM, Rabin BS, Day R, Williams JN, Choi K, Kang JD. The effect of sunlight on postoperative analgesic medication use: a prospective study of patients undergoing spinal surgery. *Psychosom Med.* 2005 Jan-Feb;67(1):156-63.

Walker M. *The Power of Color.* New Delhi: B. Jain Publishers. 2002.

Walters AS, Silvestri R, Zucconi M, Chandrashekariah R, Konofal E. Review of the possible relationship and hypothetical links between attention deficit hyperactivity disorder (ADHD) and the simple sleep related movement disorders, parasomnias, hypersomnias, and circadian rhythm disorders. *J Clin Sleep Med.* 2008 Dec 15;4(6):591-600.

Wang H, Hui KM, Chen Y, Xu S, Wong JT, Xue H. Structure-activity relationships of flavonoids, isolated from Scutellaria baicalensis, binding to benzodiazepine site of GABA(A) receptor complex. *Planta Med.* 2002 Dec;68(12):1059-62.

Watson L. *Beyond Supernature.* New York: Bantam, 1987.

Watson L. *Supernature.* New York: Bantam, 1973.

Wauters M, Considine RV, Van Gaal LF. Human leptin: from an adipocyte hormone to an endocrine mediator. *Eur J Endocrinol.* 2000 Sep;143(3):293-311.

Wayne R. *Chemistry of the Atmospheres.* Oxford Press, 1991.

Wazna-Wesly JM, Meranda DL, Carey P, Shenker Y. Effect of atrial natriuretic hormone on vasopressin and thirst response to osmotic stimulation in human subjects. *J Lab Clin Med.* 1995 Jun;125(6):734-42.

WB Saunders; 1982, Fishman HC. Notalgia paresthetica. *J Am Acad Dermatol.* 1986;15:1304-1305

Weaver J, Astumian R. The response of living cells to very weak electric fields: the thermal noise limit. *Science.* 1990;247:459-462.

Weeks BS. Formulations of dietary supplements and herbal extracts for relaxation and anxiolytic action: Relarian. *Med Sci Monit.* 2009 Nov;15(11):RA256-62.

Wehr TA, Aeschbach D, Duncan WC Jr. Evidence for a biological dawn and dusk in the human circadian timing system. *J Physiol.* 2001 Sep 15;535(Pt 3):937-51.

Wehr TA, Rosenthal NE, Sack DA, Gillin JC. Antidepressant effects of sleep deprivation in bright and dim light. *Acta Psychiatr Scand.* 1985 Aug;72(2):161-5.

Wehr TA, Sack DA, Duncan WC, Mendelson WB, Rosenthal NE, Gillin JC, Goodwin FK. Sleep and circadian rhythms in affective patients isolated from external time cues. *Psychiatry Res.* 1985 Aug;15(4):327-39.

Wehr TA. A brain-warming function for REM sleep. *Neurosci Biobehav Rev.* 1992 Fall;16(3):379-97.

Wehr TA. Sleep loss: a preventable cause of mania and other excited states. *J Clin Psychiatry.* 1989 Dec;50 Suppl:8-16; discussion 45-7.

Wehr TA. The durations of human melatonin secretion and sleep respond to changes in daylength (photoperiod). *J Clin Endocrinol Metab.* 1991 Dec;73(6):1276-80.

Wei A, Shibamoto T. Antioxidant activities and volatile constituents of various essential oils. *J Agric Food Chem.* 2007 Mar 7;55(5):1737-42.

Weinberger P, Measures M. The effect of two audible sound frequencies on the germination and growth of a spring and winter wheat. *Can. J.*

Bot. 1968;46(9):1151-1158.

Weiner MA. *Secrets of Fijian Medicine.* Berkeley, CA: Univ. of Calif., 1969.

Weinert D, Waterhouse J. The circadian rhythm of core temperature: effects of physical activity and aging. *Physiol Behav.* 2007 Feb 28;90(2-3):246-56.

Weiss RF. *Herbal Medicine.* Gothenburg, Sweden: Beaconsfield, 1988.

Weller A, Weller L. Menstrual synchrony between mothers and daughters and between roommates. *Physiol Behav.* 1993 May;53(5):943-9.

Weller L, Weller A, Roizman S. Human menstrual synchrony in families and among close friends: examining the importance of mutual exposure. *J Comp Psychol.* 1999 Sep;113(3):261-8.

Welsh D, Yoo SH, Liu A, Takahashi J, Kay S. Bioluminescence Imaging of Individual Fibroblasts Reveals Persistent, Independently Phased Circadian Rhythms of Clock Gene Expression. *Current Biology.* 2004;14:2289-2295.

Werbach M. *Nutritional Influences on Illness.* Tarzana, CA: Third Line Press, 1996.

Wesołowska A, Nikiforuk A, Michalska K, Kisiel W, Chojnacka-Wójcik E. Analgesic and sedative activities of lactucin and some lactucin-like guaianolides in mice. *J Ethnopharmacol.* 2006 Sep 19;107(2):254-8.

Wesołowska A, Nikiforuk A, Michalska K, Kisiel W, Chojnacka-Wójcik E. Analgesic and sedative activities of lactucin and some lactucin-like guaianolides in mice. *J Ethnopharmacol.* 2006 Sep 19;107(2):254-8.

West P. *Surf Your Biowaves.* London: Quantum, 1999.

Westman M, Eden D. Effects of a respite from work on burnout: vacation relief and fade-out. *J Appl Psychol.* 1997 Aug;82(4):516-27.

Wetterberg L. Light and biological rhythms. *J Intern Med.* 1994 Jan;235(1):5-19.

Wheatley D. Medicinal plants for insomnia: a review of their pharmacology, efficacy and tolerability. *J Psychopharmacol.* 2005 Jul;19(4):414-21.

Wheeler FJ. *The Bach Remedies Repertory.* New Canaan, CN: Keats, 1997.

White J, Krippner S (eds). *Future Science: Life Energies & the Physics of Paranormal Phenomena.* Garden City: Anchor, 1977.

White JP, Schilling JS. Postmenopausal hormone replacement: historical perspectives and current concerns. *Clin Excell Nurse Pract.* 2000 Sep;4(5):277-85.

White S. *The Unity of the Self.* Cambridge: MIT Press, 1991.

WHO. *Guidelines for Drinking-water Quality.* 2nd ed, vol. 2. Geneva: World Health Organization, 1996.

WHO. *Guidelines on health aspects of water desalination. ETS/80.4.* Geneva: World Health Organization, 1980.

WHO. Health effects of the removal of substances occurring naturally in drinking water, with special reference to demineralized and desalinated water. Report on a working group (Brussels, 20-23 March 1978). *EURO Reports and Studies.* 1979;16.

WHO. How trace elements in water contribute to health. *WHO Chronicle.* 1978;32:382-385.

Wildon DC, Thain JF, Minchin PEH, Gubb IR, Reilly AJ, Skipper YD, Doherty HM, O'Donnell PJ, Bowles DJ. Electrical signaling and systemic proteinase inhibitor induction in the wounded plant. *Nature.* 1992;360:62–65.

Wilkinson SM, Love SB, Westcombe AM, Gambles MA, Burgess CC, Cargill A, Young T, Maher EJ, Ramirez AJ. Effectiveness of aromatherapy massage in the management of anxiety and depression in patients with cancer: a multicenter randomized controlled trial. *J Clin Oncol.* 2007 Feb 10;25(5):532-9.

Williams E, Stewart-Knox B, Bradbury I, Rowland I, Pentieva K, Helander A, McNulty H. Effect of folic acid supplementation on mood and serotonin response in healthy males. *Br J Nutr.* 2005 Oct;94(4):602-8.

Willis GL, Turner EJ. Primary and secondary features of Parkinson's disease improve with strategic exposure to bright light: a case series study. *Chronobiol Int.* 2007;24(3):521-37.

Wilson L. *Nutritional Balancing and Hair Mineral Analysis.* Prescott, AZ: LD Wilson Cons, 1998.

Winchester AM. *Biology and its Relation to Mankind.* New York: Van Nostrand Reinhold, 1969.

Winfree AT. *The Timing of Biological Clocks.* New York: Scientific American, 1987.

Wing YK. Herbal treatment of insomnia. *Hong Kong Med J.* 2001 Dec;7(4):392-402.

Winstead DK, Schwartz BD, Bertrand WE. Biorhythms: fact or superstition? *Am J Psychiatry.* 1981 Sep;138(9):1188-92.

Winstein KJ, Armstrong D. Top Pain Scientist Fabricated Data in Studies, Hospital Says. *Wall Street J.* 2009 March 11. http://online.wsj.com/article/SB123672510903888207.html?mod=loomia &loomia_si= t0:a16:g2:r1:c0 .0270612: b22894832. Accessed July, 2009.

Wittenberg JS. *The Rebellious Body.* New York: Insight, 1996.

Wixted JT. A Theory About Why We Forget What We Once Knew. *CurrDir Psychol Sci.* 2005;14(1):6-9.

Wolfson P, Hoffmann DL. An investigation into the effi cacy of Scutellaria lateriflora in healthy volunteers. *Altern Ther Health Med.* 2003;9(2): 74–78.

Wolverton BC. *How to Grow Fresh Air: 50 House Plants that Purify Your Home or Office.* New York: Penguin, 1997.

Wood M. *The Book of Herbal Wisdom.* Berkeley, CA: North Atlantic, 1997.

Woolger R. *Other Lives, Other Selves.* New York: Bantam, 1988.

Worwood VA. *The Complete Book of Essential Oils & Aromatherapy.* San Rafael, CA: New World, 1991.

Wright ML. Melatonin, diel rhythms, and metamorphosis in anuran amphibians. *Gen Comp Endocrinol.* 2002 May;126(3):251-4.

Wyart C, Webster WW, Chen JH, Wilson SR, McClary A, Khan RM, Sobel N. Smelling a single component of male sweat alters levels of cortisol in women. *J Neurosci.* 2007 Feb 7;27(6):1261-5.

Yamanaka Y, Honma S, Honma K. Daily phase adjustment of human sleep-wake cycle. *Nippon Rinsho.* 2009 Aug;67(8):1475-82.

Yamauchi M, Hiraoka S, Imanishi T. Role of the serotonergic nervous system in anxiety disorders and the anxiolytic mechanism of selective serotonin reuptake inhibitors. *Nihon Shinkei Seishin Yakurigaku Zasshi.* 2006;26(5–6): 193–98.

Yan P, Pang QH, Jiao XW, Zhao X, Shen YJ, Zhao SJ. Genetic variation and identification of cultivated Fallopia multiflora and its wild relatives by using chloroplast matK and 18S rRNA gene sequences. *Planta Med.* 2008 Oct;74(12):1504-9.

Yang HQ, Xie SS, Hu XL, Chen L, Li H. Appearance of human meridian-like structure and acupoints and its time correlation by infrared thermal imaging. *Am J Chin Med.* 2007;35(2):231-40.

Yeager S. *The Doctor's Book of Food Remedies.* Emmaus, PA: Rodale Press, 1998.

Yellen G. The voltage-gated potassium channels and their relatives. *Nature* 2002 Sept 5;419:35-42.

Yeung JW. A hypothesis: Sunspot cycles may detect pandemic influenza A in 1700-2000 A.D. *Med Hypotheses.* 2006;67(5):1016-22.

Yi LT, Xu Q, Li YC, Yang L, Kong LD. Antidepressant-like synergism of extracts from magnolia bark and ginger rhizome alone and in combination in mice. *Prog Neuropsychopharmacol Biol Psychiatry.* 2009 Jun 15;33(4):616-24.

Yokoi S, Ikeya M, Yagi T, Nagai K. Mouse circadian rhythm before the Kobe earthquake in 1995. *Bioelectromagnetics.* 2003 May;24(4):289-91.

Yokoyama M, Yokoyama T, Funazu K, Yamashita T, Kondo S, Hosoai H, Yokoyama A, Nakamura H. Associations between headache and stress, alcohol drinking, exercise, sleep, and comorbid health conditions in a Japanese population. *J Headache Pain.* 2009 Jun;10(3):177-85.

Yoshioka M, Doucet E, Drapeau V, Dionne I, Tremblay A. Combined effects of red pepper and caffeine consumption on 24 h energy balance in subjects given free access to foods. Br J Nutr. 2001 Feb;85(2):203-11.

Young SN. How to increase serotonin in the human brain without drugs. *J Psychiatry Neurosci.* 2007;32(6): 394–99.

Yu HS, Lee SY, Jang CG. Involvement of 5-HT1A and GABAA receptors in the anxiolytic-like effects of Cinnamomum cassia in mice. *Pharmacol Biochem Behav.* 2007;87(1): 164–70.

Yuan CS, Dey L, Wang A, Mehendale S, Xie JT, Aung HH, Ang-Lee MK. Kavalactones and dihydrokavain modulate GABAergic activity in rat gastricbrainstem preparation. *Planta Med.* 2002 Dec;68(12):1092-6.

Yuan CS, Mehendale S, Xiao Y, Aung HH, Xie JT, Ang-Lee MK. The gammaaminobutyric acidergic effects of valerian and valerenic acid on rat brainstem neuronal activity. Anesth Analg. 2004 Feb;98(2):353-8.

Zadra A, Pilon M, Montplaisir J. Polysomnographic diagnosis of sleepwalking: effects of sleep deprivation. Ann Neurol. 2008 Apr;63(4):513-9.

Zafar KS, Siddiqui A, Sayeed I, Ahmad M, Salim S, Islam F. Dose-dependent protective effect of selenium in rat model of Parkinson's disease: neurobehavioral and neurochemical evidences. *J Neurochem.* 2003 Feb;84(3):438-46.

Zhang Z, Lian XY, Li S, Stringer JL. Characterization of chemical ingredients and anticonvulsant activity of American skullcap (Scutellaria lateriflora). *Phytomedicine.* 2009 May;16(5):485-93.

Zi N. *The Art of Breathing.* New York: Bantam, 1986.

Ziegler G, Ploch M, Miettinen-Baumann A, Collet W. Efficacy and tolerability of valerian extract LI 156 compared with oxazepam in the treatment of nonorganic insomnia – a randomized, double-blind, comparative clinical study. *Eur J Med Res.* 2002;7(11): 480–86.

Ziegler G, Ploch M, Miettinen-Baumann A, Collet W. Efficacy and tolerability of valerian extract LI 156 compared with oxazepam in the treatment of nonorganic insomnia - a randomized, double-blind, comparative clinical study. *Eur J Med Res.* 2002;7:480-486. 1974;24:2066-2070.

Zimecki M. The lunar cycle: effects on human and animal behavior and physiology. *Postepy Hig Med Dosw.* 2006;60:1-7.

Zimmerman J, Stoyva J, Metcalf D. Distorted visual feedback and augmented REM sleep. Psychophysiology. 1970;7:298-303.

Zou Z, Li F, Buck L. Odor maps in the olfactory cortex. *Proc Natl Acad of Sci.* 2005;102(May 24):7724-7729.

Zumiani G, Tasin L, Urbani F, Tinozzi CC, Carabelli A, Cristofolini M. Clinicostatistical study on hydropinic and balneothermal therapy of psoriatic patients using the low mineral-content waters of the Comano springs. *Minerva Med.* 1986 Apr 14;77(16):627-34.

Index

www.ingramcontent.com/pod-product-compliance
Lightning Source LLC
La Vergne TN
LVHW091215080426
835509LV00009B/1012